Bodies at Work

Bodies at Work

Carol Wolkowitz

SAGE Publications

London ● Thousand Oaks ● New Delhi

First published 2006

SAGE Publications Ltd
1 Oliver's Yard
55 City Road
London EC1Y 1SP

SAGE Publications Inc
2455 Teller Road
Thousand Oaks, California 91320

SAGE Publications India Pvt Ltd
B-42 Panchsheel Enclave
Post Box 4109
New Delhi 110 017

British Library Cataloguing in Publication data

A catalogue record for this book is available
from the British Library

ISBN 1 7619 6063 5   978 0 7619 6063 8
ISBN 1 7619 6064 3   978 0 7619 6064 5

Library of Congress control number: 2005934169

Typeset by C&M Digitals (P) Ltd., Chennai, India
Printed on paper from sustainable resources
Printed and bound in Great Britain by Athenaeum Press, Gateshead

Contents

List of Figures and Illustrations

Acknowledgements

I want to acknowledge, first of all, the courtesy of individuals and institutions who reproduced, helped me to locate or gave me permission to use a number of different photographs or other materials, including Rebecca Barnard at Solo Syndications, Gerald Beasley and Julia Toser at the Avery Architectural & Fine Arts Library at Columbia University, Anne Braybon, Jean-Pierre Durand, Jo Ann King at King Visual Archives, Bill Maguire, Palgrave Macmillan, Holly Reed at the United States National Archives, Jonathan Smith at Trinity College Library, Cambridge, N. Adam Watson at the Florida State Archives, Ed Westcott and Peggy Wilson.

I also want to thank a large number of people for the very extensive support I have had in writing this book, in particular the postgraduates who have taken my Body/Work course, as well as some of my doctoral students, for their insights and suggestions of materials, including especially Thea Cacchioni, Terence Chong, Halla Dijab, Nicola Gale, Heather Leask, Ben Lo, Pam Lowe, Emma Nelson, Julia Rayment, Nina Robinson, Lesley Spiers, Marianna Tortell and Pam Wakewich. I have benefited from research assistance from Duncan Adam, Danny Beusch, Jane Ellis and Matt Elton and conversations with Kate Sloss and Chris Massingham. I feel indebted to the support of almost every colleague in the Department of Sociology at the University of Warwick, but especially to helpful discussions with Simon Williams and to the generosity of those colleagues who read and commented on earlier drafts of all or parts of the book – Terry Lovell, Tony Elger, Christina Hughes and Nickie Charles. Karen Phillips and Anna Luker at Sage were endlessly patient. Paul Stewart kindly took the time to read the final manuscript. Members of the extended Wolkowitz family – Rhoda, Dan, Barbara, John, Rick and Barbie – not only have been consistently encouraging but also debated the ideas with me. But most of all I need to thank Martyn Partridge, without whose support this book could never have been written, and our son Tim Partridge, especially for his present of 'The Body in the Library'.

Introduction

The changed meaning of the 'body shop', from a section of a car factory – or a garage knocking wrecks back into shape – to The Body Shop, a chain of stores selling products to relax and enhance the appearance of human bodies, is now so entrenched that some younger people may scarcely remember the earlier usage. The shifting connotations of the phrase 'body shop' testify to complex changes in how we think about the role of the human body in economic life and employment relations. Because much of the production of things has been exported to countries where wage rates are lower, or environmental or other controls less strict, workers in the richer Western nations are increasingly concentrated in jobs in the service sector, in which interpersonal interactions, as compared to the making of objects, is often of greater importance.

This shift means that if we want to consider embodiment in the workplace, we need to consider changes as well as continuities in the constructions of the body and its uses that guide, empower, constrain and exhaust many kinds of workers. Based on a wide range of literatures, this book crosses conventional demarcations, demonstrating the contribution that concepts developed in the sociology of the body can make to our understanding of changing patterns of work and employment; equally important, it highlights the impact of work and employment on experiences of embodiment. It shows that the body/work nexus is crucial to the organisation and experience of work relations, and, conversely, that people's experience of embodiment is deeply embedded in their experiences of paid employment.

To date the body and embodiment have constituted a relatively minor thread in research on organisation, work or employment. Even where they are present, this theme tends to be subsumed within the focus on work cultures and identities. Research and debate have tended to follow the main drift of postmodernist approaches on the body, highlighting the production and consumption of the fluid and dynamic symbolic body as a feature of social interaction. While this perspective has succeeded in bringing the body into our picture of work, one of the problems of such an approach may be its exaggeration of the malleability of the body and its underestimation of the bodily effort work still involves. This can result in a failure to recognise that, as journalist Madeleine Bunting (2004: 177) puts it, 'human beings have finite resources, physical and emotional'. Workplaces and work identities focused around competition and long hours, a 'can do anything' culture, have ignored this, leading to the current epidemic in stress, overwork and depression. One of the key arguments of this book is the need to supplement the body as constructed by the 'cultural turn' in sociology with a fuller picture of the continuing materiality of workplace activity, including the many ways in which workers' health and safety contribute to their experience as embodied social actors. This entails making fuller use of feminist perspectives that, though long concerned to reveal the contribution of embodied sexual difference to language and culture (for example Grosz 1994; Moi 1999) need to be widened so as to encompass more aspects of embodiment, especially in the context of employment relations.

The origins of this book go back to two experiences that provoked a lot of thought about the body as a focus of diverse labour processes. The first was my observations of my father's care in an American hospice in the weeks before his death from cancer in the late 1980s. Although I was aware of criticisms of the objectification of the body by the biomedical model adopted by doctors, what struck me more forcibly at the time was the relation between the division of labour that governed work in this institution and the fragmentation of the human patient. Concern for the patients' emotional well-being was seen as the responsibility of the hospice chaplains, and seemingly completely divorced from either pain relief, which was delivered by nurses at set hours, or the physical upkeep of the patients' environment. Rooms would be dusted, tables wiped and floors swept as if the bed in the room were empty; and every time the mop handle rattled my father's bedstead he would wince with pain. Even in a hospice, a type of institution supposedly guided by notions of holistic care (Saunders et al. 1981), no one seemed to comment on this, or find it unusual, perhaps having already naturalised the division between patient care and housekeeping services that was to become so prominent in debates on the NHS in Britain. Even today, health policies recognising the links between care, cleaning and patient health are the exception, as in the current crises over the rates of MRSA infection of hospital patients in the UK, which has brought to the fore the relation between infection and nurses' overloaded timetables, the contracting out of housekeeping services, and the movement of patients from ward to ward to improve bed occupancy rates.

The second experience occurred a few years later. When my son started school I had to take him round a number of appointments to get him organised for the new venture. I took him for inoculations at the GP's, then to be measured for school shoes, for a haircut, to the dentist. It was a Foucauldian moment, when I realised my child's entry into the wider social world involved a new degree and type of bodily regulation. I was also conscious that to meet his requirements for food or clothes, I had not previously needed to have him with me, mostly choosing items appropriate for a child of his age on the way to or from work. My university term started a month later, in October, and again I made the rounds of a number of practitioners and salespeople. Like many academics, I attempt to get personal business finished before the pressure of term time makes it difficult to fit in. So I too needed to freshen up my public body, undertaking a round of visits to dentist, opticians, and hairdresser; I bought a new outfit for work and had my first mammogram. All this involved interactions with a range of practitioners and retail workers in which parts of my body, or my child's, were systematically isolated and taken up as the focus of attention. The distinctiveness of these engagements with the world of service work seemed to lie partly in the co-presence of the service provider and service user, but they also targeted the body as such and involved a degree of intimate interaction and even fleshiness that went beyond the boundaries of normal social interaction.

Yet at that time the sociology of work, to which I was linked by earlier research on gender and home-based work, made almost no reference to aspects of the body and embodiment that were beginning to feature in sociology (Featherstone et al. 1991; Turner 1984) or the study of sexuality (Foucault 1979; Walkowitz 1980), a subject on which I already taught. Term started, my colleagues and I gave our 'option talks' to postgraduate students, and it seemed that all the modules on our then Labour Studies MA programme dealt with the production of things. Vehicle assembly lines and South African mine workers were part of the curriculum, but health care was dealt with in the sociology of health and healing rather than the sociology of employment. Do we need to rethink the sociology of work, I thought, in relation to bodies' softness, individuality, responsiveness and capacity for independent growth and feeling, as against one originally constructed in relation to the 'hard', defensive social relations of industrial production and the social practices with which they were associated? It was true that we had courses in public sector unionism, but there seemed no explicit interest in considering its relation to the micropolitics of the intimate encounter between worker and customer. Sociologists could build on our understanding of gender relations, I thought, by considering not only the gender composition of the workforce in various kind of work, but also by focusing on the connections between labour processes, gender ideologies and constructions of the bodies of workers and those with whom they interacted, including their patients, customers and clients.

In the mid-1990s these reflections led me to add a new, 10-week MA module I called Body/Work to the course I already taught on Gender, Work and Employment – a course that eventually, with the expansion of research literature on the body and work over the intervening period, gave rise to this book. The course considers the relationship between the body and paid employment in a number of different areas, including changing assumptions about the body as an instrument in the labour process and constructions of the body that guide workers in their relations with clients, customers and patients. But because the literature at the time was so sparse, the students were asked to produce their own data, and this process also fed into my project. I still recommend this as a way into the subject, even now that there is so much more material available. In addition to the research publications then available on topics like emotional labour (Hochschild 1983) or healing (Lawler 1991), we tried to consider how feminist scholarship on, for instance, the disciplining of female bodies (Bartky 1990; Bordo 1990a) or sociological theories of the body (Shilling 1993) would need to be expanded if they were to comprehend women's involvement as paid workers in the remaking of the body. Each student was therefore asked to supplement the reading by conducting an interview with someone whose work involved intimate contact between bodies, for example a doctor or nurse, a tattooist, a hairdresser or physiotherapist, concentrating on the worker's experience of embodied activity and their understanding of their relation to the bodies on which they focused.

Although more literature soon became available, for instance Macdonald and Sirianni's (1996) *Working in the Service Society*, Lawler's (1997) *The Body in Nursing* and Foner's (1994) *The Caregiving Dilemma*, books which are still important on the course, we found that analysing together the transcripts the students had produced provoked new insights into workers' perceptions of their relations, as workers, to their own and others' bodies. Moreover, it helped to shift our gaze towards the kinds of labour processes in which women workers are concentrated, rather than seeing these as exceptions to patterns of work more typical of the male-dominated industrial work around which many of the questions in labour studies were first formulated. Although the evolution of the course in some ways paralleled increasing interest within sociology in areas like consumption, workplace identities and cultures, care work and new forms of labour market polarisation, coming at them 'through the body' gave them an immediacy, helped to integrate them within a common framework, and highlighted their relation to gender, race and ethnic divisions in employment.

4

Recognition of the centrality of the body and embodiment to work and employment has grown exponentially since these personal and work experiences in the late 1980s and 1990s, but rather surprisingly it has not yet been dealt with systematically as a distinct, emergent field of study. Drawing on my experience in teaching the course mentioned above, this book seeks to highlight the body/work relation as a key field for research and teaching, taking the key texts already mentioned as a starting point. It is meant mainly for undergraduate and postgraduate students, as an aid to identifying resources that can help us understand both the changing constructions of the body that accompany its instrumentalisation as a labour input and the labour processes and occupational cultures that take the body as a focus of work. I hope it will also encourage sociologists to see the potential that looking at the body/work relation has for enriching our understanding of work and employment, by focusing on the corporeality of social agents, and to give more attention to work relations in understanding human embodiment.

In considering the body/work relation I am especially concerned with questions of individual agency of different kinds. As we shall see, there are many ways that workers, as embodied agents, make space for themselves at the micropolitical level and it is very important to document these. But the agency gained at the micropolitical level may also reinforce gender stereotypes and even shift the costs onto other people, such as the paid substitutes for work traditionally undertaken, unpaid, by women in the home. Similarly, one of the key benefits of focusing on the body and body work is being able to capture the feelings of power women especially may feel 'flowing out' from themselves as givers of care or intimate services to recipients (Bartky 1990). But body work occupations and relationships are also structured by the complex, global hierarchies and polarised labour markets in which they are located. Optimistic variants of postmodernism, and also those who have distanced themselves from it, such as Giddens, place hope for change in the social relations of consumption. Pessimists, such as Bourdieu, Harvey and many of the studies I report on here, echo Adorno and the Frankfurt School in seeing the social relations of consumption and personal life stitched up so tightly with the social relations of capitalism that there is no hope in that direction. I too think we need to insist on the links between the body, which lends itself to an analysis at the micro-level, and these wider relations of inequality and domination. Although this picture would be much stronger were we able to take the story onto a global scale, there is enough evidence of the ambiguous consequences of the commodification of bodies and embodied experience here in the Western countries to be getting on with.

However, the problem is not just that one can become so enchanted with the pleasures of consumption (and I don't exempt myself) that one can lose sight of these macro-issues. It is also a question of *whose* bodies we take as a focus. Focusing on the bodies of workers contributes a vivid picture of the costs they – we – bear, which obviously vary considerably in type and extent. But there is also a problem because although we can highlight the productive, 'powerful bodies' of the workplace, the 'bodies of power' that people international finance or corporate boardrooms, which have less need to embody that power or to represent it in their own corporeality, remain shadowed. Of course many public figures, especially politicians, are advantaged as both bodies of power and powerful bodies, and those women who have got through the door to the corporate boardroom will have even more need to demonstrate their entitlement to embody both kinds of power. But we need to remember that although everyone has a body, not everyone has the same relation to its economic and symbolic significance.

Chapter 1 seeks to provide the intellectual context within which research and debate on the body, embodiment and work can be located. It seeks to sketch, with a necessarily broad brush, key concerns considered in, firstly, the sociology of work and, secondly, sociological and feminist scholarship on the body and embodiment, for readers who may be familiar with only one (or indeed neither) of these fields. As part of the review of concepts deployed in the sociology of employment, it identifies key changes in labour markets and work organisation over the past 30 years. As this book will show, research in the specialised area of work, employment and organisation is already showing that dealing explicitly with the embodied character of work does much to enrich our understanding. However, the chapter suggests that the main advocates of the sociology of the body in Britain have so far resisted taking this research on board, and considers why this has been the case so far. It argues that while we can appreciate the rich view of subjectivity provided by the anti-dualist perspectives that challenge the Cartesian mind–body binary, they cannot develop further unless they take on board the embeddedness of such dualisms in the structures and experiences of paid employment. The chapter then considers the contribution that the political economy of the body can make to this endeavour.

Chapter 2 provides historical depth through an analysis of still photographic images that vividly portray changing constructions of the body as an instrument of labour. It contributes, therefore, to increasing interest in the development of visual sociology, as well as to the sociology of work, considering the continuing legacy of representation of labouring bodies in gender, race and class-specific terms. It takes as examples particular figures in the Western imaginative landscape whose bodies have become emblematic of labour in different ways. There are three case studies:

1   the photographs collected by of A.J. Munby (1828–1910), which demonstrate the fascination of Victorian gentlemen with images of working-class women in Britain, those who worked outdoors in trousers as well as the household servants whose bodies were metaphorically stained by household labour;

2   the images produced by the American photographer Lewis Hine (1874–1940), in which are contrasted the iconic figure of the heroic, white manly worker and degraded female workers pictured as having usurped men's proper role as breadwinners; and

3   photographs produced by the American Manhattan Project during the Second World War, in which the images circulated by the project adopted the photographic conventions established by Hine and others in order to normalise the secret work of the project, making atomic bombs, and reassure prospective and current workers.

The use of still photographs as a way of highlighting bodily posture, conduct and interaction in the work environment is continued in the rest of the book, where the focus is on employment today.

Chapters 3 and 4 review the literature on aspects of embodied labour for which research is already underway. Chapter 3 considers constructions of the industrial body from several vantage points, outlining Foucault's influential analysis of the production of the 'docile body' and considering some of the limitations of this view. Chapter 4 considers newer constructions of the working body, especially in large-scale organisational settings, including managerial workers' own anxiety about their bodily self-presentation and expectations regarding the performance of emotional, sexual and aesthetic labour. It focuses on interrelational customer services, one of the areas in which there has been considerable research on the body in work and organisation. Chapter 5 considers occupational health and safety, one area which is usually omitted from scholarship on the body, reminding us of the organic moorings of work activities and relationships.

The latter part of the book considers occupations and interactions that involve a high degree of intimate contact between workers' bodies and those on which their work focuses. Chapter 6 looks at prostitution and other kinds of sex work, long crucial foci of feminist debate, but only just beginning to be considered by those with an interest in work and organisation. An important example of this development is Brewis and Linstead's (2000) *Sex, Work and Sex Work*, which considers postmodernist theories of the body as essential to understanding the place of sex in organisations and the organised sex of prostitution. In addition to providing a vivid picture of the ways some sex workers talk about their experiences, the chapter identifies six distinct constructions of the body that appear in feminist debate on sex work, in order to demonstrate the relationship between concepts of the body and political argument and social policy.

In Chapter 7 the term 'body work' is adopted as a move towards conceptualising paid work that takes the body as its immediate site of labour, involving intimate, messy contact with the (frequently supine or naked) body, its orifices or products through touch or close proximity. This kind of paid body work is a component of a wide range of occupations, for instance (in alphabetical order) care assistants, dentists, hairdressers, maids, undertakers and yoga instructors. After considering the centrality of these kinds of body work to post-industrial national and global economies, it considers four aspects of this increasingly large 'sector': the concepts of the body that guide workers and practitioners in their relations with consumers; the hierarchical divisions of labour by which occupations are ranked; the spatial organisation of work, including its relation to migration; and the micropolitics of bodily interaction that workers have to negotiate. The chapter shows how the construction of the Other's body is constitutive of work relations, especially in the employment of racialised migrants to do the invisible 'dirty work' on which the new body regimes actually depend.

Finally, Chapter 8 tries to summarise what research on work and employment may be telling us about the key themes emerging from the sociology of the body, as identified in Chapter 1. These are the body's relation to the social order, to conceptualising the self, to constructions of gender and to the political economy of contemporary life. The concluding remarks in Chapter 8 stress the recursive relationship between these aspects of social life and constructions of the body and embodiment.

ONE Embodiment and Paid Employment

This chapter seeks to provide the intellectual context within which research and debate on the body, embodiment and work can be located. It seeks to sketch, with a necessarily very broad brush, some of the main concerns considered in, firstly, the sociology of work and, secondly, scholarship on the body and embodiment, for readers who may be familiar with only one (or indeed neither) of these fields. But I also want to consider the absence of employment in the way the sociology of the body has developed as a field of study. As this book will show, research within the specialised literature on work, employment and organisation is already showing that dealing explicitly with the embodied character of work does much to enrich our understanding. Yet the main advocates of the sociology of the body in Britain have so far either resisted taking this research on board, or have done so very belatedly. The lack of attention to the world of work has many sources. As Scarry (1994) points out, we tend to associate bodies with sensuousness, play, pleasure and spontaneity rather than work, which is seen to involve mainly numbing routine. But underlying the neglect of paid employment may also be a reluctance to confront the kinds of constraints to fluidity and self-expression that work has historically represented.

What is the sociology of work and employment?

Traditionally, what distinguishes work from non-work depended on the social context within which an activity is undertaken and the value it is given in particular societies (Grint 1991). Although it is often seen as something that transforms nature, or that ensures survival, the meanings expressed by calling something 'work' are extremely variable. Feminist insistence on defining unpaid caring in the home as work demonstrates that, like other sociological categories, 'work' is a contested concept (Glucksmann 2006, 1995). Employment tends to be used as a narrower, more objective term, since the social relations within which it takes place are specified. Generally it refers to all forms of waged work in which an employee works under the authority of an employer (Edwards 2003: 1), and therefore excludes some kinds of paid work, such as self-employment, along with unpaid labour.

Three areas have dominated research. One focuses on long- and short-term changes in the structure of the labour markets that 'bring together workers in search of a wage and capitalists in search of employees' (Peck 1996: 1). Although many economists may understand labour market outcomes in terms of the inevitable logic of market exchange, in which jobs are allocated based on workers' skills and other human capital, sociologists have long stressed their socially contingent nature. If only because the choices of both employers and workers are affected not only by economic incentives but also by many features of the wider society, including state welfare systems, migration opportunities, gender roles, family and household composition, and educational aspirations, the sociology of work and employment has always had to consider the social developments and institutions within which labour markets are embedded. Moreover, the structuring of labour markets feeds back into the wider society, since the output of employment includes 'not only the production of goods and services but also the structures of advantage and disadvantage' to which employment gives rise (Edwards 2003: 4).

Much debate concerns the effects of the sectoral shift that has taken place since the early 1970s in the labour markets of Britain and other advanced capitalist societies (Peck 1996; Sayer and Walker 1992; Warhurst and Thompson 1998). Much of the employment previously required by manufacturing, mining and agriculture has now been now transferred to lower-wage economies and has been supplanted by jobs in the service sector. This has involved to some extent the upgrading of employment through the growth of job opportunities in the 'new economy', led by knowledge-intensive work in, for instance, finance and business services, product design, retail management, the professions and the creative industries. However, many commentators stress counter-trends in which jobs available to previous generations of craft and assembly line workers have been replaced by less well-paid and less secure jobs as cleaners, fast-food retail workers and carers, to take just three examples of work that cannot be readily exported. Meanwhile many jobs even in new, technologically more advanced sectors still involve routinised, repetitive tasks and close monitoring, such as customer service work in high-volume call centres.

Herzenberg et al. (1998) suggest that the characteristics of jobs available in the labour markets of post-industrial economies have to be analysed in terms of the restructuring of a whole range of different aspects of employment, for example the characteristics of business organisation (including, the expansion of franchising arrangements and outsourcing); work systems (how jobs are defined and worker effort regulated, especially the types of incentives that are available and degree of autonomy permitted); and career paths, especially the balance between long-term employment with promotion prospects and casualised, insecure work. Many of these changes reflect the increasing possibilities offered by technological changes in information-processing and surveillance, and, at least in Britain, are intertwined with the privatisation of formerly publicly owned services and assets. These changes are resulting in complex new patterns of employment inequality and insecurity among workers (Beynon et al. 2002).

In the US the particular mix of manual and non-manual, union and non-union, and high-skill and low-skill jobs characteristic of different regional labour markets has important and contradictory implications for men and women, white and racialised minority workers (McCall 2001). In Britain the previous segregation of women into relatively low-paid jobs in manufacturing and routine services (along with their concentration in the lower strata of professional and semi-professional public sector employment, for example as primary school teachers and nurses) has been succeeded by a much more polarised labour market for women, which has seen highly educated women's opportunities expand dramatically, although they still do not match those of men with the same qualifications (Walby 1997). At the other end of the labour market, jobs may be so ill-paid, insecure and dead-end, Peck (2004) argues, that at least in the US they are increasingly filled by workers effectively forced to accept them by prison parole programmes, immigration controls and the state workfare programmes, which have replaced welfare payments for the mothers of dependent children. Moreover, the monopolisation of access to jobs in the low-paid sector by temporary help agencies has made it difficult for workers to directly challenge terms and conditions of work.

These labour market changes have meant that a second area where sociologists have been especially active – the study of workplace relations – has also altered to some extent. Much of the research on workplace relations that is concerned to reveal a rich world of meaning (Cornfield and Hodson 2002: 6) has involved ethnographic case studies of particular occupations and workplaces. These initially focused on male workers, including classic studies of manual occupations, including fishermen (Tunstall 1962), lorry drivers (Hollowell 1968) and manufacturing and processing plants (Beynon 1973; Burawoy 1979; Collinson 1992; Nichols and Beynon 1977), but from the 1970s also focusing on the experience of women factory workers (Cavendish 1982; Pollert 1981; Westwood 1984).

11

Following Braverman (1974), many were influenced by the debate over the reworkings of Marx's concept of the labour process, i.e. the processes of production which transform raw materials, through the application of human labour, tools and machinery, into use values that can be sold on the market as commodities (Thompson 1989: xv). According to this way of thinking, the labour process has a dual character, since the concrete labour processes through which specific goods are made and particular types of services provided are shaped by the capitalist labour process which seeks to turn labour into profit. In the light of the sectoral shifts noted above, ethnographic study has had to be extended by new research on the organisation of work in expanding sectors, for instance the hospitality industry, retail work, knowledge work and cultural production, and the new roles, relationships and identities these kinds of work may involve (Adkins 1995; Black 2004; Kunda 1992; Foner 1994; Lash and Urry 1994; Macdonald and Sirianni 1996; Pettinger 2004). There have also been important contributions by women journalists (Ehrenreich 2001; Toynbee 2003) who have sought to capture the experience of workers in feminised, low-wage personal services and sales work by taking low-paid jobs themselves and writing about their experiences. But it has to be said that the direction of ethnographic research still lags behind the sectoral shifts in the location of paid work.

Much of the research on paid work tends to be integrated by taking presumed commonalities in the employment relation – the relation between capital and labour, employers and workers – as its starting point, and focuses on how the labour processes involved in producing diverse goods and services shape (and are in turn shaped by) conflicts of interest between employers' perceived interests (for instance, increasing profits, saving costs, controlling or monitoring workers' input, marketing considerations) and by what workers define as theirs (e.g. financial rewards, security of employment, autonomy and self-esteem). However, research increasingly draws on new theoretical frameworks that focus on the subjectivity of the worker, said to be missing from labour process analysis (Newton 1999; Sturdy and Fineman 2001), or at least broadens the interest in worker's consent or compliance to encompass with more precision? 'how corporate power and worker subjectivity intersect within social relations of organisational domination' (Fleming and Spicer 2003: 158; see also Kunda 1992). In fact, some critics argue that theorists influenced by the work of Foucault (see below) have been so preoccupied with the construction of worker identity and subjectivity that new approaches present a picture in which 'the labour process is just part of the scenery' rather than integral to the analysis (Thompson and Ackroyd 1995: 627, cited in Newton 1999: 425; West and Austrin 2002).

The sociology of employment increasingly overlaps with a third focus, the study of organisations, i.e. 'the bureaucracies that employ workers in many occupations, organise them in hierarchies and shape movement between them' (Halford et al. 1997: 3). Aspects of the organisational context within which work is undertaken are considered so important that this type of research has tended to push an earlier tradition, which focused on occupations as the building blocks of the division of labour, to the background. The biggest employers include not only private sector corporations but also public utilities and public services – the NHS is the largest employer in Europe (Culley 2001). The changing shape of organisation has become a particular concern; increasingly large organisations do not employ people directly, but obtain labour input through a variety of inter-firm contractual arrangements, such as franchising, subcontracting, reliance on temporary staff agencies and the use of project management consultants. Under such conditions the responsibilities of employers to employees, and employees to employers, become blurred, making it even more necessary to link studies of the employment relationship and organisational analysis (Marchington et al. 2005).

Organisational theorists have been concerned with non-manual employ-ment rather more than sociologists of work, especially with management as itself an employment niche and managers as a type of worker. Such research is frequently to be found in what is sometimes termed Critical Management Studies (Alvesson and Willmott 1992), which takes a more critical view of management neutrality and rationality than much applied research. Because most large organisations are divided by gradations in formal and informal access to the exercise of power, it tends to operate with a less binary model of power than those models of paid work focusing on the relations between employers and employees. It has tended to draw on postmodernist construc-tions of the plasticity of subjectivity and the mobility of power more than deterministic traditions in the sociology of work privileging structural con-straints on the social relations between groups (Fleming and Spicer 2003).

Feminist interventions have contributed to all these developments in the sociology of work and organisation. Early initiatives were concerned with explaining the then segregation of women into a narrow band of lower-level jobs in manufacturing and services (Hartmann 1979), seeing women's position in the labour market as determined by macro-systems, like capitalism and patriarchy, that were beyond their control. Feminist research also made a big contribution to workplace studies, as noted above, especially the importance of non-economic factors in the relations between workers and between work-ers and employers. Later accounts are more influenced by the poststruc-turalist focus on 'the cultural [re]production of gendered identities through practices enacted in the workplace' (Smith and Gottfried 1996: 13), thereby highlighting the role of women's own practices in the sex-typing of occupa-tions (Andermahr et al. 2000: 86–7). They have also paid special attention to the discourses of gender neutrality that obscure the unwritten, gendered assumptions of bureaucratic organisations (Smith and Gottfried 1996: 12).

Crossing these successive developments, however, has been a continuing interest in the relation between paid and unpaid work, production and repro-duction, and public and private spheres. For instance, when the women jour-nalists mentioned above undertook their studies of low-paid work, they each not only took a series of low-paid jobs themselves but attempted to set up a home and live on their earnings. Although the present volume has been unable to give the attention to unpaid work I would have liked, it does try to incorporate the paid work done in private homes (see Chapter 7) to a much greater extent than is normally the case in the sociology of employment. The paid care work now undertaken in private homes is only one example of the reconfiguration of the interconnections and overlap between work activities previously divided between paid and unpaid work or formal and informal sectors (Pettinger et al. 2006).

Bodies are not really new to studies of work, but for many reasons have been obscured till recent years. Marx, whose understanding of labour was central to the trajectory of radical approaches in the sociology of work, insisted on the mutually constitutive relationship between the body and work: bodies are both the source of labour and themselves its product. Marx saw the artefacts human beings create as 'the memorialisation' of embodied work, and the tools, land and material objects with which we labour as extensions or 'prolongations' of the worker's body (Scarry 1985: 247). 'Man' remakes his body through labour (which is therefore also a kind of artefact), providing himself with sustenance and other use-values with which to renew his body. Weber, too,who is as important to the study of organisation as Marx is to the labour relation, gave importance to the embodiment of social actors in his analysis of charisma as a form of authority. However, each of these founding fathers also recognised that in modern societies the corporeality of the worker (or members of organisations, in the case of Weber) has become less evident. Weber argued that in modern societies charismatic authority was usually superseded by impersonal bureaucratic authority, vested in the office rather than the person, while Marx stressed that the incorporation in production of the labour of fragile and feeling human bodies is obscured under capitalism, by being turned into a commodity. Moreover, in so far as consumer and producer are linked only by the market, they can remain oblivious to each other's existence as embodied beings.

The relative absence of the body from most studies of work is no doubt also due to the fact that most of the activities which directly service the body and the spaces it inhabits, to use Smith's (1988) phrase, have historically been provided by servants or slaves, or by women in their roles as wives and mothers, i.e. outside the labour market and not publicly visible as work at all. Moreover, in so far as such work is reproductive, it has not been seen as appropriating nature by transforming it through the use of human labour. A number of shifts in employment, including the entry of women into work in large-scale organisations, the commercialisation of reproductive work, the focus on worker–customer interaction, the rise of new methods for monitoring work output, and the emergence of new work-based health hazards, have made some sociologists more conscious of the need to attend to the corporeality of workers.

A phenomenological analysis of the body's 'disappearance' from everyday consciousness is also relevant to understanding its disappearance from the labour process, even when the body is patently involved, as in 'manual labour'. For instance, building on the work of Merleau-Ponty (1962), Leder argues that although the body is 'the most abiding and inescapable presence in our lives', it is also characterised by absence: 'it is rarely the thematic object of attention' (Leder 1990: 1). The disappearance of the various parts and sense modalities of the body are structured differently, Leder argues, and our conscious awareness of even our arms and legs, which are so central to human perception and motility, is limited. Instrumental activity, including labour, evokes awareness mainly of targets outside ourselves rather than the body from which we experience. To use a simple example, the archer concentrating on the bull's-eye has little conscious awareness of his eye focusing on it or his arm holding the bow. The body only makes its 'dys-appearance', according to Leder, through pain, discomfort, the awareness of disability, or when a person becomes conscious of the scrutiny of other people. This might help to explain why, until recently, consideration of the physical body in work was restricted mainly to consideration of work-related injury and ill health. Moreover, questions regarding injury and impairment have been constructed mainly as technical questions, rather than being integrated into the main currents in the sociology of work (Williams 1993), reflecting the long-standing identification of the body with scientific descriptions of its anatomical and functional properties (Leder 1990: 5).

However, as discussed below, Leder's view of embodied experience may be unduly universalistic. It may be insufficiently gendered, for instance, taking little cognisance of differences between men's and women's relation to bodily movements, as discussed below. (Women using a bow-and-arrow may have a different experience than men, for instance.) Moreover, although it is true that the heightened consciousness of one's own body that people experience while learning new skills may tend to disappear once such skills become automatic, this is not only because skills become incorporated, as Leder suggests, but also because many tacit skills, including physical strength, are so rarely credentialised that they disappear from social analysis and come to appear as entirely natural abilities.

In seeking to convert the body in the workplace from a relatively unremarked 'absent presence' (Turner 1984) to an acknowledged aspect of the construction and experience of paid work, we must take account of the body's many guises. As I discuss further below, the sociology of the body and embodiment persistently expresses uncertainty as to what the body really is or its relation to the sense of self (Howson 2004). As Terry Eagleton (1993: 7) put it, 'It is not quite true that I have a body, and not quite true that I am one either.' In different contexts we feel ourselves as fully embodied subjects, in others we become more conscious of having a body with which we do not fully identity or which confronts us with its Otherness. Bodies are physical entities, organisms located in biological and physiological processes, symbolic objects transformed by culture and represented by images of various kinds, and, *pace* Merleau-Ponty (1962), our way of knowing the world.

Where the body is present in the sociology of work, as it has become in recent years, it has been brought into view in particular ways, and these will be discussed in detail in the course of this book. For instance, as we shall see in Chapter 3, the body was at least a minor feature of some studies of male manual work, which celebrated the strength, skill and masculine presence of the male working body. More recently a focus on the body as an explicit target of sociological interest has been associated with the poststructuralist analysis of bodies, subjects and organisations as discursive constructs. This has led in two quite distinct directions, emphasising, on the one hand, the historical construction of the worker's passified, 'docile body' (Foucault 1991; Schatzki and Natter 1996b; Bahnisch 2000) and, on the other, highlighting the disruptive potential of unruly bodily pleasures, excess and play as forms of resistance (Brewis and Linstead 2000; Burrell 1992; Hassard et al. 2000; Holliday and Hassard 2001; Linstead and Brewis 2004). A very few analysts, such as Witz et al. (2003) and Black (2004), also make use of the work of Pierre Bourdieu, discussed below. But within the sociology of work there has been relatively little explicit reference to phenomenological approaches, like Leder's (1990), that are concerned with how it feels to be embodied, or to the use of the senses in employment, such as Reinarz's (2003) historical commentary on the use of the sense of smell in work.

Feminist scholars, who have been among the first to address questions about the body in work (Acker 1990; Adkins 1992; Cockburn 1986; Halford et al. 1997), relate their investigations to a range of different theoretical traditions, including materialist feminism and organisational studies. But as we shall see in the next section of this chapter, while the apprehension of the body in the sociology of work is still rather partial, it goes a lot further in considering embodiment than the sociology of the body has gone in considering employment.

The sociology of the body

In thinking about the scope of the sociology of the body, I want to start slightly sideways, noting a fictional short story by Juliet Brown (1991), in part because it helps to make evident some of the everyday assumptions about the body with which sociologists are concerned. 'Beauty' tells the story of Hazel, a woman who works as a beautician in an American neighbourhood salon. Her boss, Don, decides to take the salon upmarket, to make it more stylish, and that includes both décor and staff. The homey workstations crowded with family snapshots are due to be replaced by slate grey modular structures. Hazel herself is called to the salon for a public makeover to publicise the shop's new image. Compelled to accept the constraints of normative femininity in order to keep her job, over the course of a week she joins a gym, is given a reducing diet, a new hairdo, new clothes and a new face. The story ends with Hazel caught outdoors in the exhilaration of a sudden downpour: while she stands looking at herself mirrored in a shop window the rain washes away the traces of hairspray and make-up, leaving, one is led to assume, Hazel in her 'natural' authentic state. Hazel consoles herself that despite the trials of conforming, 'at weekends, at least, this body was hers' (1991: 177).

This story is the only piece in the three-volume collection on the body published as issues of the *Michigan Quarterly Review* in 1991 that deals with paid work, and then only by linking Hazel's problems as a paid worker to the politics of women's appearance more generally. Although the *Quarterly* concentrates on cultural critique, this lack of interest in experiences of embodiment characteristic of paid work is typical of the sociology of the body too. For instance, since its inception in 1995, the British journal *Body and Society* has published only two articles dealing with paid work (Bahnisch, 2000; Valentine 2002). Classic texts in the sociology of the body, like Burkitt (1999), Shilling (1993), Turner (1984) and Williams and Bendelow (1998) say almost nothing about paid work either. Of the many collections of articles in the sociology of the body (Fraser and Greco 2004 as a recent example), until this year only two (Hancock et al. 2000 and Schatzki and Natter 1996a) had included any mention of the embodied experience of the workplace. The same is true of feminist classics, compendia and textbooks, such as Brook (1999), Evans and Lee (2002), Grosz (1994), Jaggar and Bordo (1989), Price and Shildrick (1999), or Weitz (1998, republished 2003). In fact, it is striking that the phrase 'body work' tends to refer to techniques of the self, including dieting, exercise or the consumption of services like cosmetic surgery or other beauty treatments (e.g. Black 2004; Gimlin 2002; Howson 2004) and is rarely used to refer to work by paid workers on others' bodies. While the situation is improving (for instance the publications of Shilling (2005), which includes a chapter on 'working bodies' and the volume of essays edited by Morgan and Brandth (2005)), we have to be careful that we do not simply tack work and employment onto existing approaches in the sociology of the body but consider how far its concepts and agenda might need revising.

The neglect of paid work in the sociology of the body has any number of sources. It is, of course, part of the wider 'cultural turn' in sociology and feminism, the focus on 'words not things', the association of identity with consumption rather than production, and a view of the body as the product of consumer choice (Barrett 1991; Featherstone et al. 1991; Giddens 1991). Feminist theory has in part contributed to, as well as reflected, this trend, having argued that the 'production paradigm' excluded many of the issues of most concern to women (Andermahr et al. 2000). Before returning to this absence of work in the sociology of the body, however, I want to sketch, again in the broadest manner, what I see as its three main concerns.

The first of these is the relation between body and society. Almost invariably sociologists of the body reject the model of the body implicit in the short story summarised above, which rests on what Shilling (1993) calls a 'naturalistic' view of the body, one that presumes a pre-social body that exists outside the power relations that impact on it. Instead, for most social theorists, 'individuals and their identities are constituted through the social shaping of bodies' (Schatzki and Natter 1996b: 2). As John O'Neill (1985: 24) puts it, 'we have – we must have – society in our bones' (cited by Schatzki and Natter 1996b: 2). However, theorists vary between those social constructionists who see the body as produced by, contained within, and struggling to exceed discourse and others who, while rejecting naturalistic views of the body, have been concerned to bring the flesh-and-blood prereflexive body (malleable and subject to power though it is) into the picture of embodiment (Williams and Bendelow 1998). Indeed, recently there has been renewed debate over whether we should give more weight to the 'biological body' (Birke 2000; Newton 2003; Williams 2003), including by some disability theorists concerned that the social model of disability does not preclude some attention to physical impairment (Thomas 2002), suggesting that there are more limits to the plasticity of the body than much poststructuralist theory implies.

Underlying the debate about the social shaping of bodily being is the longstanding opposition between structure and agency that has dogged the history of sociology, and that is brought into play once again with the introduction of 'the body'. Sociologists who are most concerned with the defence of agency, against the determination of action/actors/practices by social structures, might well be concerned that the 'society in our bones' thesis may undermine human agency. Sociologists of the body have usually been concerned to pre-empt this line of criticism, in part by deconstructing the structure/agency opposition, arguing that structure is a function of agential practices that are largely habitual. This does not necessarily satisfy the critics, who argue that 'practice' that is a function of institutional structures and instituted 'practical schemas' learned and embodied in childhood secures only the appearance of agency. Of the theorists I now want to introduce, both Foucault (in his early writings) and Bourdieu have been the focus of this 'anxiety over agency'. On the other hand, the third influential sociologist of the body considered here, Erving Goffman, has been accused of 'bending the stick' too far in the opposite direction and, through the idea of the performance of the self (Goffman 1969), exaggerating the extent of individual agency and underestimating the determination of structure.

Probably the single most influential figure in the sociology of the body has been Michel Foucault. This is because his theorisation of the management of social life sees power targeting the individual primarily through their body. Whereas Marx identified the key moment in the constitution of society as the appropriation of 'labour power', Foucault's focus was what he called 'biopower': the increasingly rationalised management of biological matter through technologies of surveillance, expert knowledges and corrective measures (Foucault 1979). Much of Foucault's early work is concerned with the operation of technologies that dominate the individual through the construction of a 'docile body', a passified object of regulation and surveillance (Foucault 1991). For Foucault, however, docility does not equal weakness. In taking hold of the body, power is productive rather than repressive in its effects, working through individuals rather than against them (Garland 1990). One of Foucault's (1991) examples is the training of the soldier, especially the processes whereby the loutish, loose-limbed lad is reshaped through the disciplinary regime of boot camp. Although subjected to power, by coming to act as a part of a unified troop, his capacities are enhanced rather than attenuated. For Foucualt, therefore, in modern societies the exercise of power does not repress or take power away, it is not what is called a 'zero-sum game'.

In Foucault's later work, he attempted to make room for conceptualising resistance to power through his notion of embodied 'practices of the self', through which the subject constitutes himself, attributing therefore 'a certain degree of autonomy and independence to the way in which individuals act' (McNay 1992: 61). However, McNay (1999) argues that because Foucault did not attempt to integrate his earlier thoughts on biopower with later work on the practices of self, he never considers the obstacles to the transformation of the self, including the materiality of the body.

A second, increasingly influential theorist of the relation between the body and the social order is Pierre Bourdieu (2001, 1990a; Bourdieu and

Wacquant 1992). Bourdieu's approach is synthetic. It is influenced by the structuralism of Claude Lévi-Strauss in particular, but his sociology is equally deeply influenced by Merleau-Ponty, Sartre, phenomenology and existentialism. He attempts to carve out a position that avoids both structuralism and voluntarism, based on a reconceptualisation of 'the self' through the concept of *habitus*. This concept puts the body at the centre of the negotiation of structure and agency, the social and the individual. Bourdieu says that 'To speak of habitus is to assert that the individual, even the person, the subjective, is social, collective. Habitus is socialized subjectivity' (Bourdieu and Wacquant 1992: 126).

As compared to Foucualt's focus on knowledge/power, Bourdieu proposes a prediscursive inscription of social structures into bodies' tacit, practical sense. For Bourdieu the social is indeed 'in the bones', or, rather, in the habitus, the structured, structuring dispositions that frame bodily conduct, hexis, or bodily stance, bodily skills and competence, the embodied aspects of language in speech habits, vocabulary, accent and so on. Habitus changes as individuals find their place, and as they subsequently move across the social field.

The key resources in this development of the social actor in social space Bourdieu conceptualises as 'capitals', the principal being economic, social and cultural capitals. It is the 'capital holdings' of the primary social group in which the child is socialised, with social class taking priority, that determine the child's initial capital holdings as his/her habitus is formed. Not only does this framework, very schematically presented here, suggest how society can be 'in the body' without being imposed upon it, it also connects the cultural dimension of contemporary social life, on which many social theorists increasingly focus, to the economic order in a non-reductionist way. Bourdieu also recognises that habitus is gendered. Although he had some interesting things to say from time to time, he did not focus specifically on the gendered habitus until his essay 'La domination masculine' (Bourdieu 1990b), developed into a short book in 2001. His approach to embodiment has been explored in a number of ways by feminists, for example Adkins and Skeggs (2004), Lovell (2000), McNay (1999), Moi (1999) and Skeggs (1997).

The third of the numerous theoretical initiatives linking the body and society that I wish to introduce (see especially Shilling (1993) and Williams and Bendelow (1998) for a much fuller account) is Erving Goffman, who saw people's management of their bodies as a necessary and constitutive element in the maintenance of social order (Crossley 1995). For Goffman the body 'plays an essential role in mediating the relationship between people's self-identity and social identity' (Shilling 1993: 82–3); individuals have to manage the social meanings of their individual embodiment, such as the stigma of disability, and anticipate and repair social infractions of polite interaction that would otherwise risk the continued respect of others (Goffman 1972). Whereas a theorist like Norbert Elias (1978 [1939]) had explored the historical emergence of the 'civilised', bounded body in the rituals that came to govern behaviour in the feudal court, Goffman was more interested in deciphering the 'feeling rules' demanded by social interactions of contemporary social actors and the effort people made to conform to them through 'face work' (Goffman 1969) and, by implication, 'body work' (Shilling 1993: 84). However, while Goffman sees social actors as mediating social identities through embodied performances, they do not bring them into existence through their activity, a view sometimes associated with the notion of performativity later advanced by the poststructuralist feminist theorist Judith Butler (1993, 1991, 1990). Rather, Williams and Bendelow (1998: 60) consider Goffman as strikingly similar to Bourdieu in seeing social structures gearing into the interactional order through the body, with symbols of class status 'literally embodied and enacted during routine social interactions'.

As noted above, critics of poststructuralist theorists – Archer (2000, 1988) being a foremost example – identify the risk of completely collapsing structures and actors, leaving too little room for conscious choice, resistance or even conscious alliance with power. The danger is a double one, however. The danger in structuralism of determinism, in which the actor is 'oversocialised', is all the more pressing when the social order is embedded in the body, so that what the actor does 'freely' simply reproduces social structures. But there is a matching danger in the emphasis on agency, of underestimating 'society in the bones'. Judith Butler's undermining of bodily identities through the concept of performativity has been frequently subject to this latter critique.

We need to make a few distinctions, therefore, between (a) the agency that everyone has, except in the most extreme conditions, however curtailed and constrained it may be; (b) resistance, or agency exercised against the grain of lines of domination; and (c) progressive social transformation. Foucault, Bourdieu and Goffman all recognise the agency of social actors, but agency is not the same thing as resistance – it may be, as some critics have pointed out, an agency that is allied with power. Secondly, concepts such as Bourdieu's habitus in no way preclude resistance; Bourdieu makes it explicit that 'there exist dispositions to resist' (Bourdieu and Wacquant 1992: 81). But he goes on to say that there are specific conditions under which these dispositions 'are socially constituted, effectively triggered and rendered politically efficient' (ibid.). This does not snatch back the agency that is vested in habitus, but guards against the overly optimistic habit of seeking resistance everywhere among the dominated and then assuming that it necessarily presages social transformation. It also suggests that transformative possibilities are not evenly distributed across social fields, being perhaps more available in the domain of sexuality and gender, as Harvey (1998) argues, than in the labour process.

The second main theme in the sociology of the body is the relationship between body and self, which is particularly prominent in Goffman's (1969, 1963) conception of the presentation of self in everyday life as well as his conceptualisation of stigma. Foucault's concern in his later work with the production of subjects through their 'practices of the self' could also be seen as an example. However, much contemporary scholarship would reject the dualism involved in setting up the issue in terms of an interaction or relation between the body and self.

The critique of body–self dualism, like the distinction between mind and body, often draws, like Bourdieu, on the phenomenology of Merleau-Ponty (1962), who rejected the Cartesian construct of the mind and body as separate or even interacting systems (Crossley 2001 and Leder 1990 are particularly useful accounts). For Descartes the self is equated with the mind ('I think therefore I am'), because, he argued, only the mind could be conscious of itself, i.e. is able to know what it thinks, whereas the body is part of the external world of objects (Crossley 2001: 10). For Merleau-Ponty, in contrast, 'our bodies are our way of being in and experiencing the world', not 'objects of experience' but rather 'our very means of experiencing' (Crossley 2001: 16). Hence, as Wacquant says of Bourdieu's anti-dualist conception, corporeality is intrinsic to the contact between the subject and the world (Bourdieu and Wacquant 1992: 20).

Williams and Bendelow (1998), like many others, reject what they see as an impoverished view of subjectivity associated with mind–body dualism. Critics argue that it reduces the body to a living corpse (Leder 1990), for instance, or to meat, or constructs the body as the slimy site of dangerous desires of the flesh from which the objective mind struggles to escape (Williams and Bendelow 1998: 1). Of course, as Crossley (2001) points out, we can (and do) sometimes treat our bodies as objects, or attempt to distance ourselves from them, but this will still be part of our embodied experience, not something outside it. In the same vein, Williams and Bendelow (1998) argue that we should distinguish between dualism as an ideology, which legitimates the mind–body divide as natural, rational and unconditional, and the concept of duality, which would enable us to explore and understand different ways in which we experience ourselves as embodied subjects. The latter might include pain or illness, for instance – or the different ways the self–body relation is imagined, experienced and shaped among different groups and at different times. Ultimately, however, they look forward to a stage at which we can transcend mind-body duality, too, 'through a unifying notion of the lived, experiential, body – an active, expressive, 'mindful' form of embodiment' (Williams and Bendelow 1998: 209). However – and I shall return to this point below – it is not really clear how this might come about, or how it relates to the social practices in which long-term dispositions (including, presumably, ways of experiencing the mind–body relation) are sedimented.

A third concern in the sociology of the body, the relationship between the body and gender, crosses the other two foci already noted. Although the body has always been a central political concern of feminist campaigns around women's health and fertility, sexual violence and other aspects of body/ politics, much of feminists' recent scholarly work has argued that any attempt to understand and transform the power relations of gender has to rethink the relation between gender and the physical, sexed body. Many feminists have followed Foucault in giving particular attention to the regulatory discourses and mechanisms that construct and passify the female body (Bartky 1990; Bordo 1990a, 1990b; Smart 1992). Others, like Judith Butler, argue that although we perceive bodies through the lens of gender, gender is troubled by the ultimately rather shaky basis which bodies provide for it. Whereas these theorists follow Foucault's interest in the historical and discursive construction of bodies, other feminists have been more interested in phenomenological approaches and interpersonal contexts, but taking the female body as their model of embodiment. For instance, in her path-breaking essay 'Throwing like a Girl', philosopher Iris Young analysed gender differences in the 'basic modalities of feminine body comportment, manner of moving and relations in space' (Young 1990: 143). Following Merleau-Ponty, she points to the 'ordinary purposive orientation of the body as whole towards things and its environment that initially defines the relation of a subject to its world' (ibid.). Still others, noted above, are exploring the evolution of the gendered habitus through dialogue with Bourdieusian concepts.

The main drift in feminist philosophy of the body and embodiment is summarised in Andermahr et al. (2000), who see it as rejecting the sexually undifferentiated body of Western theory as implicitly male. Instead it develops its understanding of the relation between subjectivity, gender and sex through the deconstruction of the dualisms of Western discourse in which the body is embedded in binary oppositions (Grosz 1994). Feminists argue that such dualisms are deeply gendered, in the sense that one half of each dichotomy is identified with the male self (mind, culture, rationality) and the other with the female Other (body, nature, emotionality). Williams and Bendelow (1998) are effectively following one of the main directions in feminist thought by refusing to associate subjectivity with mind as against body. Corporeal feminists go even further, though, in seeing (sexed) corporeality as the bedrock of social identity and subjectivity. Unlike the short story outlined above, for instance, which seems to see femininity as laid down over one's authentic self, corporeal feminists build on the notion of the lived, sexed body as experienced 'from the inside' (Grosz 1994).

The major foci of corporeal feminists are the embodied experiences – sexual pleasure, pregnancy and childbirth – most intimately linked to sexual difference. Drawing on French feminists like Kristeva, Cixous and Irigaray (see especially Grosz 1989), they reject the vision of the unified subject constructed by mainstream philosophy as a projection of the experience of male embodiment. Instead, pregnancy challenges the division between immanence (being) and transcendence (transformation and control) (Battersby 1997, 1989; Young 1990), while women's experience of multiple sites of sexual pleasure can form the basis of an alternative libidinal economy which they see as challenging our containment in and by the phallic male logos, or language. In particular, they point to Irigaray's (1991) revaluation of the open, leaky body rejected by the masculine ideal, and the reclamation of the abject that transgresses the boundaries installed by Western thought. Corporeal feminism therefore emphasises 'fluid boundaries, connection rather than separation, interdependence rather than autonomy' (Andermahr et al. 2000). The rejection of firm boundaries dividing the self from its environment can also be seen in Haraway's (1991) rejection of the boundaries between the human and the animal, the organic and inorganic.

We are now in a position to consider more fully the absence of work in the sociology of the body. The approaches outlined above provide a gamut of ideas through which to explore the body/work nexus, but their application is not easy, since none brings work or employment into view as a central concern. In the first place, none of the key influences is particularly interested in the workplace as a distinctive environment. For instance, Goffman drew his examples from a wide range of encounters, including the workplace, but used them to illustrate the skill required for the performance and interpretation of embodied symbolic interaction across the institutions of public life. Similarly, while Merleau-Ponty's phenomenology of instrumental activity could be applied to the workplace, this could be at the cost of losing any distinction between the types of constraints (and the shaping of experience) that are associated with remunerated employment as compared to unpaid activities. Bourdieu, too, despite his identification of the relevance of embodied capitals to social domination, is not particularly interested in tracing the contribution employment makes to the accumulation of capitals by individuals and groups. And while Foucault recognised the workplace as one of the domains in which power is exercised (as shown in his analysis of the surveillance made possible by the invention of the modern factory), its mechanisms of power were not seen as different from those of other disciplinary institutions of modern society. Moreover, although Foucault says that power always implies resistance, because he sees it located in discourses it is often difficult to 'see' human agents, or the interactions between social actors, such as employers and employees, who are conceptualised as 'nodes' through which power passes in a 'capillary' fashion. As Bell (1993: 27) says, albeit in quite a different context, Foucault considers individuals in relation to discourses, 'but not in relation to each other; the interaction between people . . . does not seem to be there'.

While appreciating the richer view of subjectivity provided by anti-dualist perspectives on the body–self relation, there is a problem, I would argue, in attempting to develop anti-dualist perspectives that ignore the embeddedness of dualism in the timetables, policies and contracts that structure everyday life, including those of paid employment. Until anti-dualist perspectives take on board the fact that, as journalist Madeleine Bunting (2005: 17) says, 'For most people in white-collar jobs for eight hours a day, the office is where they experience most directly other people's power over their lives', they will not be able to recognise the extent to which dualism is reproduced, day by day, in the heart of our everyday experiences as embodied agents. One can only suspect that this is one of the reasons why employment seems to be so studiously avoided as an area of concern. Taking employment on board would mean recognising that challenging mind–body dualism means taking on board the other dualisms that structure social life and pervade the workplace.

Dualisms do not just pervade but organise working life, beginning with the taken for granted distinction between manual and mental labour and the pay differentials, working conditions and status hierarchies that distinguish between them. Moreover, 'making workers' (Peck 1996) is itself a complex, contradictory process, seeking to treat workers as commodities like any other work objects, on the one hand, but forced to recognise labour's unique social character on the other. Although many of us may enjoy work and throw ourselves into it willingly, it is also true that firms and other workplace organisations instrumentalise our capacities for their own ends, and in order to make a go of it we learn to instrumentalise (parts of) ourselves too. The long-standing model of the labour market that dominates economic and managerial thinking treats capacity to work as effort that can be exchanged for a salary or wage, and many people find that they can only defend themselves against assaults on the self by deploying dualistic conceptions in their own defence. It is not only that capitalism alienates workers from the product of their labour, they may develop a divided sense of self as a survival strategy (Collinson 2003). Hazel, for instance, in the short story discussed above, is a good example of someone whose response to the power of her employer is to treat her own body as an object, separate from herself, at least some of the time.

Locating a sense of self outside of and in contrast to one's role as a worker, while not quite the same as the distinction between mind and body, overlaps with it in everyday experience, because the mind–body distinction is such an important idiom for talking about alienating experiences ('I was there, but my mind wasn't really in it'). Manual workers talk of being able to do their jobs with their hands, while letting their minds roam freely; knowledge workers may in contrast seek to defend their sense of self through hidden tattoos and piercings, while displaying apparent commitment to organisational goals in what they say. And many people speak of their resentment of the greedy workplace demanding their loyalty 'body and soul' (Baxter and Hughes 2004). In other words we should recognise that dualism may be so intractable not only because of its centrality in Western discourse, but because it is imposed on us as workers and even becomes a feature of the reverse discourses, to use Foucault's term, through which much resistance to power is expressed.

However, it is possible that shifts in work cultures are changing the relation between work and self. It is increasingly argued that employers no longer allow the Hazels of this world their 'own' bodies even at the weekend, expecting them instead to manage their embodiment with work in mind, a move towards the involvement of the 'whole person' in work (Bunting 2004; Fleming and Spicer 2004; Thrift 2005; Warhurst and Thompson 1998). Maybe, therefore, we need to question whether the blurring of binary boundaries between self and others, for instance, or mind and body, is as radical as some imagine. As this book will attempt to show, the role of different kinds of boundaries, and the interests their maintenance or dispersal may serve, is one area in which the study of employment can make a necessary contribution to the sociology of the body.

Corporeal feminism may have much to offer the sociology of work and employment in so far as it challenges many of the assumptions about workers' interests and self-understandings, which are arguably constructed around a not-so-implicitly male body and take for granted autonomy as a universal criteria on which to evaluate jobs and their rewards. Feminism has long challenged the boundaries assumed by some workers and trades unions, for instance the assumption that 'work' is separated, temporally and spatially, from the private sphere of the home. Corporeal feminism could go even further, though, in identifying the assumptions about the body built into the organisation of paid work. There are hints of this, for instance, in Kahn's (1989) explicit contrast between the temporality of the breast-feeding mother and the industrial time of paid employment. But in most cases writers would rather explore 'women's time' (Kristeva 1989) outside the tempo of the wider society. So they are never forced to confront the constraints that the requirements of the labour market, as presently constituted, present to the fluidity and libidinal economy they seek.

The exception is in the sociology of health and healing, where the interaction with people's bodies is sometimes considered within an institutional context. As compared to the discussion of caring by other postmodernists influenced by the work of Deleuze and Guattari, such as Fox (1999), which makes little attempt to consider the organisational and financial considerations that structure caring in bureaucratically organised and/or profit-oriented settings, some feminist researchers influenced by corporeal feminism have given more weight to the institutional contexts in which caring takes place (Chatterji et al. 1998; Parker 1997). But while they privilege the social relationships that are associated with tactile care, they may pay scant attention to what can replace the professional and other boundaries that have seemed to offer the care worker some protection against emotional and physical exhaustion, injury and exploitation (Menzies-Lyth 1998).

One final resource for considering the body/work relation that we need to consider is new developments in political economy. These give much more emphasis to the underlying structuration of social life by economic relation than any of the perspectives noted above. Yet political economy resembles in a surprising way the sociology of the body developed by Bourdieu in so far as it follows Marx's concern not just with the body as a source of labour, but also with the body as the product or 'artefact' of labour. This conception of what might be called the 'worked on' body is thus a common thread.

Towards a political economy of the body

So far I have been making the case for, on the one hand, incorporating work and employment within the sociology of the body, and, on the other, identifying work and employment as a crucial domain that studies of the relationship between corporeality and subjectivity need to take on board. A third literature to draw on in bridging the gap between these two fields is that of largely American scholars who have begun to develop a political economy of the body that takes more account of the economic organisation of society than has so far been the case in the sociology of the body in Britain, even though most do not give as much attention to employment relations as one might like (for example, Brown 2003; Ebert 1996; Harvey 1998, 1989; Haraway 1991; Harvey and Haraway 1995; Lowe 1995). As Schatzki and Natter put it in the introduction to essays discussed in detail in Chapter 3, they are attempting to relate the consolidation of 'bodies sociopolitical' to the production of sociocultural bodies 'cut to certain specifications' (1996b: 2). Other commentators, especially Harvey (1998, 1989) and Lowe (1995), draw on Marxist traditions, in particular the Regulation School developed by Aglietta (1979) and Lipietz (1987), which highlights the interdependence of production and reproduction under Fordist and post-Fordist 'regimes of accumulation'. Rather than rejecting outright the emphasis on consumption that currently dominates academic constructions of the body, they attempt to understand it in the context of broader changes in the mode of capitalist accumulation.

Harvey's (1990) analysis of the concordance between mass production, standardised consumer products and practices and the family-based household that typified the accumulation regime of the Fordist era, and its succession by a more individualised, diversified regime of flexible accumulation, is frequently cited. In a later essay that should be better known, Harvey (1998) explores the implications of 'the body as an accumulation strategy' (a phrase borrowed from feminist theorist Donna Haraway (Harvey and Haraway 1995)) for the politics of the body. While bemoaning the failure of contemporary social theory to consider Marx's writings on embodiment, Harvey draws on an eclectic mix of scholars whom he sees as relevant to analyses of capitalist accumulation 'in the deepest sense' (1998: 401), including Butler and Haraway as well as Foucault and Bourdieu.

Rather than rejecting the contemporary focus on the body, Harvey recognises that the lived body has become the 'one referent apart from all the other destabilized referents' (Lowe 1995: 14): the measure of all things. However, rather than highlighting its potential to signify resistance to social determination, as Butler argued, he stresses that it too is subject to social construction, making it a highly contested reference point. Precisely because it is open, unfinished, malleable and relational, the body is not irreduceably there in a final sense. Rather, being porous to its environment, its performative practices 'are not independent of the technological, physical, social and economic environment' or the representational practices of the wider society. To return to the body is therefore to return to a body shaped by the very processes it rebels against (Harvey 1998: 404) – an insight, incidentally, very much in accord with Bourdieu.

Harvey argues that Marx provided a still relevant analysis of how bodies are socially produced, through his concept of variable capital. Bodies are inserted into the circulation of variable capital, labour power being abstracted from them in return for a wage that allows for the purchase of (capitalist produced) goods to survive. The exigencies of capitalist production push the working body to the limit in contradictory ways, capacities of the human body being reinvented as well as extinguished. The formation of the body under capitalism does not stop with production, however, but extends also to its consumption, which we should be wary of seeing as a domain of transgressive performativity in which resistance to power takes place. Although with money to spend the worker is free to spend it as s/he likes, consumption is, as Marx put it, as much an aspect of capital 'as the lifeless instruments of labour are' (Harvey 1998: 211). The social relations of consumption take the form of lifestyle, neither insignificant nor purely personal, but as much a battleground under capitalism as the sphere of production. They involve not only the reproduction of worker as the carrier of the capacity to work, i.e. of labour power, but also the maintenance of status-conferring embodied capital in the Bourdieusian sense.

In developing a framework for understanding the relationship between capital accumulation and the body at the present juncture, it seems to me one could push this argument even further. Seeing the body as the focus of an accumulation strategy might also infer that 'new bodies' - e.g. new bodily needs and new uses for the body and body parts - are produced by and taken hold of by capital's drive for profits. As an entrepreneur who had invented a new kind of chair told television interviewer Louis Theroux, all his design and marketing strategies for new products were based on the realisation that 'Everyone has a body'. Something like this - but on an infinitely larger scale - seems to be going on at the present time, where new technologies in surgery, human reproduction and genome research provide scope for new investment and profit. At the same time other entrepreneurs, often large-scale criminal groups, have become involved in the employment of sex workers, people trafficking, and act as intermediaries in the sale and purchase of body parts. Moreover, shifts in the employment of women and changes in household structure have meant that much of the work of recruiting and organising reproductive labour, that is the caring of bodies, has been marketised and undertaken by waged workers.

This new economic value of what Foucault calls 'biopower' is explored by Lowe. Lowe's starting point is the way that

> the body is socially constructed by the work we do, the commodities we consume, the ways we procreate and socialise the next generation, the politics of gender and sexuality, and [a domain he is particularly concerned about] the promised healing of impaired bodies by psychoanalysts and psychotherapists. (Lowe 1995: 1)

In particular, Lowe is interested in the increasing commodification of body practices, including not only production and consumption, as these were previously understood, but areas like gender construction and sexuality. Like myself he is struck by the body as a target for direct appropriation by capital and he tries to relate high-tech health care, transplants, assisted reproduction, genomic research, sex reassignment and other body technologies to the expanding 'exchangist' practices of subjectification. Because, as Foucault suggests, sexuality has been freed from family and gender (and gender itself desolidified), it too presents a domain for commodified exchangist practices. Ultimately the social pathologies that result from the pressures of flexible accumulation are redefined as individual psychic dysfunctions and treated/disciplined by experts, to whom people have access in class-differentiated ways. Hence rather than (or as well as) the body being 'our own', it has become 'the other to late-capitalist development', which represents precisely the kind of dualism entrenched in economic structures of everyday life mentioned above. 'The satisfactions of bodily needs are currently the means by which the end of late-capitalist accumulation is accomplished', he argues, and 'bodily needs change for the sake of capital accumulation' (ibid.: 174). While one should question the totality of capital domination this picture presumes (providing, for instance, little opportunity for conceptualising either gender power or the professional interests of experts 'separately'), Lowe's argument suggests that we should be wary of seeing body practices as simply technologies or practices of the self. Rather, the agency of the body is appropriated by the demands of capital accumulation and is therefore intrinsic to the construction of production, consumption and social reproduction in late capitalism.

However, because scholars like these are concerned to contest poststructuralism on its own ground, they tend to focus on consumption, like those they criticise, but setting it in the context of regimes of capital accumulation. This can imply that we already know how the body figures in production, something that is actually far from the case. Moreover, one also gets a sense of the body as an abstraction, a necessary site in the circulation of capital; we have no sense here of the meeting of bodies, the sensuous activity of bodies or the stigma, pain or pleasure they feel. This may in part be due to the assumed separation of production and consumption as moments in the circulation of capital (or into separate times of the day), ignoring their connectedness and articulation in, for instance, the interactional service encounter (Glucksmann 2006).

The contribution a more fully embodied analysis could make can be seen in the example Harvey (1998) discusses at some length, namely the campaigns for a living wage that emerged first in the US, and, more latterly, in Britain (Purser et al. 2004; Wills 2005, 2001). He concentrates on the campaign led by mainly African-American women working as low-paid cleaners for the university, corporations and privately owned employment agencies in Baltimore. Harvey's point – and it is no doubt the crucial one – is that their struggle for a wage adequate to their physical reproduction needs to be considered as much an aspect of the politics of the body as the body politics more conventionally studied by feminists and postmodernists. Yet the body could enter into this story in even more ways than Harvey suggests. For instance, there is a considerable literature on paid cleaning (for example, Anderson 2000; Ehrenreich and Hochschild 2003a; Glenn 1996) that could be used to highlight other aspects of the embodied social relations in which cleaning is located. Harvey does not mention the longstanding racialisation of cleaning and other stigmatised activities which Hughes (1984) labelled 'dirty work', nor, at least in this article, the relevance of diurnal body cycles to the construction of cleaning as nightwork. We might recognise also the intersubjective element in the relation between workers and consumers, even in cases where they do not actually meet. Although night cleaners probably rarely talk to the people whose offices they clean, this is not to say that the cleaners do not talk about and experience the bodies of the office workers, through the detritus and stains they leave behind. According to the interviews my students have conducted with university cleaners on our campus here in Britain, the cleaners are intensely aware of the students, 'about how they're messy and rude and inconsiderate', and of the dirt students leave behind them. And in addition to the hidden, overnight work of hiding (dirt produced by) the bodies of students and professional workers, we should make more of the bodily injuries and ailments which cleaners routinely experience (Pai 2004a, 2004b).

My approach to the body and work overlaps with that of Teresa Ebert (1996, 1993), who is also critical of the absence of work and exploitation in contemporary feminist theory and its omission of 'bodies in and of labor'. Her self-conscious positioning outside the mainstream of writing on the body is not dissimilar to Lowe's (1995: 1), who notes that his take on the body is 'not about the body as that term is usually understood', i.e. in terms of literary representation or photographic images. Ebert's target is the feminist politics of representation – the discursive construction of practices – which has superseded socialist feminism among academic feminists. Although she is more sensitive to the ins and outs of feminist theory than Harvey or Lowe, she does not go nearly as far as many in recognising the new importance of the economics of signs and space (and the issues of personal identity they involve) to contemporary capitalism developments (Lash and Urry 1994). Moreover, because her argument for the *'primacy'* of women's and men's productive and reproductive practices – their labour process – in the articulation and development of human history and in the construction of their own subjectivities' (Ebert 1996: 37, italics added) is developed through a contrast to the current theoretical focus on language, pleasure and play, she is unable or unwilling to explore the role of representations of labour processes or how they shape perceptions and experience of work and of bodies. (In Chapter 2 I shall be analysing a series of photographic representations with this aim in mind.) Given the political impasses that she herself would recognise as underwriting the turn to culture on the left, it is hard to see how theory guided by her invocation of an almost unchanged conception of revolutionary historical materialism is going to understand or transform the position of embodied workers.

Incorporating the sociology of work and employment

Harvey's much reconstructed political economy is a move in the right direction, not only for understanding the body/work nexus but also for any transformation of relations of domination that have been the focus of feminist critique. The aims of this book are much more modest. It seeks to build on some of the ideas already broached here to consider the diverse constructions of the body involved in the recruitment, management and recompense of many kinds of workers and the ways these enter into our experiences and identities as embodied workers. I am inevitably influenced by the theoretical stance adopted by empirical research on these subjects, which has been much influenced by Foucault's understanding of the discursive construction of workers as subjects. But I want also to consider the ways in which much of workers' 'physical doings' (Crossley 2001: 20) might be (better) understood in Bourdieusian terms. Agency and 'resistance' are not necessarily socially transformative – indeed, as we shall see, some of the strategies whereby workers carve out a space for themselves that allows some degree of control may actually contribute to the reproduction of relations of domination. Which is not to say that the 'small dignities' and degrees of control they facilitate are not exceedingly important.

Obviously the body/work nexus is a potentially enormous field, and this account is constrained not only by space restrictions but also by my familiarity with research conducted in this area so far. The areas I have chosen show that focusing on the corporeal aspects of work particularly enriches our understanding of changes in labour processes and employment relations, representations of the body, and the corporeal as an aspect of work. These were summarised at the end of the Introduction.

TWO Picturing Embodied Labour

If we want to comprehend the working body, then its representation in photography is a useful starting point. Photographic representations of people at work have historically played important roles in constructing 'work'. For example, scientific management utilised the possibilities of still photography opened up by Eadweard Muybridge's pictures of moving human and animal bodies to measure, compare and objectify workers' gestures and movements with a new precision (Callan 2005; Lalvani 1996; Pace 2002; Sekula 1983). As interesting, though, are the ways that different types of work, social identities and social divisions are linked through the depiction of working bodies. Certain bodies are shown to be dignified by their labour, for instance, whereas others are degraded.

The production of photographs by sociologists and their informants is gradually becoming a more popular method through which social researchers are exploring experiences of work and employment (e.g. Bolton et al. 2001; Coover 2004; Dant and Bowles 2003; Harper 1987; Strangleman 2004). But we need to remember that informants, as well as sociologists and photographers themselves, are already imbued with ideas about work and workers that may influence the pictures that they produce. Middle- and upper-class perspectives on the labouring class have been historically evidenced through their representations of the latter's bodies. For instance, speaking of eighteenth-century representations, Jordan (2001: 62) suggests that 'to most comfortable-class writers, the bodies of the so-called "idle" poor were grotesque, objects of fear and revulsion, while the bodies of the industrious were rhetorically reduced to their useful parts.' By the end of the nineteenth century, Van Gogh could still say of his painting of *The Potato Eaters* (1885) that he had sought to give 'the impression of a way of life quite different from that of us civilised people' as well as to convey something about the honesty of the manual labour through which they had earned their food, by highlighting their hands 'that have dug the earth' (Treuherz 1987: 123–4). Indeed, Callan (2005) suggests that in the nineteenth century the figures of working-class men, even when highly eroticised, were pictured as distorted by their work, as compared to classical masculine ideals, as in the elongated chests and arms of the workers pictured in Caillebotte's painting of *The Floor Scrapers* (1875). Scarry (1994), however, points to a more sympathetic strain in pictorial and verbal depictions of working bodies, commenting on their possibilities for representing the transformative capacity of work's movement and effort.

A particularly systematic analysis of the relation between work and gender, class and race in the representation of bodies is Lutz and Collins's 1993 examination of a sample of photographs published in the American magazine *National Geographic* between 1950 and 1986, which they coded for a large number of variables, including the apparent skin colour of photographic subjects. Lutz and Collins found that the magazine was much more likely to show non-Western people at work, rather than at play, arguing that such photographs 'idealize through focusing on people's industriousness' (Lutz and Collins 1993: 106). More problematic was the association of activity level with different figures, with those coded as black most likely to be pictured in high levels of activity, those coded as white engaged in low-level activity, and those coded as bronze pictured in activities between these two extremes, such as walking or herding animals. Lutz and Collins say that 'people of colour (both black and bronze) were most likely to be portrayed at work in the photographs . . . while people with white skin were most likely to be found at rest' (ibid.: 161).

As Lutz and Collins remark, this could reflect 'events in the real world', with photographers finding dark-skinned peoples at work more often than lighter-skinned people, or it could reflect the editors' wish to counter Euroamerican stereotypes about the 'laziness' of non-white people. The more troubling possibility, they say, is that 'deeply ingrained notions of racial hierarchy made it seem more "natural" for dark-skinned peoples to be at work and engaged in strenuous activity' (ibid.: 162). In this way these photographs perpetuated assumptions about black people's 'tremendous capacity for work' that were crucial to the creation of wealth in the colonial and slave-holding era. Such examples suggest from the outset that considering representations of work and working bodies is a useful way of accessing wider constructions of the relation between (different) bodies and work, but also important in its own right in so far as such images keep particular constructions in circulation.

After a few other general comments about photography and the representation of workers, this chapter seeks to explore the social construction of labouring bodies by focusing on particular figures in the Western imaginative landscape whose bodies have become emblematic of labour in different ways. This chapter considers three case studies from the nineteenth and twentieth centuries. While I hesitate to generalise from these few examples from still photography – especially since counter-instances come to mind – I want to demonstrate not only that bodies have been inscribed historically by ideas about the work which people do, as well as by the work itself, but also that particular constructions of labouring bodies then come to signify (and sometimes assuage) anxieties about the nature of work and employment. 'Race' and 'gender' in particular come to play important rhetorical functions in debates about the meaning of work, the adequacy of its rewards and the nature of its dangers at particular historical conjunctures.

Photography and power

Social scientists wanting to utilise photography in new ways recognise that we need to engage with debates about how to reconcile the photograph's appearance of 'surface validity' and the indeterminacy of its meaning (e.g. Chaplin 1994; Harper 2003; Rose 2001). Until recently, making sense of the body using photographic archive material has been concentrated in cultural theory, in which work inspired by photographic theory (Burgin 1982) has rejected the apparent literalness of documentary photographic representations for an exploration of the social relations of their construction. Rather than seeing such images as providing an objective picture of workers or working conditions, we can read them for both explicit and unconscious assumptions about the classed, gendered and raced bodies that they project.

Photographs of working people have tended to be seen as part of the documentary tradition, separate from representations of the (often nude) body as art. They have been influenced by conventions that structure many of our images of work, in painting as well as photography, such as the going-to-work-at-dawn and returning-home-in-the-evening-light pictures which are a staple of both genres. The nostalgia that reflects the photograph's unique relation to the passage of time (Sontag 1979) deeply permeates photographs of work, many of which seem to have been occasioned by awareness of the rapid disappearance of particular labouring communities. These include most notably Salgado's (1993) *Workers: Archaeology of the Industrial Age* but also the Depression-era photographs of American tenant farmers, or even earlier pictures of male craft workers taken just as their trades were disappearing with the onslaught of mechanised production. Another example is Breman and Shah's (2004) images of Ahmedabad, in western India, which show how the closure of the textile mills employing organised labour decimated a working-class community.

Many key writers follow Foucault in seeing photography as an example of the 'material elements and techniques that serve . . . and support . . . the power and knowledge relations that invest human bodies and subjugate them by turning them into objects of knowledge' (Foucault 1979, as cited by Schatzki and Natter 1996b). For instance, Tagg's (1988) well-known study of the power relations of representation concentrates on the development of photography in relation to the surveillance of the bodies of subordinate peoples, especially the sick or insane, the orphaned, the criminal, the colonised or enslaved. Other commentators suggest that understanding the power relations of representation has to include the study of the social institutions within which photographs are made, chosen, edited, printed, circulated and experienced by viewers. For instance, the research by Lutz and Collins (1993) noted above considers different kinds of evidence about the idealisation, naturalisation and sexualisation of difference in *National Geographic*. This included not only analysis of the images but also interviews with editors and photographers and observations at editorial meetings at which decisions were taken about which images to publish, how to caption them, and so on. They also interviewed readers about their opinions of the photographs.

Others see photography as a more overtly contested space, for instance some writing on industrial photography exploring the relationship between photographic culture and economic life. It stresses that images are interpreted differently depending on the viewer's individual and classed relation to the image. For instance, a photograph produced in line with the instrumental interests of the entrepreneur still might have sentimental significance for workers who remember the particular individuals in it; the picture of a company football club that forms part of an imaginary landscape, the harmonious community projected by industrial capital, might be seen differently by members of the team (Benjamin and Wilkie 1983).

Feminist photographic theory has been particularly concerned with the centrality of fantasy to the construction of photographic meaning, including pictures of working people. Reading photographs for the unconscious fears and anxieties they evoke or contain for spectators has been central to the work of Kuhn Mulvey (1975), Pollock (1993) and other cultural theorists. As Pollock (and also Trachtenberg 1989) comment, whose bodies are pictured is as important as how they are represented: leading personages are usually figured in portraits showing only their subjects' head and shoulders. Their bodies do not need to be figured as powerful bodies, nor even to be figured at all. Indeed, the use of such portraits to line the boardroom is not accidental; one could say that they naturalise and legitimate the absence of the capitalist's bodily labour from th e production process. Even when the entire body is shown, images never document the actuality of the subject but rather represent the 'fantastic bodies' produced by unconscious desire. This makes them an especially rich way of tapping into constructions of working bodies.

The 'fantastic body' of Hannah Cullwick

If we want to understand the bodily aspect of labour in class, gender and race-specific terms, the fascination of bourgeois Victorian men with the bodies of working-class women, especially women who worked out of doors in 'masculine' manual jobs, is a good place to start. As Davidoff (1983), Pollock and others highlight, 'images of laboring women's bodies circulated from Parliamentary report to popular journalism to the walls of official galleries and the pages of private albums' (Pollock 1993: 5). Just as the body of the prostitute was a contested site, a terrain for the playing out of Victorian class and gender anxieties (Nead 1988; Walkowitz 1980), so too the bodies of female manual workers were a subject for 'the bourgeois deployment of the technologies of sexual regulation of the body of the proletariat' (Pollock 1993: 5).

An important resource for examining the era's obsessive interest in working-class women's bodies has been the collected papers of A.J. Munby (1828–1910), a Victorian civil servant who moved at the fringes of London artistic circles of his time (Hiley 1979; Hudson 1972; Stanley 1984). He left his papers to Trinity College Cambridge, with the reservation that they not be revealed for 40 years. His secret relationship with and marriage to a domestic servant, Hannah Cullwick, with whom he lived but briefly, is documented through their correspondence; the diaries she kept for him, in which she described – indeed celebrated – her gruelling day-to-day tasks in obsessive detail; his own diaries; and his sketch books. Munby's papers also contain his collection of 600 photographs of working women – for example, colliers, fisherwomen, mill workers, acrobats and servants. Although the eroticised master–servant relationship between Munby and Cullwick raises a huge number of questions, especially in so far as it was played out in terms of gender and class symbolism, my main concern here is the way in which writers using the archives have illuminated the complex and highly contradictory connections between social structure and the construction of labouring bodies.

Leonore Davidoff's 'Class and Gender in Victorian England' (1983), first published in 1979, concentrates on Munby's obsessions with the construction of the classed female body through certain kinds of manual work. Davidoff's use of these documents to explore the ways both class and gender were inscribed on the bodies of female domestic servants gives a lie to the idea that scholars have become interested in 'the body' only recently. The continuing popularity of the Munby–Cullwick relationship as a subject of study is also due to the readiness with which we can assimilate the construction of Cullwick's clearly eroticised classed body to the concepts through which bodies and their representation have been theorised more recently. The labouring body is brought within the domain of psychoanalysis, performance and sexuality, where current thinking simply assumes the body belongs. But we should not allow it to disappear as a body of labour either.

Davidoff explores the ways Victorian working-class women literally embodied class difference, through, for instance, diet, labour and the learned postures of deference. Munby himself was fascinated by working women's physical features – their 'rude strength', broad backs, 'ruddy countenance' and sun-tanned skin and, especially, their hands and feet, which contrasted greatly with the dainty white hands and smaller, more delicate feet of the middle-class girl. He wrote approvingly, for instance, of a colliery girl in boots, 'shod like a horses hoofs' (Davidoff 1988: 42). The photograph of Hannah Cullwick in Figure 2.1, in which she is polishing boots, is one of many that show off her strong forearms and forceful yet deferential posture. Davidoff's analysis thus highlights, to begin with, the extent to which bodies are worked on by the work they do.

Equally compelling is the way in which bodies are polluted, metaphorically as well as actually, through work, especially through the demeaning nature of domestic labour and the confinement of domestic servants to the 'back passages' of the house. In this sense the situation of Victorian domestic servants resembled that of the prostitutes of the same era, who, as Nead (1988) demonstrates, stood at the nexus between classes: whereas the prostitute was in close body contact with the bourgeois male, the labour of the domestic servant preserved the privacy of the middle-class household. By bringing water indoors for the family to wash, dealing with stained linen, and removing rubbish and body wastes from the house, the servant enabled the middle class to keep their own bodies out of the public eye. She was a kind of conduit between the private and the public, a kind of sewer.

[The servants'] most important job was to remove dirt and waste: to dust; empty slop pails and chamber pots; peel fruit and vegetables; pluck fowl; sweep and scrub floors, walls, and windows; remove ash and cinders; black lead grates; wash clothes and linen. (Davidoff 1988: 44)

It was not surprising therefore that working-class women had a particular place in the Victorian map of the social body. As Davidoff says, the middle-class male was its head; the 'unthinking, unfeeling' working-class man its hands; the middle-class housewife was responsible for the emotional, tender side of life, its heart. The working-class girl in turn represented the 'nether regions' of bodily functions, sexual and cloacal. Her degradation was constituted by both the work she did – it was only her labour which allowed the

Figure 2.1   Hannah Cullwick blacking boots. Photograph by J. Stodart of Margate, 1864. With the permission of the Master and Fellows of Trinity College Cambridge.

middle-class woman to develop an image of disembodied purity, to signify femininity for the age – and the servile social relation in which it was embedded.

Ann McClintock (1995), like Davidoff, stresses the extent to which through the equation of dirt, sexuality and blackness the working-class woman's body

39

was racialised and the middle-class woman whitened. Racialisation was explicit in the then current understanding of heavy labour, for instance in 'representations of sweating, glistening bodies' (Bordo 1993: 195; Cranny-Francis 1995) belonging to slaves and colonised peoples. Hannah Cullwick called Munby 'Massa' in imitation of her idea of a 'Negro' slave word for master. She had her photograph taken for him posing as slave (as well as in other roles). In Munby's own sketches his working-class women appear to be racialised as well as masculinised. The figure of Boompin' Nelly, for instance, 'is entirely blackened: she squats hunched and brooding, her colossal arms resting on enormous, widespread, foreshortened legs' (McClintock 1995: 107).

However, analyses of the particular relationship between Hannah and Munby and the photographs of her have undergone significant shifts. Although some commentators agree that his fantasies of masculinised working-class women allowed Munby to enjoy his unacknowledged homosexual desires, the further question arises: who was empowered by these images? (Mavor 1996: 980). Tagg takes it for granted that Munby's collection of photographs embodies 'the procedures of objectification and subjection' (Tagg 1988: 92) and Davidoff assumes not only that Munby himself took the photographs, but that Cullwick was a passive victim of Munby's obsessions. More recent analyses challenge what they see as the problematic equation of woman with victim. It appears that the photographs of Hannah Cullwick were not taken by Munby himself, but by professional photographers either in their shops, to which Hannah often took herself and her props, or outdoors by a passing photographer seeking commissions.

McClintock argues that the power relation between Munby and Cullwick can be best analysed using the model of sadomasochism, in which the scenarios directed by the S/M couple are orchestrated and controlled as much by the 'bottom' as the apparent master. Although the symbols they used in their games are drawn from the wider social structure, Munby did not always play the master; for instance he liked to be held by Cullwick in scenarios now associated with the practice of 'babyism'. McClintock insists therefore that the ways in which the photographs and diaries make Hannah Cullwick's work visible should be seen as her own achievement; Cullwick makes visible, through the photographs that she organised, the labour that was supposed to remain hidden. The servant's work was supposed to be undertaken before dawn or late at night, dodging the employer when 'in her dirt', opening the door to guests only when wearing clean clothes. Because the Victorian middle-class obsession with dirt symbolised a refusal to acknowledge the source of their wealth, when Cullwick guided Munby around the household, showing him the sites of her labour, or counted out for him the number of boots she had blacked, this was her way of claiming a presence and making her labour visible. According to McClintock,

Smeared on trousers, faces, hands and aprons, dirt was the memory trace of working class and female labor, unseemly evidence that the fundamental production of individual and imperial wealth lay in the hands and bodies of the working class, women and the colonized. Dirt, like all fetishes [e.g. money] thus expresses a crisis in value, for it contradicts the liberal dictum that social wealth is created by the abstract, rational principles of the market and not by labour. (McClintock 1995: 154)

The idea that the photographs and diaries give us a sense of Cullwick producing herself as a subject through reiterated labour echoes Butler's (1991) analysis of the performativity involved in doing gender. The photographs show Hannah Cullwick in what looks like a dramatised performance of her domestic duties, partly because the pictures look so staged, due to long exposure times and the use of props in studio photography, but there is more to it than this. The photographs of Cullwick as lady, milkmaid, slave and so on prefigure the work of the American photographer Cindy Sherman (1990), who photographed herself in different classic cinematic female roles constructed through props, dress and expression. In this context the photographs Hannah had taken of herself as a domestic servant imply that this was only one of several possible roles, all equally illusory. But of course we have to ask whether (working) class identities should be seen as performative in the same way.

In another interpretation of the archives, Pollock (1993) sets the Munby–Cullwick relationship in the context of the other images of women manual workers that Munby collected. Many pictures were taken by local photographers and sold to visiting businessmen as curiosities. From Pollock's point of view, this obsessive interest demonstrates the role that fantasies about working-class women played in the construction of the subjectivity of the middle-class male.

The context of Munby and Cullwick's relationship was widespread concern about the female labouring body, and especially her relation to sexual difference. This was part of wider semiotics in which 'hardship and poverty signified in and on the bodies of miners' and other working people. Their bodies stood for 'the radical alienness of industrial labour', constructed through an anthropological gaze which naturalises the social Other, picturing difference not as an effect of capitalism but as an inherent bodily trait (Pollock 1993: 24). While at first sight Pollock's discussion seems to imply that the body is only a textual construction, she does not deny either the material effects of social relations or indeed the social effects of particular representations.

The most obsessive concern was for females, and among them the Wigan colliery pit-brow women who, because they wore divided skirts, were seen as half girl, half man. For instance, Figure 2.2 shows a female mining worker

Figure 2.2 *Carte de visite* portrait. One of many carte portraits of pit-brow workers in Wigan and Shevington. Photographed by John Cooper of Wigan, 1867. With the permission of the Master and Fellows of Trinity College Cambridge.

in the trousers that so exercised Victorian gentlemen. In this and others of photographs of its type, the young women are so often pictured with the shovel and sieve that were the tools of their trade that one cannot help but read them also as male and female symbols connoting the women's ambiguous gender identity. As Pollock and Davidoff both argue, the otherness of the worker is signified by her unnatural sexuality.

There was a fear that these girls' work and costume led to the revealing of their sex, as well as, paradoxically, anxiety that their work de-sexed them. In either case moral outrage was saturated with disgust. One famous passage in the 1842 Parliamentary enquiry into labour conditions in mining noted that:

> The chain, passing high up between the legs of two of these girls, had worn large holes in their trousers and any sight more disgusting, indecent or revolting can scarcely be imagined than these girls at work. No brothel can beat it. (Cited in Davidoff 1983: 51)

Pollock argues that the obsessive disgust these working women generated also has to be understood psychoanalytically. For Pollock the fascination of the photographs of mining women to Munby and other collectors was related to the way they played on their unconscious anxieties. The artifices adopted by the middle-class lady, the wide skirts and corsets, meant safety; although they confirmed gender difference they hid the female's sexed body. In contrast, the trousered legs of women manual workers challenged the inevitability of men's difference from and superiority over women; their trousers both reveal the artificiality of gender difference and make evident 'what happens between their legs', sexual difference. Since it is recognition of the girl's lack that precipitates the boy's fear of castration and the Oedipal stage, the female genitals are seen in psychoanalysis to excite male anxiety, deflected through fetishisation. Pollock argues that along with the more usually cited reasons for seeking to get women out of the workplace, we have to consider the unconscious anxieties the sight of these women produced in middle-class men of the time. She argues that working women were experienced as threatening not only because they challenged notions of male social and economic privilege but also because their bodies challenged the stability of masculine psychic structure.

These are not so much competing accounts of the Munby–Cullwick relationship or of the obsession with the bodies of working-class women as attempts to uncover further layers of meaning. What they share is the perception that gender and (fantasies about) sexual difference were essential to the representation of the labouring body and its alterity. The gender, class and race-specific connotations of the working body are equally clear when we consider the photography of a key twentieth-century figure like Lewis Hine.

The manly worker as sign

If Hannah Cullwick's work, and that of domestic servants generally, was domestic, demeaning, servile, repetitious, ideally invisible, what work represents the opposite of all these – the heroic triumph of man (!) over nature? Although images of the heroic worker go back to at least Victorian times, for instance the famous painting 'Work' by Ford Madox Brown (Treuherz 1987), some of the most interesting examples come from twentieth-century United States.

Barbara Melosh (1993) outlines the inflection of work with nobility through images of masculine bodies in the classical heroic mould in some detail. She focuses on the public art sponsored by the American New Deal's Treasury Section of Fine Arts in the US, which from 1935 to 1943 awarded commissions for paintings and sculpture for new buildings. As she documents, the broad, bare-chested, heavily muscled figure of the 'manly worker' became a key icon precisely at a time when male unemployment was at its height, skilled craftsmen were being replaced by semi-skilled operatives, and manual workers by clerical and professional employees in the growing service sector. Unlike the iconography of Soviet socialist realism, which along with Mexican murals was a key influence, the representation of work as mastery, 'the ability to reshape the material world and to make one's own destiny' (Melosh 1993: 156), was always represented as male, and almost always as white male. African-American male workers were not infrequently portrayed, but never cast in such a monumental role (see also Natanson 1992). Women were never represented as emblematic of work; although occasionally included as factory workers in one part of a large mural, they were more typically figured as members of families.

In the American documentary photography of the Depression era, however, this manly worker does not figure very strongly. The best-known photographs of the period, by Dorothea Lange, Walker Evans, Margaret Bourne-White, Russell Lee and Arthur Rothstein, who were employed by the Farm Security Administration under the tutelage of Roy Stryker, more often dealt with migrant, tenant, dispossessed *families*, serving, Tagg (1988) argues, to legitimate their status as dignified but passive recipients of state financial support.

In some ways more vivid and interesting comparisons with the Victorian images of working women come from an earlier period, in the well-known photographs by Lewis W. Hine (1874–1940), especially in two sets of pictures. The first is his series of photographs of the paid homeworking done mainly by women and children, which Hine undertook as the staff photographer for the National Child Labor Committee. As Boris (1994) highlights, American campaigners wanted to stop homeworking entirely, campaigning not just against child labour, but also against the paid work women undertook at home, which they saw as undercutting men's wages. Their most famous poster, 'Sacred Motherhood', for instance, made the point that the exploitation of women by suppliers destroyed family life, keeping mothers from their appropriate duties and rendering the husband-father idle (Boris 1994).

Hine's photographs convey this definition of the situation well. As Trachtenberg (1989) says, although these photographs show work being done, the women and children doing it are not accepted as workers. This is highlighted in the particular ways the work is pictured. Photographs intended to document the existence of homeworkers and the condition of their families had to be taken on site, in tenements where there was little light. The photographs show heavily shadowed, gloomy interiors, slovenly housekeeping and degrading work. As Trachtenberg (1989) says, they show in a 'frozen moment' how unabsorbed the women and children are in the work, lacking in joy or satisfaction. Men are either absent, idle or out of place.

After the First World War, however, Hine published another series of photographs which could not be more different. His famous series of photographs of the making of the Empire State Building in New York City were commissioned by the building's owners and published in 1932 as the main part of Hine's book for children, *Men at Work: Photographic Studies of Men and Machines* (1977). The book also included some of the 'work portraits' of male workers that he had begun producing in the 1920s. These bodies in motion are everything Hine's homeworkers (or Victorian working women) were not: work makes man transcendent. A feeling of space and light and movement shows them embodying positive values of work. As Trachtenberg says, the explicit message in the accompanying text as well as in the photographs identifies industrial workers as modern heroes. This notion 'finds its realization in the display of the working body in motion, in acts of concentration, muscular co-ordination, balance, strength, a repertoire of spontaneous gestures that show the body's experience, skill, training' (Trachtenberg 1989: 210).

Whereas Hine's homeworkers are bound down by their bodies, literally sagging in their chairs, the men atop the Empire State Building are existential giants, transcendent figures flying through space. In some shots (for example, Figure 2.3) the worker looks almost like a flying angel; in others, in which workmen are pictured at the edge of mile-high platforms, they resemble the statues which sometimes ring the roofs of urban buildings.

These different images, the homeworking mother and the male worker, were deployed at different political moments and in relation to different critiques. According to Trachtenberg, the earlier photographs come out of a more radical, albeit reformist, politics than the later ones. Hine's earlier work

Figure 2.3   Icarus Atop Empire State Building, New York © The Estate of Lewis W. Hine, 1931. Courtesy of the Avery Architectural and Fine Arts Library, Columbia University in the City of New York.

was located within the institutional framework of the American Progressive reform movement, which critiqued and sought to control the destructive forces of urban industrial capitalism. Although a bourgeois movement set against socialist politics, it sought to shift public opinion in favour of legislative change. However, by the late 1920s, with the intensification of corporatist links between state and the owners of industry, former radicals now sought only recognition of the contribution of labour to the capitalist system. The 'moral realism' of the period sought to overcome the fissiparous tendencies of the increasing industrial division of labour by spiritualising labour. The recognition of – indeed the glorification – of the manly worker was part of this attempt at symbolic integration.

One is tempted to generalise and argue that when photographs figure employment within a critical frame, this takes the form of focusing on women (and children), whereas the bodies of (white, skilled) male workers signify social solidarity. However, as is seen so clearly in the case of the Victorian photographs examined above, it is not only male and female bodies but gender-stereotyped feminine and masculine poses and dress which connote the character of a workforce or which comment upon their relation to the wider society. For instance, in a posthumous collection of

Hine's photographs, *Women at Work* (Doherty 1981), packaged as a companion volume to *Men at Work*, some of the photographs do show respect for women as workers. But the women workers are most frequently photographed sitting down, heads bowed to their handiwork or machine, which effectively replicates the postures of demure femininity typical of portraits of women in domestic settings. When pictures show male workers in such poses, such as in some photographs of clothing factories, they tend to be read as pictures of docility. It is surely significant that the photographs produced during the Second World War (and also images in Soviet socialist realism) that seek to project women's integration into the industrial workforce in positive terms often do so through masculinising women's dress and body shape. For example, Dorothea Lange's pictures of wartime California shipyards (for two examples, see Tagg 1988) show women workers wearing overalls and hard-hats, as mainly masculine in stance and staring straight at the camera.

Normalising work

I want to consider one more case study, in which pictures of the American wartime production of the atomic bombs ultimately dropped on Japan show what by then had become conventions guiding the photography of work being used in new ways. Geoffrey Batchen (1997: 93, cited by Pace 2002: 325) suggests that we need to consider 'what the photograph actually does in the world', and its rhetorical role is especially evident in this later deployment of images of working bodies that had been central to many of Hine's photographs. As I shall try to show, such images of working bodies were used during the Second World War by the US Government in order to render innocuous what was dangerous and potentially strange by representing it through the by then commonplace iconography of 'ordinary' working life. (There is also, it should be stressed, an important history of photography's involvement in opposing the production of nuclear weaponry, for instance Tredici (1987) and Gallagher (1993); see also Blackmar (2001) and Davis (1993)).

The Manhattan District Project was the wartime code name (now usually shortened to Manhattan Project) for the invention and production of the atomic bombs dropped on Hiroshima and Nagasaki in 1945, organised under the aegis of the US Army Corps of Engineers. From 1943 three completely new townships were established by the Army as part of this process: Los Alamos in New Mexico, where Robert Oppenheimer led the most famous of the scientists in working out how to make and test the bomb; Oak Ridge, Tennessee, where industrial installations were built to produce uranium isotopes through several different methods of production; and Hanford,

Washington, where another method for producing fissionable material was developed. Whereas the Los Alamos and Hanford sites were run by the Army, it had contracted with existing private corporations to build and run Oak Ridge, where the population exceeded 20,000 people by the end of the war. Much of the work was hazardous and the possible effects of these untried process on the future health or well-being of those working there was not allowed to interfere with the programme (Hacker 1992; Hales 1997).

Thorpe and Shapin, like many others, see the Manhattan Project as bringing into being 'a new form of modern technoscientific organisation' along with 'a new precariousness of global human existence' (Thorpe and Shapin 2000: 546). Peter Hales (1997) documents the thoroughness with which the Army and its contractors planned the townships, evolved new systems for hiring and managing civilian personnel, and organised the infrastructure of security measures, housing, public eating halls, schools, site newspapers and so on as well as the plants and laboratories themselves. The construction of what were effectively total communities sought to redirect social relations and manage social space. This was never entirely successful, since many workers, especially the white technical and scientific staff, were able to bring their families with them and the unusual circumstances produced very distinctive communities that, although they supported the war effort, were suspicious of military authority and resisted it in what small ways were available to them. (Hales (1997) and Wolkowitz (2000a, 2000b) give more details about the Manhattan Project 'nuclear families' and the communities they formed.)

In considering the visual material produced on the three sites, the extreme secrecy of the projects is crucial. The purpose of the project was hidden, not only from the outside world, but even to most of the people who worked there, who struggled, usually unsuccessfully, to find out what its real aims were. The people working in the laboratories and plants were not permitted to discuss their work with other people on the site. Even if they knew, they were not supposed to tell their spouses what was going on. Letters to family off the site were censored and residents were not permitted to mention where they lived. Of course, people still tried to make sense of what they were doing. For instance, I have been told that the library at the Oak Ridge townsite had to repeatedly replace their dictionary, since fingers searching for the definition of the word 'uranium' wore a hole in the page on which it was listed.

This secrecy also affected the production of visual images. In Los Alamos most residents were not allowed to use or own cameras, according to Hales (1997). Judging from the photographs included in published personal narratives or other sources (Wolkowitz 2000a, 2000b; Fermi and Samra 1995), family photography was limited to the most senior scientists or to a few family snapshots taken with an officially borrowed camera for a special occasion. At the same time all the sites employed a professional photographer to document the enterprise. Some of these images must have been intended as a historical record, or for publication only after war, but others were used for advertising or internal consumption. The Project faced a number of problems in this regard. For instance, the sites needed to advertise for civilian workers without telling them anything about the project itself, and they also had to provide images for people on the sites, perhaps to discourage people from trying to produce their own.

Hales argues that the Army's monopolisation of the making of photographs on the sites, along with the billboards, printed notices and other visual material, reinforced the Manhattan District's 'hegemony' over the sense of place (Hales 1997: 261). Reading the photographs produced by the official photographers, he says, one can recognise the District's 'grammar . . . imbedded in visual form' (ibid.: 261). The extraordinary, carefully staged pictures by Ed (James E.) Westcott, the official photographer in Oak Ridge, for instance, are often exceptionally bland. Indeed, however clear the image, the faces are not really distinguishable as recognisable individuals: 'faces have that washed-out generality that allows the specific people to become Everyman and Everywoman' (ibid.: 264). One of the effects of these images is to render causality invisible; no one in particular can be held responsible for anything.

Some of the images produced by Ed Westcott and his colleagues at the other Manhattan Project sites closely mirror those of Lewis Hine, in so far as the photographs construct their human subjects as symbols, rather than attempting to capture individual subjectivity. The poses and arrangements of the pictures also seem to follow Hine's images of workers and the conventions these had established for picturing work. This would have the effect of normalising the work on the Project, likening it to ordinary civilian employment. The similarity between Hine's images and those later produced by the Manhattan Project is especially clear if we compare Hine's photograph of 'Machinists at work' (Figure 2.4) with Westcott's picture of two men repairing a K-25 Gaseous Diffusion Cell (Figure 2.5). Other Manhattan Project images mimic the upright manly white worker. For instance, the poster entitled 'Highlights of Hanford: Work for Victory' (reproduced in Hales 1997: 271) was used to recruit civilian craftsmen for work at Hanford. It pictures three comradely men standing to attention, two in overalls or protective gear, their faces apparently lit by sunlight. The line of tall smokestacks in the background literally heightens their attractiveness as tall, manly figures.

The most extraordinary image is Westcott's picture (Figure 2.6) of the Control Desk in the Master Control Room at K-25 in Oak Ridge. As Hales

Figure 2.4   Machinists at work, one of Hine's photographs for *Men at Work* *(1932)*. Courtesy of the Avery Architectural and Fine Arts Library, Columbia University in the City of New York.

Figure 2.5   K-25 Gaseous Diffusion Cell, Oak Ridge, Tennessee. Photograph by James E. Westcott. Courtesy of the US National Archives and Records Administration.

Figure 2.6   Control Desk in the Master Control Room, K-25, Oak Ridge, Tennessee. Photograph by James E. Westcott. Courtesy of the US National Archives and Records Administration.

explains, although the picture is obviously managed, the 'obsessive orderliness' of the room is made to look natural: the banks of switches, the paperwork on the supervisors' desks lined up parallel and neatly diagonal to the walls, and 'the people, too – two men, two women . . . are nicely symmetrical' (ibid.: 261). As Hales says, bringing the women into the control room enabled all four figures to act out the comfortable roles of men and women in the workplace, with the men as bosses and the women as secretaries. The naturalised assumptions about gendered work roles in the choice and positioning of these gendered bodies is one of the ways the image reassures the viewer that 'Everything's under control in the control room' (ibid.). Although Hales does not put it quite this way, we can say that it is the heterosexualisation of relationships in the control room that normalises it – and if one couple isn't enough to do the trick, we get two.

It is worth adding that although images like those above played a normalising role at the time they were produced, the imagery produced at and by the Manhattan Project can also be deployed differently, to examine the Project's history more critically. For instance, Rachel Fermi and Esther Samra's (1995) *Picturing the Bomb* evokes the story of the Manhattan Project through counterposing the 'human interest' pictures of workers and their families with pictures of the effects of the bombs in Japan. Moreover, the authors' reproduction of an image of Girl Guides playing outside one of the Oak Ridge plants on the cover of the book, however intended at the time it was produced, is surely meant to be read ironically now. Another striking image is a picture of Harry Daghlian's hand (ibid.: 113) taken, presumably by medics, in the days before he died of radiation disease following an immediately postwar accident in Los Alamos. Its inclusion can be seen to symbolise, although this is not necessarily Fermi and Samra's intention, the strange sacrifice of those who laboured in the making of the bomb, harking back to the hands of Van Gogh's *Potato Eaters*, noted above.

Conclusion

This chapter has considered photographs of men's and women's work and male and female workers, differences in how their bodies are represented and the use of their bodies as representations. It suggests that the use of working bodies as signs often reflects and comments on changes in the organisation of work and intervenes in political debates about work in many ways. This is particularly so when the gendering and racialisation of bodies is central to the visual image. Generally men's bodies are taken to signify respect for labour's strengths. White men's bodies in particular tend to be used to deflect anxiety, for they signify the positive virtues of work and the incorporation of the worker into the social mainstream. These men are pictured using skill and courage to enable them to use their work to shape the world, and as a route towards their own transcendence. Such images celebrate work and, sometimes, the sacrifices it involves. So strong are these connotations that they could be readily appropriated in the images made on the Manhattan Project.

The uses made of women's work and women's bodies is more varied. In the main the bodies of white working-class women are pictured as curiosities, scrutinised for evidence of actual or potential social ills. Women's bodies that have been already physically 'masculinised' through the work they do may trigger anxiety; women's maternal bodies, as in the case of Hine's homeworkers, may render their status as workers unnatural. In either case the interest is in the subjects' alterity: we are invited to inspect the bodies of the women in Munby's collection of postcards and intrude into the homes of Hine's homeworkers, who appear too discouraged and passive to tell us to go away. The immanence/transcendence of these raced female and male bodies is paralleled by other binaries – between flesh and spirit, shame and pride. The Manhattan Project pictures only seem to be different in their assumptions, for it is through the assumed vulnerability of women's bodies that we are invited to notice that since women are doing the work it *must* be safe. The whiteness of the subjects in Figure 2.6 is exaggerated by the use of lighting and exaggerates too the ease, safety and superior status of the work.

We obviously want to free ourselves from such constructions of working bodies by making them visible. There are dangers in concentrating on the bodies of workers if this risks saturating ourselves in sexual and racial difference, thereby reproducing rather than challenging the notion that one has to be 'defined by one's body' (Dyer 1997: 5). To this it can be countered that we need to show the extent to which the bodies by which we are defined are in any case partly imaginary. This is not to say, however, that the bodies of workers are simply the product of representational practices. Indeed we could say that one reason the bodies in such images are so important as a subject for analysis is because they are doubly constructed, shaped not only by representational practices but also by their actual labour and position in the social structure. It is this second aspect of the ways in which bodies are worked on to which we now turn.

THREE Industrial Bodies

The fact that relatively few people in the West are still engaged in heavy manual labour has led some commentators to assume that in a knowledge-based society the body is less implicated in the labour process than it was in the past. For instance, Catherine Casey's (1995) concentration on the constitution of the self in and through organisational discourses ends up ignoring the continuing centrality of the organisation and surveillance of workers' bodies to working life. She argues that one of the ways in which post-industrial differs from industrial work is that 'the primary impact is no longer on the body' (Casey 1995: 86): work no longer requires demanding bodily exertion or physical prowess nor does it lead to bodily fatigue. Indeed, when the primary requirement is the quick, attentive, trained mind, she says, the worker's body need not be present at the workplace at all, and laser tools can do better quality work than the workers' hands. Even in the most routine service sector work, such as in fast food outlets or portering, she adds, the additional skills of personality, congeniality and good humour are also required.

Is this view of the disappearing body (a rather surprising one given Casey's (2000) later writing on the body) really adequate for understanding the relation between work and the body in post-industrial societies? The comments quoted above illustrate some of the assumptions that have led to the naturalisation of the body in employment debates in the past. Casey seems to be arguing that employers now construct workers' 'selves' by shaping them discursively, rather than, as previously, using (up) their bodies physically. But this implies a rather binary distinction between exertion, strength and dexterity, which are seen as embodied, and therefore naturalised, and what Casey calls 'social inputs' (ibid.: 184). In contrast to the kind of gender-neutral 'social inputs' she highlights, such as 'personality, congeniality and good humour', the body appears as a pre-social entity, given in and by nature. The question is whether as a starting point this can do justice to the social character of manual labour, the embodiment of social relations, or the undiminished, if changing, impact of work on bodily health.

The alternative view, to which I hope this book contributes, suggests that human body continues to be deeply involved in every aspect of paid work, and, moreover, that paid employment continues to play a large role in building what Schatzki and Natter (1996b) call 'social and political bodies' – rather more so than the body building people do in their local gym. Our bodies are built out of and through our roles as paid workers, and the organized bodies of employees in turn contribute to the making of the corporation and its profits; we monitor and manage our own bodies with work obligations in mind and feel its effects in fatigue and impairments as well as satisfactions. We should not forget that the worker's body is always still present when he or she is working, even when the work is not directly supervised nor undertaken away from the employers' premises. Consequently, although we need to recognise the kinds of changes in the nature of employment to which Casey (1995) draws attention, we also need to examine, rather than sideline, their implications for embodiment.

Over the past 20 years considerable research has gone in to making visible what used to be naturalised and taken for granted, the corporeal basis of work and its construction and reconstruction in the light of shifts towards a post-industrial economy. This and the next chapter pay particular attention to changes in the ways corporations target our bodies, as employees, which cannot help but have implications for the ways in which we understand the relation between our 'selves' and our bodies in everyday life. The labour process never takes the body 'as found'. Whereas industrial production constructed a 'useful' body, one trained to act as a cog in the wheel, a 'body segment', in Foucault's terms, the post-industrial economy of the rich OECD countries targets instead the 'whole person' (Thompson 2003). Because the capacities now targeted and the identities now formulated are conventionally understood to be more closely related to the individual sense of self, their instrumentalisation raises crucial questions regarding the proper boundaries (if any) between the self and the employee role. For instance, in one of the few other attempts to consider the construction of working bodies across the occupational structure, Hancock and Tyler (2000b: 115) see the recruitment and management of employees as increasingly commodifying embodied capacities previously seen as private: 'new modes of organisation may require new modes of embodiment'. They imply that whereas previously the body was configured as productive, valued for what it could do, new expectations distort valued aspects of the embodied self by rendering them expressive but empty signs of corporate branding. Gender is a hugely important dimension of these changes. As discussed by Adkins (2001) and McDowell (1997), changes in the kinds of bodily attributes employers seek, including the aestheticisation of workers to be discussed in Chapter 4, are often understood in terms of a 'feminisation' of employment.

While there is much to be said for this way of understanding very broad-based change, it does present problems. For instance, it may lead to an overly schematic view of the transformation of advanced industrial nations into post-industrial economies and from Fordist to post-Fordist methods of production and marketing. This may exaggerate the differences between 'then' and 'now' as totalities or 'isms', something queried by commentators who emphasise capitalism's continuing interest in profits and control, the continuing importance of manual labour, and/or the degradation of many workers' conditions of work (Callinicos 1989; Clarke 1990; Ebert 1996; Pollert 1991; Thompson 2003). It may also exaggerate the feminisation of the employment, by paying too little attention to organisations and sectors where attempts to reconstruct the body have been less pronounced, or which continue to organise work around the presumed capabilities of the men's bodies and the exclusion of women's (Greed 2000). For instance, one man in the construction industry cited in a report by the EOC in Britain is said to have commented that 'This is a job for big strong men. We don't want women coming in here with their hormones' (Ward 2005). Comments like this suggest that we need to see working bodies as severally constituted, considering not only their construction by employers but also the role people's own practices play in the development of and differentiation between embodied identities.

In this and the next chapter I examine several types of work discussed by researchers whose explicit focus is the shaping of the working body. This chapter considers the construction of industrial bodies, especially in and through manufacturing, while Chapter 4 considers key areas of employment in service sector organisations, especially front-line customer services and professional and managerial work. While necessarily restricted to a limited number of examples of types of work, this should still enable us to consider the diverse and contradictory constructions of working bodies that are emerging in different types of employment. The research I review (and occasionally critique) should be seen as a point of departure for the wider explanation of embodied labour that this book advocates.

The political anatomy of industrial bodies

Although it can be argued, with Pateman (1988), that the involvement of the (sexed) body in paid work is obscured by the 'political fiction' of labour power as an abstract commodity, with some exceptions the body of the industrial worker has been consistently subject to the more or less explicit gaze of the employer on its potential for production, deviance and resistance. But whereas industrial sociology has tended to take for granted the embodied nature of human labour, locating its reproduction in the private sphere, Foucault's writings, especially *Discipline and Punish* (1991), made the historical construction of the industrial body an explicit focus of analysis. The evolution of manufacturing moulded the body of the worker to fit the production process and, conversely, developed industrial processes that could exploit the passification and subjectification of the worker's body. Scholars drawing on the Foucauldian vocabulary have gone a long way towards putting the working body on the sociological agenda, but at the cost, as I discuss later, of a rather partial account.

Foucault saw the rise of the modern age not in terms of a new political economy, but in terms of the 'invention' of a 'new political anatomy' (Foucault 1984: 182). The human body, he argues, enters a 'machinery of power that explores it, breaks it down and rearranges it'. Discipline increases the utility of the body; it does not repress or take power away from the body, but turns the now 'docile' body into a new, more compliant and more productive carrier of aptitudes and capacities.

Although Foucault treats the transformation of the organisation of work as part of the wider inauguration of a disciplinary regime that included the school, the prison and the asylum, the development of the factory was no less important. This disciplinary regime positioned workers' bodies in time and space in ways that made evading surveillance pointless. Several mechanisms were involved. Through the creation of the late eighteenth- and nineteenth-centuries workshop, formerly separate workers were brought together in a single, enclosed workplace, distributed across space so that a few observers could survey the many. Here supervision developed as a central function of the factory, as an integral part of the production process. The individual became an element that was 'placed, moved, articulated on others' (Foucault 1991: 164), the timing of each adjusted to the timing of the whole. Commands take the form of simple, brief and clear signals (like the factory bell). Moreover as E.P. Thompson (1967) had already pointed out, time-discipline comes to govern non-working as well as working hours, ultimately extending throughout the whole of society. Some capitalists even set up whole townships, in which the behaviour of the working class could be monitored and improved, and family and community life regulated more closely, for instance, Bourneville in Birmingham and Saltaire in Yorkshire, although these were exceptions. The result was the constitution of a labour force that was more productive than the sum of its parts.

Yanarella and Reid (1996) put the 'mind–body percept of the new worker' at the centre of further developments in industrial production methods, labour management relations and other facets of industrial employment. Frederick Winslow Taylor is credited with articulating, at the beginning of the twentieth century, the 'scientific management' of shop-floor operations, which fragmented the labour process so that the different jobs, now devoid of intellectual content or discretion, could be undertaken by a 'trained gorilla'. As Yanarella and Reid put it, Taylor sought to break apart jobs requiring the use of intelligence, imagination and technical dexterity into their component parts, reducing 'productive operations to their exclusively mechanical or physical aspect'. The 'old psycho-physical complex' characterising the worker who knew what he was doing was replaced by a division of labour in which the worker performed a small part of the larger process, mechanically, but more efficiently than ever before.

All this demanded intensive, explicit attention to the labouring body. By the 1920s workers' bodies were extensively analysed through time-and-motion studies, for instance, using a stopwatch to measure and eliminate extraneous movement or unnecessary expenditure of energy. The organisation of factory work also explicitly sought to design labour processes that would control the fleshly, animal desires of the worker and appropriate workers' tacit and explicit skills into the production process, leaving only a kind of purified body as the instrument of production. What Merleau-Ponty (1962) terms the 'body schema', the subject's taken-for-granted sense of where his or her body is, in time and space, and the use of tools as an extension of the subject-body, are investigated, measured and objectified by capital and incorporated into machines that pace the work day. Such apparently technical ways of disciplining the worker's body reconstructed workers' bodies as docile, 'passive objects in the service of capitalist production' (Bahnisch 2000: 55).

Ford's assembly line and his experiments in human engineering developed these trends even further. Ford sought to create a 'new sort of worker' who would thrive under the new conditions of production he set in train (Yanarella and Reid 1996: 182). Developed first in meat processing, where once living animals are disassembled and converted into things, the assembly line went even further in constructing the human worker as an appendage of the machine, as one of its limbs. While Fordist vehicle production never entirely eliminated craftwork, it dominated the imagination of twentieth-century managers.

The arrangement of workers in time and space was part of a wider discursive framework that also involved the subjectification of workers. As Rose (1989) documents, by the 1920s the worker was increasingly addressed as a new kind of subject. At least in its US version, the discipline of scientific management strove to effect a revolution in which the worker accepts higher wages and consumption in return for the binary division of the productive body into brain (management) and brawn (labour). But as Yanarella and Reid (1996) comment, industry also tried to deal with the resulting fatigue, industrial accidents and 'lost time' by beginning to talk to (and about) the worker through personnel policies that went beyond appealing to his economic interests as a wage earner.

The standardisation of the worker, along with the technology and product, was essential to Fordism. Because Taylorism works by designing machinery, processes and products according to the law of averages, difference is not a positive contribution, as Banta (1995: 167) puts it, but a problem to be dealt with. The bodies of workers in general were seen as anarchic, dangerous and politically threatening (Bahnisch 2000). Hence, industrial psychology, as Rose (1989) documents, developed as a way of fitting the man to the task with greater expertise, through testing and other kinds of psycho-technology.

By the 1980s, however, further trends were apparent in the ways that industry shaped workers' bodies. Two ways of conceptualising these new reconstructions of the body in industrial production have been mooted. Yanarella and Reid (1996: 200) suggest the term 'humanware', first mooted by MIT management consultants, as a way of denoting the 'unfolding of an increasingly integrated production system' in which humans are increasingly adapted to the capacities of microelectronics, rather than vice versa. The expanding use of robotics implies an increasingly porous boundary between human beings and technology; the use of prostheses that extend human reach and precision adapt the human being and begin to dissolve the distinction between human and non-human.

A second, related way of thinking about the reshaping of working bodies is through the concept of 'flexible bodies' (Martin 1996, 1994). This notion highlights the connections between the labour market flexibility sought by employers and the construction of new subjectivities and modes of embodiment. As Emily Martin puts it, the flexibilisation of production and the labour market, instigated in response to globalisation, are being 'registered' as 'challenges' to the 'individuality and bodily integrity of the person' (1996: 145–6).

Martin locates the construct of 'flexible bodies' firstly in new models of human health and then, by extension, in new ways of directing production. Corporate restructuring, along with biologists' conceptions of the body and ordinary people's ways of understanding diseases and epidemics, all evidence a perception of the collapse of rigid structures (including firms, bodies, cells, etc.) and/or the boundaries between them. As compared to the 'invisible shield' that we used to fantasise protected our families and jobs (and, as in the advertisement for Colgate toothpaste, our teeth against decay), we now presume that boundaries are so porous that we can only fight AIDS or cancer, or protect ourselves against unemployment, by making ourselves, our immune systems and skills, mobile and flexible enough to adapt to the unpredictability of these threats. Sustaining a livelihood is no longer possible through loyalty to a long-term employer; rather, workers are expected to continuously reskill themselves as they move from job to job and task to task. Meanwhile, the safety-net for those who cannot be flexible, who can't or won't reinvent themselves, has been eroded, resulting in their exclusion from the new 'organically' integrated body politic. As Richard Sennett (1998) concludes, consistency of character, attachment to one's past, now looks like rigidity and no longer counts for much.

The flexible body is also a self-regulating body. Total Quality Management (TQM) and other managerial practices imagine a worker who has so absorbed the need to meet the demands asked of her or him that there is little need for external surveillance or rigid timetabling. Culture change policies try to construct new subjectivities that can best find satisfaction through identification with corporate goals. 'Gone are the piece rates, quality inspectors, first line supervisors' (Martin 1996: 155); instead, self-managing workers are expected to operate as members of a team. Although these changes may be seen as an intensification of labour through alternative modes of control, they seem to involve some qualitative changes. These include flexibility in work rules and labour markets and a movement away from a predominantly technical and task-based definition of skills towards the utilisation of broader social competencies, leading to 'an increase in the duration and intensity of work and the investment of more of the "whole person"' (Thompson 2003: 363). Therapeutic discourses 'involving the saturation of the working body with feelings, emotions, and wishes, the transformation of work, mental and manual, into matters of personal fulfillment and psychical identity' (Rose 1989: 244) are supposed to replace economic incentives. Lower-level workers are now asked to identify with their jobs to an extent previously expected only from managerial and professional staff (Edwards and Wolkowitz 2002). As one informant told Taylor (1998: 13), albeit in a different context, 'They train you to put the stress on yourself.'

Although the historical trend towards internalised or invisible surveillance has long been noted (Sturdy et al. 1992: 5), Martin highlights the extent to which such moves target the body. In so far as these new regimes seek to appropriate the whole self, they involve 'new forms of work integrating mind and body' (Martin 1996: 156) that make thinking in terms of, much less defending, the boundary between work and non-work seem outdated. New organisational identities and capacities are instilled in part through bodily exercises, including especially the Outward Bound type training courses targeting, at least in the US, line workers as well as managers, and involving experiences of fear, vulnerability and interdependence. Such programs are intended to bond participants through inculcating trust in each other's abilities as well as providing social occasions.

The former rigidities and defensiveness are also seen to be undercut by an informalisation of work, including for instance the introduction of practices like dress-down Fridays (and the wearing of more casual work clothes at work generally) as an encouragement to be 'ourselves' (Fleming and Spicer 2004). The apparent breakdown of formerly rigid gender distinctions has been seen as part of this wider process. As Adkins (2004) summarises this approach, a more self-conscious or reflexive attitude towards work performances involves a scrambling of gender characteristics, especially a revaluation of characteristics formerly associated with women rather than men. This is a point we return to in more depth when considering service sector employment in Chapter 4, where these trends are more apparent. But even in the case of 'manual work', there is fragmentary evidence that stereotypically feminine traits are coming to be valued over stereotypical masculinity. For instance, in the British meat and livestock industry some business leaders have pushed for an increase in the employment of women, in order to soften the public image of the industry, dissuade consumers from turning to vegetarianism, and, incidentally, improve the taste of the meat by ensuring that the animals are in a calm state when they are killed (Leask 2000).

The body as working-class habitus

These Foucauldian accounts of the continual reshaping of the working body are very helpful in highlighting the interest employers take in workers' embodiment, and the extent to which the 'body–mind precept' is targeted by employers and challenged by changes in the labour process. By the same token, however, they may overplay the sway of (employers') power and the centrality of external and internalised surveillance to these developments and underplay their embeddedness in the wider framework conditioning workers' embodiment. They may also exaggerate the uniformity and scope of recent trends.

Theorists exploring Bourdieu's theory of the body would argue that he provides an alternative to the 'docile body', through the notion of the embodied habitus, which is better able to explain the evolution of industrial bodies by considering their location within the wider context of class and other social relations. While allowing for more agency on the part of workers than Foucault, his approach also recognises its limits. This is because for Bourdieu habitus represents an accommodation between bodily dispositions and power relations (McNay 2004). Indeed, one advantage of Bourdieu's theory of embodiment, as compared to Foucault's political anatomy, is that it both points to the existence of a more autonomous, class-based, embodied habitus than the 'docile body' envisioned by Foucauldians, but also recognises that the evolution of embodied practices is constrained by their relation to the exigencies of the social field.

One of the problems with the Foucauldian account of the early history of the making of the industrial body, for instance, is its implication that the 'docility' inculcated through the surveillance of factory workers was characteristic of industrial employment as a whole. All the classic British sociological studies of 'men at work' suggest that, historically, male workers in a position to choose have weighed up the relative advantages of different kinds of work, with many preferring the rigours of the coal face, fishing vessel or construction site, where work was not so directly supervised or observed by the employer, to working indoors (Blackburn and Mann 1979; Dennis et al. 1956; Hill 1976). In the absence of close supervision, workers' productivity depended as much on their solidarity with, and concern to maintain, the respect of their co-workers as on the Taylorisation of tasks.

Another implication of these classic studies is that we should not see the bodily capacities of manual workers as natural attributes, as Casey's comments imply, but, rather, as social inputs like humour or appearance. For instance, in a section entitled 'Man and Job', Dennis et al. (1956) suggest that one aspect of men's identification with their jobs was their perception of bodily capacities as tacit but learned abilities, because a worker had to learn to do heavy work in a way that would not damage him. The development and deployment of bodily strength and skill was pre-eminently social. Rotella's American cultural history of 'urban body work' – the work of the body in the skilled trades, assembly line, boxing ring – also stresses that '"a good pair of hands" implied a thick tangle of connections to the world' (Rotella 2004: 1). To have a 'good pair of hands' was both a personal virtue and a social identity, involving technical 'skill and finesse, craft mated with strength' (ibid.: 2). The implication is that workers' (socialised) bodies function as a form of workers' cultural capital to which they are strongly attached.

Although obviously Foucault's idea that a 'machinery of power' explores, breaks down and rearranges the body is more plausible in the case of manufacturing than in some other occupational sectors, we need to recognise that work that looks from the outside as if it rests on the worker's docility may actually depend on the worker's tacit embodied skill and agency. Over the years sociologists have challenged the implication, in Braverman's (1974) account of historical change, as well as Foucault's, that the capitalist labour process actually succeeds in turning human beings into trained gorillas.

Ethnographies of assembly-line production suggest that the most fragmented, deskilled work still requires human 'living labour', the title of a

Figure 3.1   Content of workstation 'strengthening of rear floor' in MV (1/100ths of a minute)

Stamp confirmation of having fitted an anti-torque rod (insert quality-control checklist into printer connected with screw-driver, then withdraw)	14
Stamp confirmation of having fitted the anchorage of front right shock-absorber (insert quality-control checklist into printer connected with screwdriver, then withdraw)	14
Lock screw on the anti-torque rod in the engine compartment (using a servo-controlled electrical screwdriver)	27
Position 2 of 3 front right shock-absorber screws	35
Screw home 3 front right shock-absorber screws, in engine compartment (using a second servo-controlled electrical screwdriver)	36
Connect pipe to water pump, when this is fitted in high position, in engine compartment (using special hand-pliers)	40
Fasten fixing-stud of the airbag logic-controller, between front seats	7
Position and fasten with 3 rivets a reinforcing plate for right side rear floor, beneath back seat (using compressed-air rivetter)	57
Movement, handling and miscellaneous allowances	26
Total	254 = 2.54 mins

Source: Extracted from the documentation of the shop's organisation and methods office, defining the work to be carried out at this workstation, January 1996, Automobiles Peugeot, Carrosserie Sochaux.

Source: J.P. Durand and N. Hatzfeld, *Living Labour: Life on the Line at Peugeot France*, 2003, Palgrave Macmillan. Reproduced with the permission of Palgrave Macmillan.

recent ethnography of a Peugeot plant in France. Durand and Hatzfeld (2003) show that the workers' ability to survive the fiercely timetabled production cycles that pace car assembly at Peugeot as elsewhere depends on the workers' acquisition of shared, embodied skills. Figure 3.1, reproduced from Durand and Hatzfeld (2003: 33), specifies the tasks for one workstation that must be undertaken, in order, every four minutes. It demonstrates the extreme fragmentation of the production cycle at each workstation, and just how tightly and densely prescribed it is. Even so, according to Durand and Hatzfeld, it is only the worker's individual interpretation, gestural care, monitoring attention and selective eye for the differences between car models that enables him (or, less frequently, her) to achieve a 'smoothing-out and purification' of the sequence that gives the cycle coherence and enables it to be completed effectively. Although taking up one's post on the line involves a drastic restriction in one's field of mobility, it is only by sticking to his or her post that the worker will eventually be able to relax and extend their space of mobility. Moreover, the worker's learned capacity is a shared knowledge, as shown when the experienced worker training someone taking over their workstation passes on to him 'the right gesture', meaning one that 'not only conforms to the operations sheet' but also one that allows the worker to save himself and his strength: 'safety and economy of effort are priorities for the worker' (ibid.: 36). Like Bourdieu, it can be argued, Durand and Hatzfeld see the relations of production embodied in the worker's habitus, and in this case reconstituted, cycle by cycle, in the worker's struggles 'between subjection and self-affirmation' (ibid.: 31).

Durand and Hatzfeld's picture of workstations at Peugeot also shows that Martin overstates the extent to which TQM or other policies have increased the scope for factory workers to set their own goals or monitor their own performance. Human Resource Management (HRM) policies are supposed to foster autonomy, mutuality, high commitment and teamwork as an alternative to Taylorist approaches to work organisation, breaking down the division between mental and manual labour, design and execution. They are also supposed to encourage workers to seek fulfilment through new, positive identities offered them by and within the corporation. But most research shows that in practice most firms regulate manufacturing workers through a mixture of Taylorist and HRM policies that have been less than successful in constructing the worker as a new flexible subject (Elger and Smith 2004). Durand and Hatzfeld (2003) say that even in the wiring room at Peugeot, where the firm had experimented with alternative ways of enriching job content, these were decided without any direct participation of its (female) labour force (ibid.: 222); Delbridge suggests that in the two UK plants he studied, workers experienced a harsh Taylorised production system in which HRM policies are put in place in a perfunctory manner, if at all, and workers comply because they 'have to', not because they identify with, or accept, managerial goals (Delbridge 1998: 11). Kunda (1992) suggests that policies compelling workers to identify with the employer rapidly come unstuck when workers in the greedy organisation burn out.

We also need to emphasise both the social differentiation among working-class bodies and workers' own contribution to the maintence of status hierarchies among themselves. When men evaluate jobs in relation to the demands of hegemonic masculinity, Morgan says, the dimensions they invoke are very divisive, as well as embodied, such as the polarities between skilled and unskilled, heavy and light, dangerous and less dangerous, dirty and clean, and mobile and immobile work (Morgan 1992: 80). The shaping of the working-class trade union movement was also deeply dependent on the assumed whiteness of its members, to the exclusion of others (Roediger 1999).

The industrial body as identified by Foucauldian accounts is actually a white male working body. This is in part an accurate picture, since according to Banta (1993), the exclusion of both women and racialised minorities was central to the constitution of the Taylorised body. Not only was Frederick Taylor's work rife with animal metaphors that demonstrate a fear of the animal, the irrational and the sexual, but these abhorred qualities were seen as particularly evident in 'second class labour' – women, blacks, immigrants. Although (white) men could be co-opted by appeals to reason and self-interest through higher pay, women represented the human element, imbued with 'wayward womanness'. Although offering many advantages to potential employers, women's inherent emotionality and physical frailty were seen to present problems for those who employed them (Banta 1993). Managers who did employ women, seeking to profit from women's docility (and lower wages), were warned by contemporary writers to adopt policies carefully tailored to dealing with the woman's 'physical nature, her temperament, her social and her economic experience', similar to warnings about trying to handle a metal without knowing its properties (ibid.: 162). Women get 'headaches and crying spells, have the vapours and go hysterical', suffer from fatigue, and have to be provided with facilities for when they feel indisposed' (ibid.: 162–3). Accounts like Banta's indicate the extent of concerns for the required boundedness of the industrial body, not unlike the anxiety expressed by the construction industry spokesman quoted at the beginning of this chapter.

Bourdieu's notion of habitus is especially helpful for teasing out gender as an embodied living relation, not just a social location in a gender hierarchy (McNay 2004). The notion of a habitus formed in the struggle for survival is particularly pertinent for understanding the formation of the traditional male working-class habitus. In the case of working-class men, Lovell (2000: 18) argues, it reflected the generation of 'a culture of necessity . . . which cele- brates the physical body and the attributes of bodily strength: the form of cultural capital most readily available for accumulation in these circum- stances'. Research by Claire Williams (1993) on the experience of male and female workers in the very dangerous environment of the Australian timber industry provides an excellent example. Williams argues that the men's atti- tudes to the serious hazards they faced have to be seen as a response to the exigencies of social class oppression. If men rarely acknowledge the risks they run, this is because 'a class imperative to take risks is fundamentally built into certain men's jobs' and 'comes to be part of the masculine self- identity of the man (ibid.: 66–7). Rather than seeing men as indulging in risky behaviour through mere masculine bravado, she argues that a man's body is inscribed by working-class masculinity through undertaking the hazardous work that the necessity of earning a living demands of him. A particular habi- tus is an outcome of work and not just a requirement for it.

Simon Charlesworth's (2000) explicitly Bourdieusian ethnography of working-class life in Rotherham raises the question of what happens to that male working-class habitus when its necessity is over. The culture in which the male working-class body developed as an artefact, through self-practice, has been decimated by the decline of heavy industry: the habitus that once carried cultural capital has now become dislocated from its field. Charlesworth argues that these older modes of comportment continue as class-based survival strategies among unemployed men; we should also note the popularity of activities that can provide a field in which their habitus still commands respect, such as body-building, boxing, and even the male stripping that revived the fortunes of the male workers in the film *The Full Monty*.

If ethnographies like those of Williams (1993) and Charlesworth (2000) suggest that we would be wrong to see the male industrial body as simply an effect of power, we also need to consider whether the presumed maleness of the industrial body ever gave an adequate picture of industrial work. If one considers factory production as a whole, rather than concentrating on heavy industry, it is clear that women have played a major role in British and American manufacturing. Women's role in the history of manufacturing in Britain was particularly crucial. In the nineteenth century, although Foucault's own account ignores it, industrialisation was accompanied by shifts in the sexual division of labour that led women, if they could afford it, out of long-term paid work (Brenner and Ramas 1984). But they remained in particular industries, such as textiles, and the poorest women depended on work involving noxious substances (Harrison 1996).

In the twentieth century British female workers re-entered factory production in large numbers. Glucksmann (1990) argues that, in part because in England the mass production of automobiles using male labour did not take off until the 1950s, it was women workers who led the way in the production of mass consumption goods. During the interwar years soaring factory production of domestic goods depended on the recruitment of female workers as line operatives, even if men monopolised all the other positions on the shop floor. Women were in the vanguard of new production techniques in the assembly of electrical goods, food processing, textiles and even motor components. In Britain therefore the development of mass-assembly methods depended on the deployment of women's labour for the most regimented, mechanically paced Taylorised production processes. Women's employment in manufacturing increased still further in the 1950s, when white working-class women's employment began to be supplemented by women immigrants from the New Commonwealth, and did not start to fall off until the 1970s and 1980s.

The now classic feminist ethnographies of women factory workers in Britain in the 1970s and 1980s (Cavendish 1982; Pollert 1981; Westwood 1984) did not consider embodiment as such. Nonetheless, it is clear that in many factories women's bodies were positioned differently than workers in factories dominated by men, sitting (rather than standing) in two parallel lines, heads bowed to their work (Glucksmann 1990), an exaggerated version of the constricted movement and occupation of space that so often embodies women's constrained social position (Young 1990). That the comportment required by the way work was organised so clearly required a gendered, feminine habitus surely helps to explain why so few men even thought of applying for these jobs, despite high unemployment, as it would have undercut the embodied cultural capital of contemporary manliness in which many men had invested. We should also note how the position of these women workers indicates a kind of double conditioning, whereby not only were women's bodies conditioned by their labour, at least in the new assembly plants production was being reconstituted in line with a working-class female habitus, as clean as against dirty, light as against heavy, physically constrained rather than mobile. The entry of women to 'light' industrial work from the interwar years also suggests that the 'feminisation' of work relations, usually associated with the service sector, is not all that new.

The repetitive 'light' manual work once dominated by first white and later New Commonwealth migrant women in the interwar and postwar years now depends in large measure on recent migrants employed, without contracts, in labour-intensive, insecure jobs in low-wage sectors of the economy. This includes light manufacturing in the clothing industry, as well as food processing, agricultural work, cleaning and care work organised around fragmented, repetitive tasks, performed under close supervision, often by migrants and other racialised groups who are relatively invisible within the economy as a whole (Anderson and Rogaly 2004; Ehrenreich 2001; Pai 2004a, 2004b; Phizacklea 2005; Sassen 1991; Wills 2005, 2001). Their invisibility is heightened by their overrepresentation in nightwork and night shifts, their ineligibility for health care or housing. In Britain employers of such labour gain additional flexibility through the use of gangmasters who supply undocumented, migrant workers as and when needed. Rarely permitted to establish a permanent home, such workers are seldom addressed by managment gurus; they seem to be treated as (disposable) bodies rather than reconstructed as subjects.

Finally, the ethnographies of manual workers, male or female, suggest that we also need to give more attention to workers' resistance, through the obvious examples of strikes, work-to-rule and other industrial actions, again challenging the assumption that industrial bodies are necessarily 'docile' bodies. The neglect or invisibilisation of resistance is a frequently made criticism of Foucauldian approaches. Ethnographies have usually been careful not to exaggerate the transformatory potential of workers' agency, but do usually highlight the many ways in which workers seek to carve out a space within oppressive contexts, sometimes with ambiguous consequences. Resistance against an employer often takes gendered forms that reproduce, rather than challenge, conventional gender ideology or other hierarchies among workers. Women sometimes bring what Halford et al. (1997) call an emphasised femininity into the workplace as a way of carving out their space or asserting some independence from workplace rules: the women factory workers who wore bedroom slippers at the workbench and festooned their work area with photographs of their families (Westwood 1984), for instance, or women warehouse 'pickers' who wear make-up and high heels at work (Clarke and Neale 1998).

Cockburn's (1983) study of the printing trade documented an almost paradigmatic case of male workers resisting plans to adopt new printing technologies that would erase their privileges as male workers. The male-dominated trades unions were defending printing technologies that had been constructed around stereotypically male physical strength, arm span and technical skills that effectively excluded women from the industry and defined the workplace as space in which 'personalised masculinity' could flourish. While such examples highlight workers' agency and even resistance, however, they indicate the difficulty of naming any given piece of resistance as radical or conservative in its effects.

Conclusions

The purpose of this and the next chapter is to highlight the centrality of the body and embodiment in the organisation of paid work, and to explore some of the changes in their construction. This chapter considered, historically and at the present time, the relevance and adequacy of Foucault's analysis of the dependence of factory production, and by implication wider industrial employment, on the construction of a docile passified body. Scholars influenced by Foucault's exacting attention to the body as a target of power have been able to enrich our picture of capitalist logic by highlighting the continuing reconstruction and extension of the capacities of the body through expert knowledges, including scientific management, industrial psychology and later developments in the techniques of surveillance and robotics. As we shall see later, this approach has also been very influential in considering the ways in which bodies are arranged in Taylorised 'non-manual' employment, where many workers are subject to continuous surveillance.

While these approaches have been successful in bringing the constitution of the social and political bodies of industrial life to the fore, it may be that the Bourdieusian concept of the habitus is better able to capture the complexity of the shaping of industrial workers than Foucault's notion of the docile body, especially in so far as it gives more emphasis to explaining the logic of their practices in terms of their social location. Locating workers' bodies within the wider class habitus also helps to explain their contributions to and investments in the maintenance of divisions between working bodies.

Although there are no doubt many other examples in the empirical studies of industrial employment that could have been raided for a fuller picture of the changing relation between embodiment, gender and industrial employment, one is surprised that there are not more. One reason for this is because consideration of the relation between work and the body has been often hived off into the field of occupational health and safety and effectively buried in what is seen as a separate field, dealing with questions of bodily health, injury and impairment mainly as technical questions, rather than being integrated into the wider sociology of work relations. So after considering new constructions of bodies in parts of the service sector, we need to consider the chequered contribution of occupational health and safety to the construction of industrial bodies.

FOUR Customer Services

In this chapter we move on to consider occupations and settings associated with the service sector. This is the main area where, as we saw in the last chapter, some commentators have argued for the increasing importance of discursive constructions of workers' subjectivity, as against the focus on the body typical of industrial work. Yet at the same time a number of contributions have been concerned to show that new ways of subjectifying both workers and managers target the body in new ways, so that the organisational body, like its industrial predecessors, becomes more productive. In fact Thrift, who is optimistic about these developments, has recently suggested that 'Much of contemporary capitalism is concerned, in a touchy-feely replay of Taylorism, with producing new kinds of managerial and worker bodies' (Thrift 2005: 12) that can work harder and more attentively.

The study of employment in service sector organisations is often embedded in different research traditions than the sociology of work that developed around industrialism. When Linda McDowell says that what is distinctive in customer relations is that as compared with manufacturing jobs, 'the labour power and embodied performance of workers is part of the product in a way that was not the case in the production of manufactured goods' (McDowell 1997: 32), this scarcely does justice to Marx's understanding of the incorporation of workers' living labour in commodities that forever 'memorialise' the blood, sweat and skill that originally went into their making, even if it is obscured by the commodity form (Scarry 1985). Nor does it sufficiently recognise the tacit but learned embodied practices that are central to industrial workers' relationships to their workmates, tools and objects of labour. But McDowell is surely right to emphasise that the co-presence of worker and customer in an expanded service sector means that interpersonal, embodied interaction with customers contributes more directly to the labour process in customer servicing than in industrial work.

Much recent debate on contemporary employment centres on what is argued to be the increasing importance of the formation of self-identities in the regulation of employment relations. Through new discourses and practices, managers are said to construct subjects eager to respond to different kinds of incentives than previous generations of workers. Instead of assuming that workers are motivated mainly by economic incentives, it is argued, even workers in routinised employment are offered the carrot of positive self-image and choice, even new ways for people to be at work, not that different from the identities we seek to realise through consumption (du Gay 1996). Workers without loyalties to collective occupational, trade union, class or religious identities are much more likely to accept the satisfactions on offer, or at least to cynically play along (Fleming and Spicer 2004; Collinson 2003).

Although du Gay does not bring the body into his formulation, other scholars draw attention to the individualisation and stylisation of the body as part of this process. They draw on a range of theoretical traditions, introduced in Chapter 1, to understand the construction of embodied selves, beginning with Goffman's (1971) dramaturgical model of the presentation of self in public interactions. More influential recently in considering organisational life has been Judith Butler's (1991, 1990) analysis of the 'performativity' of gender (and by extension other social identities), which she sees as being produced 'through the gesture, the movement, the gait (that array of corporeal theatrics understood as gender presentation)' that lead to 'the illusion of inner depth' (Butler 1991: 28). Others draw on Foucauldian approaches, or Bourdieu's (Bourdieu and Wacquant 1992) notion of *habitus*, the embodied dispositions formed initially as part of one's primary socialisation and further developed through the life course.

This chapter begins by considering writings that attempt to identify and define what has been termed the organisational body. I pay particular attention to the role of feminist analyses in making this aspect of corporate life more visible. I then consider as examples two areas of service sector employment that have received the most attention from researchers interested in changes in the body/work relation, interrelational customer services at frontline and management level.

Defining the organisational body

Broadly speaking, there are two different but overlapping foci in analyses of the organisational body: the organisation as a body and the body in organisation. The first of these has been the province of organisational theorists, who adopt the human body as a metaphor for thinking about organisational structures and processes, connoted most obviously in words like corporation or organisation. As Dale and Burrell (2000) comment, the organisation, like the body, is typically understood to consist of a bounded structure of organs held together by self-sustaining, systematic connections. From this point of view, the model of the organisation follows the Cartesian binary dividing mind and body, 'separating the mind as the source of Reason from the merely material body which allows the "objective" mind to cut up and examine (and direct) the body's structures and functions' (ibid.: 15–16).

Some commentators posit the existence of a new, postmodern organisa-tion based on a conceptualisation of the organisational body in which what was previously feared as threateningly fluid flushes out static structures and blurs the inhibiting boundaries between and within organisations that are said to stifle change and growth. Examples include the new kinds of short-term contractual and other relations between firms and between the state and private sector, greater movement of personnel between firms, and also the ways in which new communication technologies blur the boundaries between paid work and other spheres. However, Dale and Burrell (2000) argue against assuming that such changes necessarily challenge Cartesian rationalism or open up more opportunities for individual entrepreneurship or self-expression. 'Post-bureaucratic', apparently boundaryless organisations, they argue, may in fact be *redrawing* boundaries, expanding control of employees over wider geographies of space and time or containing diversity by bringing it inside the organisation. Forms of control and surveillance may be just as intense, but different in character. Gabriel (2003) for instance suggests that discipline characteristic of Weber's 'iron cage' of bureaucratic containment is being supplanted by a 'glass cage' governed by unseen structures.

The ways in which the body of organisation is understood have an impor-tant gender dimension. A very influential article by Acker (1990) argued that the presumed gender-neutrality of bureaucratic organisation was a fiction, because it was based on the exclusion of values associated with women, such as emotionality, embodiment and concern for the particular person rather than the general rule. What is left supposedly governing organisational deci-sion-making are stereotypically 'masculine' traits, such as abstract thinking, analytical abilities, the ability to set aside personal or emotional considera-tions and so on. In recent years some theorists have recognised in contrast the emotionality and sexuality of even conventional organisations (Fineman 2000, 1993; Hearn and Parkin 1995). Whether this represents fundamental change is debatable, in so far as emotions are still seen as interfering with organisational activities or as needing to be harnessed to rationally defined organisational goals (Fineman 2000: 11).

The employees' bodies that are constructed within and by organisations have come in for much more discussion, and are the main focus of this chapter. The organisational body has been defined as 'the mode of embodiment which must be presented, performed and maintained in order to become and remain an employee of a particular organisation or in a particular occupation' (Tyler and Abbot 1998: 440), a definition that reflects from the outset the use of performance theories in conceptualising organisational bodies. In many settings the preferred organisational body may be still shaped by the discourses of desexualisation and disembodiment that idealise the worker as a rational agent mechanically following its bureaucratic rules (Holliday and Thompson 2001: 117), excluding the embodied charisma and passions that are seen to interfere with unbiased judgement. But it is the newer constructions of organisational bodies that have been the subject of most recent research.

The 'discovery' of organisational workers' embodiment, like the organisation's shape, was closely linked to feminist recognition of its gender specificity. The increasing academic interest in the organisational body can be traced not only to poststructuralist theorists, but also to the perception of men as a gendered category. Women's consciousness of the effort they have to put into conforming to or otherwise dealing with previously taken-for-granted masculinist constructions of appropriate workplace commitment, comportment and relationships is one of the main developments that has challenged the invisibility of the normative organisational body (Adkins 1995; Cockburn 1991; McDowell 1997). As Acker argued, organisational and economic theories built around abstract categories, jobs and hierarchies that 'assume a disembodied and universal worker' (Acker 1990: 139) mask the expectation that 'in the real world it is the male body and its relationship to sexuality and procreation that best fits the specification' (Acker 1990: 139, cited by McDowell 1997: 27). Since the development of critical men's studies, however, conceptualising men as a gender category is no longer restricted to feminists' perceptions of 'men as women see them', as I once heard Cynthia Cockburn put it, since a growing literature within men's studies now historicises, pluralises and problematises the masculinities at work in organisational life (Collinson and Hearn 1994; Connell 2002; Morgan 1992; Roper 1994).

As compared to gender, with the exception of Cockburn (1991), the construction of organisational bodies around 'race' and ethnicity has been much less studied. The relative absence of 'race' in the study of organisation requires comment, especially because it contrasts to the centrality of racial divisions to conceptualising segregated labour markets (Edwards et al. 1975). The problem is that the whiteness of organisation is as taken for granted, as its maleness used to be. This is a consequence not only of the invisibility of whiteness as a racial category, but also of the historical construction of the 'inescapable corporeality of non-white peoples', which has left 'the corporeality of whites less certain' (Dyer 1997: 24). The disembodied picture of organisational workers noted by Acker (1990) results as much from the historical projection of corporeality onto black people as a group, as well as onto women as a sex. Conversely, conceptualising some people as more 'bodied' makes it difficult to see their (hidden) contribution to a social form that is defined by its (fictive) rationality. As Puwar (2001) says in a similar argument, imperial ideology has long seen the black body as a sign of the 'natural', i.e. the primitive and sexual, which, again, puts it outside the rarefied ranks of bureaucratised structures. As we saw in Chapter 2 (and take up again in Chapter 7), the mutually reinforcing character of racial divisions and mind–body dualism have ramifications that percolate throughout the study of organisations as well as other aspects of paid work.

The 'discovery' of the constitution of the organisational body is now encouraging researchers to build on existing, if somewhat implicit, conceptions of organisational bodies and to investigate the extent to which organisations attempt to 're-define and manipulate the body's time, space and movements' (Hancock and Tyler 2000b: 109). As we will see, this often involves the commodification of embodied capacities previously considered private (ibid.: 115). The corporation now defines as use-values the body's capacity for emotional responsiveness and emotional control, its sexuality and its appearance, not just its physical movement or skill.

Customer services work: the front line

Much of the research focusing on embodiment at work concentrates on the management of front-line workers (Frenkel et al. 1999), whose work consists of face-to-face (or voice-to-voice) interaction with customers. This is not incidental, for most of the interaction with consumers is assigned to front-line staff at the bottom of the customer service hierarchy (Steinberg and Figart 1999). Since their interaction with customers is seen by employers to be central to keeping up with the competition and meeting profit and other objectives, their embodied presentation may be more explicitly targeted by management than workers further up the hierarchy.

Front-line service work illustrates the potential that growth of the service sector presents for refiguring workers' bodies along with those of their customers. Just as there were parallels between the body of the standardised Fordist assembly-line worker and the standardising constructions of the mass-market consumer (Banta 1995), post-industrial services invoke new figures. Whereas mass-production techniques gave rise to standardised clothing sizes (as against tailors' measurements) and houses and cars for

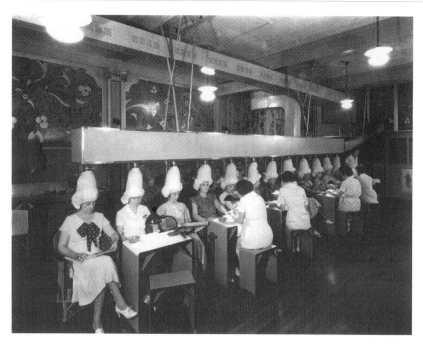

Figure 4.1   Beauticians at Chez Maurice, Miami, 1939. Photograph by William A. Fishbaugh. Courtesy of the Florida State Archives.

standard-sized families, post-Fordism claims to cater for more variegated markets and individualised choice. A nice example of this apparent transformation can be seen by comparing two photographs of hairdressing establishments (Figures 4.1 and 4.2) published in Wilson's (1989) *Floridians at Work*. In the first picture, of an American beauty salon in the late 1930s, the centralised system for drying hair requires the clients to be treated en masse. Mass production techniques govern the arrangement of the bodies of both workers and customers and the relationship between them, and one somehow knows that clients will leave the salon with identical hairdos. The later photograph demonstrates a much more informalised, democratised and individualised relationship, embodied in the dress and postures of both worker and client. However, this does not mean that the relationship is not often stage-managed, whether by the worker or her employer, since once services are produced for a mass market, the relationship of worker to client can no longer be left to the socially sanctioned class deference so evident in Figure 4.1. Indeed, as seen in the short story about Hazel (Brown 1991), discussed in Chapter 1, in hairdressing and other personal services, the relationships between workers and customers are subject to repeated reformulation that requires workers to deploy new styles of the flesh in

75

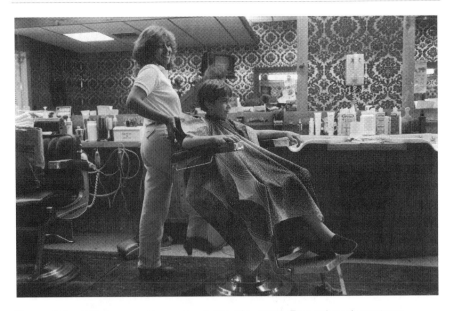

Figure 4.2   Hairdresser, Homestead, Florida, 1984. Reproduced courtesy of the photographer, Bill Maguire.

their interactions, including, nowadays, a cooler, more stylish presentation than that implied in Figure 4.2.

Sociologists identifying and commenting on the possibilities for reforming worker identities have tended to go in two directions. The more optimistic or 'empowerment' approach highlights the potential for benefiting workers, employers and customers alike, through unleashing the 'natural' sociability and vitality of workers who enjoy their interaction with customers. The other, more pessimistic view, points to the instrumentalisation of 'private capacities' like 'demeanor, expression, mood and thought' through customer services organised, in reality, around the 'industrial logic' of the production line or bureaucratic forms of control and accountability, albeit customer oriented (Korczynski 2002; Macdonald and Sirianni 1996; Ritzer 1997; Segal-Horne 1993; Warhurst and Thompson 1998). Three aspects of these private capacities have been seen as of most importance to employers, and most significant for research purposes: emotional work; gendered, sexualised performances; and aesthetic labour.

Emotional labour

The first aspect of customer-oriented relational work to be identified and analysed was what Arlie Hochschild's (1983) ground-breaking book, *The*

Managed Heart, called emotional labour, i.e. the effort employers require workers to put into evoking or shaping, as well as suppressing, feelings in themselves and others. Hochschild took a largely pessimistic view of the harm entailed by the commercialisation of feeling, for workers and for the society as a whole. Developing her ideas through a detailed ethnography of the training of mainly female airline cabin crew, she feared the commercialisation of human feeling made it increasingly difficult to remain in touch with our 'true' emotions or sense of self. What happens, she asked, to the ways a person relates to her feelings or to her face

> when rules about how to feel and how to express feelings are set by management, when workers have weaker rights to courtesy than customers do, when deep and surface acting are forms of labour to be sold, and when private capacities for empathy and warmth are put to corporate uses? (Hochschild 1983: 89)

Three key issues have emerged from subsequent research, all leading to a more 'multidimensional' (Bolton and Boyd 2003) view than Hochschild's. The first is the relation between emotional labour and social hierarchies. Some commentators stress, like Hochschild, that the effort required by emotional labour is pushed downwards, onto lower-level workers, especially women, who have to deal directly with customers without the 'status shields' that professional and managerial workers can hide behind (Macdonald and Sirianni 1996; Pierce 1996; Steinberg and Figart 1999; Taylor 1998). They argue that the construction and management of emotional labour exploit gender ideologies, reproducing naturalising assumptions about women's innate caring capacities. But others argue that the 'emotional labour' workers put into charming or mollifying customers is only one aspect of emotion in organisation, which also includes the emotional control skills managers deploy in managing subordinates and the mutual emotional support that forms part of the 'coping strategies' adopted by co-workers (Bolton and Boyd 2003; Fineman 2000, 1993; Korczynksi 2003).

A second area of dispute is the degree of discretion workers can exercise in their relations with customers. Whereas critics stress the absence of genuine autonomy in how to engage with customers, even under 'empowerment' schemes, the more sanguine point to the sense of achievement or satisfaction workers gain by demonstrating emotional expertise, as Paule (1996) notes with respect to waiting tables. I am reminded here of an acquaintance, a hairdresser, who told me of the 'buzz' she gets by dealing successfully with the challenge of 'winning round' a grumpy client who has had to be kept waiting. She says she does this by trying out different topics of conversation until she can make a 'connection', a phrase also used by one of Taylor's (2001) call centre interviewees.

Much clearly depends on the constraints under which interactions with customers take place, since the productivity goals set by management often conflict with customer demands. This can be frustrating for workers if the pace of work prevents them from helping customers as they would like (Ashforth and Humphries 1993; Bone 2000; Korczynksi 2003, 2002; Taylor 1998, 2001). It seems that while differences in interpretation inevitably reflect the weighting different researchers give the capital–labour relation in setting limits to worker autonomy, most agree that there are important differences between workplaces.

The third issue concerns the effects of emotional labour on workers. Hochschild assumed that workers evolved various strategies, not all of them very successful, for dealing with the distress occasioned by the dissonance between their 'true feelings' and the emotions they are required to display. But others have questioned Hochschild's assumption that we experience a clash between our 'authentic self', associated mainly with the private sphere, and the emotions required by work roles, arguing that we are well able to deploy and distinguish between the 'multiple selves' appropriate to different situations (Wouters 1989). Much empirical research seems to suggest that such dissonance causes people less distress than Hochschild (1983) thought (possibly, I suspect, because we have become so much more adept at it). Bolton and Boyd (2003: 301) suggest that their interviews with airline cabin crews provided little evidence of what Hochschild called 'deep acting', since flight attendants are able to provide appropriate support for customers without 'buying-in' to the norms set by the company. Ordinary politeness carries them through most encounters. For passengers they empathise with, they may go the extra mile, but for 'philanthropic' rather than 'pecuniary' motives. Nor do they pretend to themselves or alter their feelings towards the 'obnoxious'. Yet other research, even in the same sector, has come to different conclusions, stressing the emotional exhaustion customer servicing entails (Forseth 2003; Williams 2003).

One factor too little mentioned in evaluating these different claims, I would argue, is the changes in lifestyles and the wider culture that blur the division between work and home as places we can be 'ourselves'. In 1983, when *The Managed Heart* was first published, Hochschild could scarcely have imagined the proportion of people of working age who live alone, or who choose not to have children, and who look to the workplace for the kind of emotional support or continuity in relationships previously associated with family life. Moreover, as Hochschild (1997) recognises in one of her later books, subtitled 'When Work Becomes Home and Home Becomes Work', in dual career households, the unpaid caring of children and partners in the nuclear family can lead to as much conflict and competition as work obligations in the public sphere.

Nor could Hochschild have imagined the extent to which the commodification of self would be normalised through the growth of jobs in the leisure and tourist industries (Crick 2004, 2002; Sosteric 1996; Warhurst et al. 2004), or of jobs such as group leaders and motivators for commercial weight loss programmes (Stinson 2001), never mind reality television.

The more interesting question, in relation to the themes of this book, is why the embodiment of workers is so rarely mentioned in the emotional labour debate, and has been, as Witz et al. (2003) put it, 'conceptually retired'. For instance, although Fineman's (2000) introduction to *Emotion in Organizations* includes a brief discussion of the 'emotional body', of the 15 articles that follow, only one – on schoolchildren rather than paid workers (Bendelow and Mayall 2000) – makes any reference to it. Similarly, Korczynski's (2002) comparison of nursing, call centres and the hospitality sector makes no reference to either the different demands on the body made by these kinds of work or the different degrees of intimacy with the bodies of 'consumers' that these types of work entail.

The invisibility of the body in the debate on emotional labour is the more surprising because, although Hochschild's original account rejects any idea that emotions can be explained away biologistically as merely physiological states (racing heart, sweating, and so on), for Hochschild feeling still has a bodily component 'not unlike the sense of hearing or sight'. We experience emotion, she says, 'when bodily sensations are joined with what we see or imagine' (Hochschild 1983: 17). Hochschild sees emotional work as having several aspects, including not just cognitive techniques but also the bodily techniques that attempt to change somatic and other physical symptoms of emotion (2003b: 96). Moreover, body and face are involved not only in the production of the observable facial and bodily displays involved in surface acting, but also because of the depth at which deep acting takes place. Indeed, in her later *Commercialization of Intimate Life* (2003), Hochschild revisits Goffman's (1974) analysis of the presentation of self, on which she drew in the earlier book, and comments that although Goffman's social actors manage outer impressions 'they don't feel too much' (Hochschild 2003b: 90). To Goffman's quip that 'When they issue uniforms they issue skin', she suggests he also should have included 'two inches of flesh' (ibid.).

The relative invisibility of the corporeal in the employment-oriented literature on emotion is in direct contrast to the sociology of the body, where the relation between emotion and embodiment is a key concern (Burkitt 1999; Shilling 1993; Williams and Bendelow 1998). Linking the body and emotions as the denied abject of Western rational thought, the phenomenologically inclined in particular see focusing on emotions as a way of transcending mind–body dualism. Rejecting on the one hand a biologistic view of emotions, and a discursive, constructionist view on the other, they favour social interactionist perspectives, like Hochschild's, that interlock biological and social factors in a 'dynamic, rather than reductionist, monocausal way' (Williams and Bendelow 1998: 136). For Burkitt, for instance, 'the idea that emotions are cultural and historical is not inimical to an understanding of how emotions involve bodily processes . . . [S]ensations may well be necessary components of emotion while not being the defining feature' (Burkitt 1999: 116). Burkitt argues that emotions are produced through social relations and (drawing on Elias's (1978)[1939] well-known exegesis on the civilising of the body) that it is only because emotions frequently have to be concealed that we have come to think of them as 'inside' ourselves. But this does not mean that they are purely discursive either, since the means of emotional expression are acquired through the techniques of the body learned in childhood, in the context of communication within class-specific groups and communities. If emotion involves 'embodied modes of being in the world' (Williams and Bendelow 1998: 132), it follows that emotional labour involves both the body and body work, even when employers do not explicitly pick out the body as a medium through which emotions are experienced or displayed.

With very few exceptions (e.g. Sturdy 2003), the sociology of employment has not pursued this kind of approach. A disembodied understanding of emotion at work is particularly pronounced in the conceptualisation of emotional labour as emotional intelligence (Fineman 2004), i.e. a purely mental trait. However, it is also evident in the interpretation of emotional work as mainly a cognitive skill involving the management, rather than the feeling, of emotion, as in Bolton and Boyd (2003). Bolton and Boyd (2003) also tend to focus on relatively superficial emotions, as against the more visceral, one reason they do not see much deep acting going on. Nor does it need to, they argue, for workers have already internalised the necessary emotional competence for engaging with customers and workmates long before starting their jobs, as part of earlier processes of socialisation or in the inculcation of professional codes of service, so that it does not necessarily involve extra effort.

The question is how best to bring the body out of retirement. One possibility is to put more focus on the dependence of emotional work on the presence of a 'culturally intelligible body' (or at least a voice), a phrase frequently used by Butler. This would put the emphasis on the presence or absence of bodies, their location in space and differences between bodies, or at least between our various expectations of them. The actual presence of a body sometimes plays a vital role in the control of emotion, for instance in the case of night club bouncers (Monaghan 2002a, 2002b), police and other emergency workers, and health practitioners. Moreover their bearing and location in time and space help to shape customers' emotional expectations and the resources that workers can deploy to deal with them, as we can see in the photographs discussed above. In the case of the airline industry, expectations regarding the service passengers can expect from workers is conveyed partly through workers' location in space: passengers are informed about expected interaction with airport and airline staff through workers' placement at desks or counters of different heights, whether they are standing or seated, and whether they are stationary (as in the airport), move around amongst the passengers, such as flight attendants, or are curtained off like the pilots (Forseth 2005). Moreover, as passengers we are led to expect a different level of service from female than from male cabin crew (Williams 2003).

Bolton and Boyd's (2003) presumption that the flight attendants they studied had already internalised the necessary emotional competence hints at another possibility, the use of a more explicitly Bourdieusian account which focuses on the dispositions workers bring to their work rather than their labour or performances they put on. As we will see later in the chapter, this is one of the directions researchers are taking.

Sexual labour

Hochschild's groundbreaking research was soon followed by research that brought to the fore her consciousness of the specifically gendered aspects of customer service work. Of the enormous literature on the gendering of work relations, those interested in the embodiment of gender in paid work have highlighted especially the (hetero)sexualisation of women's bodies. Materialist feminists influenced by Delphy (1984) stress the appropriation of women's sexuality by men, whereas poststructuralist feminism sees sexuality as more mobile, providing opportunities for women as well as men to exercise power.

As we saw in discussing emotional labour, commentators disagree about the balance between the frustrations and satisfactions of customer servicing work. Feminists have by and large identified with the more pessimistic perceptions, arguing that the packaging of customer services exploits the expectations of normative heterosexuality and locks women into subservient, hyper-feminine roles focused around 'being nice to jerks', as I once heard it described. Research on customer services is particularly important because it shows how in many cases employers expect female workers to use their gender and (hetero)sexuality to increase custom and profits by flattering male customers, although this is much stronger in some sections of customer services than others.

Adkins's (1995) case study of women's work in the hospitality and leisure industries in the North of England was one of the first to look at the deployment of gender and (hetero)sexuality in the service sector in this

81

regard. She drew in part on Carole Pateman (1988), a political theorist who argued that the appropriation of women's labour, sexuality and fertility by men was underwritten by an implicit 'sexual contract' at the heart of the modern polity, using prostitution as one of her examples. Adkins (1995) developed Pateman's (1988) ideas in relation to more conventional kinds of work, arguing that where the quality of the interaction is part of what is sold as 'service', as in the hospitality sector, heterosexist assumptions about gender define the worker's obligations. As Brewis and Kerfoot (1994: 16) put it, employers 'tacitly contract not for a disembodied capacity to type, serve drinks or whatever, as simply "housed" within a female body, but for selved labour that gives this work a particular meaning and value'. Adkins suggests that women's jobs in the hospitality and leisure sectors require work that men's do not: women are expected to serve as a repository for male desires, in turn necessitating particular ways of dressing and making-up that ensure that they are seen as heterosexually available. Adkins was mainly concerned with the appropriation of women's sexuality by men in their roles as employers, customers or co-workers. However, as will be discussed later, Adkins's (2002, 2001) more recent work considers the extent to which women are able to trade on their gender performances in their own interests.

Tyler's research on the deployment of women's bodies by the airline industry stresses the appropriation of women's bodies by the employer to increase custom and profits, but puts more weight than Adkins (1995) on their interest in scripting women's embodied (hetero)sexuality as a marketable aesthetic capacity (Hancock and Tyler 2000b; Tyler and Abbott 1998; Tyler and Taylor 2001). She extends Hochschild's (1983) recognition of the gendering of emotional labour to identify what she conceptualises as an additional obligation on the part of women (and only women) flight attendants to present the particular, decorative 'organisational body' required by management. Throughout the recruitment, training and supervision processes women flight attendants are constituted as the embodied material signifiers of an organisational ethos. Fulfilling this specification requires 'body work' (Shilling 1993) on the part of flight attendants, that is, the time, effort and resources dedicated to maintaining a particular state of embodiment, additional to her other work obligations. Repeated instruction in 'body techniques' forms part of their training, for instance they are taught to 'always *walk softly* through the cabin, always *make eye contact* with each and every passenger and always *smile* at them' (Tyler and Hancock 2001: 31). The women workers are required to produce a feminine aesthetic, to look 'polished' and sexually attractive, not just clean and presentable, as is the case for men. Tyler argues that the body work this takes is naturalised by being equated with what women are, by nature, rather than something (extra) they do.

Tyler made particular use of feminist appropriations of Foucault's conceptualisation of internalised surveillance as a form of power (Bartky 1990; Bordo 1990a, 199b, 1989). Because flight attendants are in sight of passengers almost continually during a flight, the flight attendant's body work is particularly taxing, since in addition to the maintenance work she does off stage, in terms of diet and grooming, she has to 'remain constantly "body conscious" so as not to make a spectacle of herself, by inadvertently disclosing or exposing parts of her uncontrolled and undisciplined "natural body"' (Tyler and Abbott 1998). The flight attendant has to internalise the gaze of others in managing her own body.

Anyone who wants further illumination of the importance of both external and internalised surveillance of women's appearance has only to watch British television make-over programmes like *What Not to Wear* (McRobbie 2004). Here we see, first of all, chilling invitations to a woman's employer and colleagues, as well as her family and friends, to scrutinise her looks. The women participants are then instructed by the programme presenters in how to look at themselves, how to assess their good and weak points, and how to choose their clothes. In the penultimate scene of each programme the women are permitted to see (and glory in) the mirrored reflection of themselves as transformed women, and to look at themselves, in effect, through other eyes. The existence of such programmes perhaps should lead us to question the extent to which women's performance of a gendered aesthetic is really as naturalised as Tyler says. As Bartky (1990) says in a Foucauldian essay on the politics of women's self-surveillance in everyday life, most women recognise and openly acknowledge other women's body work; *What Not To Wear* is hardly intelligible outside the shared assumptions of female culture. *What Not to Wear* goes rather further in so far as it trains the women in 'propertising' (Skeggs 2005) their embodied appearance, reminding them that with respect to employment what you look like matters more than who or what you know.

Tyler and Adkins's analyses emphasise the economic value of heterosexualised gender performances to the employer in attracting customers and providing them with service they enjoy. Tyler and Hancock (2001) suggest that the airline companies (and by implication corporations more generally) use women's bodies as what they call 'material signifiers' to brand their product in a segmented product market, or perhaps to successfully segment the market based on relatively few substantive differences between firms. Not only are new embodied identities and capacities constructed and absorbed by the corporation, Hancock and Tyler suggest, but new modes of embodiment *distort* the body by turning it into an empty sign of corporate branding.

This role of female bodies is especially apparent in fashion retailing, where, as Leslie (2002) points out, the bodies of the sales staff form an important link in the fashion commodity chain that links production, distribution and consumption. Not only are sales staff required to buy and wear the clothes sold by their employer, the retailers also believe that the workers have to be 'the right type' for the client or the clothes (Pettinger 2004). Although the workers' bodies cannot be directly managed, expectations about the workers' bodily self-management is overt, detailed and anxiety-producing. Staff not only recognise the need to conform, but may share the employer's criteria for how they should look. Leslie's interview with one 23-year-old Canadian retail worker describes this complex picture extremely well. Discussing her fears concerning the consequences of not conforming to the regulatory regime, the sales assistant says,

> At home I'm more relaxed in the clothes I wear. Whereas [at work] I'm always concerned about the way I look … like I've been gaining weight. Yesterday I went out and bought two new pairs of pants one size bigger because I was so upset.

It seems that one of the things that exacerbates her anxiety is that, as a consumer herself, she knows only too well how the customers think:

> I look horrible. No one is going to buy anything from me … I get all paranoid about the way I look … because people are looking you up and down as soon as you are working in the store. They are saying 'Who do I want to help me? Okay. She looks my style. She looks the way I would like to look. Okay, I will go with her.' And I find that's true a lot. The girl who looks the best in your store's clothing is the one that gets most of the customers. (Leslie 2002: 69)

Whereas analyses like these emphasise the appropriation of women's appearance and sexuality by men, employers or both, other analysts put more stress on women's active participation in the gendering of work through their choice of jobs and the way they construct them once in the post. For instance, Pringle (1989) found that secretaries are not without office influence, but in the absence of institutionalised sources of power, it has to be produced through sexualised interactions or relationships modelled on familial roles. Similar conclusions have been drawn from studies of secretarial workers in Japan (Gottfried 2003; Ogasawara 1998). As Halford et al. (1997) point out, commentators who identify opportunities for female sexual power in the workplace tend to separate the deployment of sexuality from gender positioning, enabling them to conceptualise it as a distinct, mobile form of power that can challenge as well as reproduce gender hierarchies. Brewis (2000) and Brewis and Linstead (2000) also argue that the conflation of sexuality at work with sexual harassment positions women as forever the victims of sexual aggression rather than sexual subjects. Others see the unruliness of embodied sexuality breaking through and to some extent challenging the disembodiment of organisational life (Burrell 1992; Holliday and Thompson 2001). However, this approach has not been developed vis-à-vis interrelational customer services (except, ironically, in Brewis and Linstead's (2000) analysis of prostitution, which will be discussed in Chapter 6).

Although the preponderance of literature on gendered customer service work has concerned women workers, there is an increasing interest in deployment of different masculinities in the workplace. Young men too may be subjected to sexual harassment (Guerrier and Adib 2000) as part of their jobs, and as discussed later, men's bodies are also aestheticised. But in some service sector jobs an aggressive, implicitly heterosexualised masculine presence, as noted in Hochschild's discussion of the emotional labour of debt collectors, is a requirement of the job. For instance, Lee Monaghan's (2002a, 2002b) research on nightclub bouncers documents these workers' dependence on body building and 'body techniques' (a term, originating with Mauss (1973) which Tyler also deploys. The 'body capital' required to obtain and carry out their jobs is organised around a gendered conception of embodied competence and a masculinist hierarchy of values. Less explicitly, Monaghan also recognises bouncers' dependence on the ingrained (usually white) working-class habitus in which they grew up, as well as their body maintenance workouts in the gym. Monaghan also notes that the moulding and presentation of their bodies 'for the purposes of territoriality', through the use of uniforms and body and facial idiom to indicate impenetrability, is especially important to doorstaff who have to keep some customers out and manage the 'fallout' from the encouragement of heavy drinking.

It is important to consider how the centrality of the sexuality and gender of workers in some sections of the customer service sector, as an implicit requirement in the job specification, is reconciled with the principles of equal opportunities, especially the longstanding legislation that forbids discrimination along the lines of sex or race or more recent legislation forbidding discrimination on the basis of sexual identity. As Collinson et al. (1990) and Cockburn (1991) pointed out in the beginning of the 1990s, the gendered culture of some organisations is so blatant that equal opportunities discourse has had little purchase on recruitment practices. Increasingly, though, in certain kinds of organisations, men may be recruited to women's jobs, and women to men's, if they are happy to accept the masculinised or feminised habitus that governs a particular occupation or workplace. This applies to the female bouncers who, according to Monaghan, share their male workmates' respect for the attributes of hegemonic masculinity, including a forceful body build, even if they themselves 'seldom matched the physical proportions of their male colleagues' (2002a: 341). It may be the case that the maintenance of strongly gendered work cultures in an era of equal opportunities is made possible only by the blurring of the links between biological sex and gendered *hexis* in the wider culture, especially the more open performance of gender-bending masculinities and femininities. But before entertaining such hypothetical presumptions, we need to consider whether in fact gender is still as central to the definition of work roles in the customer services sector as Adkins, for instance, claimed.

Aesthetic labour

In the last few years, research on the gendering of service sector work roles has been complemented by a new conceptualisation of 'aesthetic labour' that marginalises the gendering involved in the aestheticisation of work roles. This is concerned with analysing what are seen as employers' attempts to make the body more visible in customer service work through a focus on the body's aesthetic qualities, including deportment, style, accent, voice, and sexual desirability. Indeed, this concerns all the aspects of the body that appeal to the senses, and not just a concern with 'beauty', as the term 'aesthetics' is sometimes understood. The publications and papers emerging from the research programme at the University of Strathclyde (for instance Nickson and Warhurst 2003; Nickson et al. 2002, 2001; Warhurst et al. 2004; Witz et al. 2003) do not see the gendered body as integral to the construction of what they term 'aesthetic labour', and instead give much greater importance to embodied dispositions linked to social class. The context is the concentration of job growth in the 'high style' sector in Glasgow in the years since its nomination as the European City of Culture for 1990, in style-intensive bars, restaurants, hotels and retail outlets. They argue that in this setting workers' bodies are treated as a kind of animate hardware, contributing to the design landscape in much the same way as the inanimate decor or gourmet food. In this sector, at least, a large part of their work consists of 'looking good' and 'sounding right', as these attributes contribute directly to the popularity of the venue with its targeted clientele and thus the profitability of the enterprise.

According to Witz et al., 'increasingly modes of worker embodiment are being corporatively produced or "made up" in new and different ways in today's service economy' (2003: 35–6) so as to embody the aesthetics of the service organisation. Such an approach foregrounds the 'sensible components' of the service encounter, which depend on 'styles of flesh', not just, as in Hochschild, the manufacture of feeling. Although recruitment criteria stress the kind of person being sought, with the expectation that practical skills can be inculcated during post-recruitment training, management's concern with aesthetics does not stop with recruitment. One Glasgow hotelier apparently tries to sensitise new workers to 'what successful looks like, what confidence looks like' by sending them out to photograph examples of these qualities (Warhurst et al. 2004). Examples like these indicate that the worker's style is treated as an explicit requirement of the job.

As already seen, similar evidence comes from the fashion retail sector, in the UK and elsewhere, where workers' 'look' – their dress style, hair colour and cut, and 'attractiveness' – play an important communicative role in conveying the brand image of different chain stores (Leslie 2002; Pettinger 2004). At the top, designer end of the market aesthetic labour is strongly inflected by social class, demonstrated by the recruitment of workers with middle-class accents, confidence and familiarity, as consumers, with the environment in which they work. These developments are highly discriminatory, and have tended to favour (middle-class) students seeking temporary or part-time work, as against working-class or older workers. The involvement of some of the Strathclyde researchers in a Wise Group pilot training programme suggests that while working-class young people might gain these 'competencies' through training, they will remain at a disadvantage (Nickson et al. 2002).

One of the strengths of the way the concept of aesthetic labour has been developed is the adoption of aspects of Pierre Bourdieu's social theory, especially its sensitivity to the importance of social class inequality to the sociology of the body. Witz et al. (2003) argue that the reason the concept of emotional labour gives too little attention to the corporeal is because it is associated only with the display aspects of surface acting. Like Bolton and Boyd (2003), Witz et al. challenge the distinction between surface and deep 'inner selves' by suggesting that what employers seek are workers with embodied dispositions sedimented in childhood, as part of what Bourdieu calls the *habitus*, as defined in Chapter 1. Habitus is learned and exemplified partly through durable ways of standing, speaking, walking and other aspects of deportment, what Bourdieu calls *hexis*. Witz et al. (2003) argue that although Bourdieu himself linked habitus to class structure, and did not explore its relevance within the workplace, employers target exactly the class-specific dispositions that interested Bourdieu, dispositions that are part of the (embodied) self rather than displayed in particular situations.

Nonetheless from my point of view there are some problems with 'aesthetic labour' as a concept, especially a definition of aesthetic labour that is, on the one hand, too broad, but, on the other, too selective in bringing corporeality into view. The very broad definition of aesthetic labour as the 'mobilisation, development and commodification of the embodied capacities and attributes of employees to produce a favourable interaction with the customer' (Nickson et al. 2001: 178) is confusing, in so far as it is not clear whether the social and technical skills that aesthetic labour supplements (Nickson et al. 2002: 13) are also envisioned as embodied. Presumably other, more utilitarian aspects of the embodied subject, such as stamina, health and relative sobriety, as well as emotional competencies, continue to feature as recruitment criteria, even though they do not feature so much in the style sector's marketing-led discourse. The problem here is partly whether we are talking about the criteria set by the employer that relate to appearance, or an aestheticisation of labour, which implies that all aspects of the body are reduced to their signifying value as objects of pleasurable regard. There is a danger here, as West and Austrin (2002) note in a more general discussion, of 'reducing work [and the body] to style'.

A second problem is the failure to integrate gender into the analysis or even to engage with Bourdieu's understanding of gender as integral to the individual hexis developed through self-activity in childhood (Lovell 2000). The absence of gender analysis is never explicitly justified, but presumably is to be explained by the fact that the young men working in the high-style sector, and not only the young women, are selected on aesthetic criteria and trained in self-presentation. To say the work is not confined to either men or women is not to say it is not gendered, though, especially if sexual attractiveness is one of the attributes employers look for. The Strathclyde findings may point not to the absence of gender as a key attribute, but rather to the dependence of employment in this evolving sector on new constructions of gender and sexuality. In particular these reflect the construction of new, style-conscious masculinities circulating in the realm of consumption (Mort 1996; Nixon 1996), which are said to be blurring traditional constructions of British masculinity, including the homosexual/heterosexual, male/female binaries. One suspects that the employers are not after unisex bodies but seek to recruit particular masculinities and femininities and exclude others, such as the loutish man and the procreative or ageing woman. In so far as body images constructed in terms of the (changing) constructions of gender are built into and reproduced by the labour of aesthetics, gender cannot be seen as outside or even separate from the commodification of aesthetics, even if the employers leave their constructions to the wider culture.

The suppression of gender is not unrelated to a third problem, the failure to consider the kind or amount of effort and/or expense that providing aesthetic labour entails for workers. The definition of aesthetic labour as the supply of embodied capacities and attributes possessed by workers *at the point of entry* into employment (Nickson et al. 2001) has the downside of making the ongoing labour of aesthetics once in post seem rather inconsequential.

The effect is to render the effort that goes into appearance maintenance work relatively invisible, as Tyler and Abbott (1998) suggest is the case for female flight attendants. It might be argued that this shadow work is more extensive for women than men. For instance, as Black and Sharma (2001: 100) put it in another context, although some forms of masculinity require intensive work, such as body building, on a routine basis 'men are not required to paint, moisturize, deodorize and de-hair their bodies in order to appear masculine'. But the main point is the amount of reproductive labour that a fully aestheticised body requires; this includes not just the labour of the workers themselves but the paid body work of the various body-workers we will be looking at in Chapter 7. Think of how much continuing labour a David or Victoria Beckham must take to produce!

The final point to be made about aesthetic labour is the lack of reference to 'race' or ethnicity in the development of this concept. This is as much a problem of many of the feminist accounts of the gendering of customer service work summarised above. Macdonald and Sirianni (1996: 14–15), whose book is among the few on customer services to highlight the racialisation of its division of labour, point out that traits with a 'signalling function', indicating to the customer and employer important cues about the tone of interaction, include race as well as gender, age and sexuality. Racialised distinctions have always been central to customer service provision. When the American commercial air travel industry began to expand in the 1950s and 1960s, the employment of young, Hollywood-beautiful white women was one of the ways through which air travel was distinguished from other modes of travel, and the glamorous role of the flight attendant from the menial work of the waitress (which in fact it much resembles). It gave flying a certain status. Had the airlines recruited as cabin crew black women or men (paralleling the recruitment of Pullman car stewards on American railways, at the time a job monopolised by black men), the image would have been different yet again. Thankfully, black identities may no longer count against the aesthetic criteria established in (most of) the travel, hospitality and leisure industries. Yet in so far as 'race' or ethnicity still signal qualities a firm might wish to emphasise, their connotations remain important to aesthetic labour. As an example, certain black urban body stylisations may carry a cache for firms seeking to present a cool image or street fashion credibility and others may be ruled out entirely.

Professional and managerial workers

Turning to a consideration of managers and professionals, still mainly within customer services, puts a different slant on some of the issues already addressed. First of all, as compared to the (hetero)sexualisation of lower-level customer services, women managers have been required to present a more desexualised persona, so as not to call attention to their embodied difference. However, research by McDowell (1997) and Holliday and Thompson (2000) suggests that this may be changing to some extent, especially among younger women, although a different kind of gendered performance than for non-managerial employees is still required. Secondly, class politics contextualise gender politics in important ways. Both men and women in what Goldthorpe (1982) called the service class may have better opportunities for accumulating cultural capital and benefiting from their investments in the long term than their subordinates. The deployment of classed embodied identities as cultural captial (Skeggs 2004) among upper-level managers has to be seen within this class context.

Halford et al.'s (1997) study of three sites of organisational employment (hospital nursing, local government and banking) takes us outside the realm of private sector customer services, identifying the centrality of gender and (hetero)sexuality to the tacit rules that govern workplace interaction and organisational life. It usefully conceptualises three distinct dimensions of body politics (ibid.: 258–9) that have been important in large-scale organisations governed by explicitly gender-neutral discourses that desexualise workers, although less so in the traditionally more overtly gendered and heterosexualised occupation of nursing.

Halford et al. (1997) identify, first, a spatial dimension to the body politics of the organisation, which draws attention to the management of transgressions of personal space, like sexual harassment. However, they also call attention to the need to negotiate spatial proximity. Nursing is a particularly interesting example because this aspect of body politics is intrinsic to the doing of the job, caring for patients, rather than revolving around questions of identity. Second, Halford et al. note the importance of the verbal dimension of organisational gender politics, especially the 'calling up' of women's sexuality and reproduction. They echo Cockburn's (1991) insistence that what is at issue as regards workplace sexuality is not prudery/laxity but who has the power to call up embodiment (and to what purpose).

Halford et al.'s third dimension, viz. implicit organisational rules concerning the presentation of the body, suggests that in organisational life, women's dress and general appearance are important visible markers of their difficulties in negotiating power hierarchies. As noted above, the organisation has been seen as particularly problematic for women, because the dualisms structuring both organisation and gender (mind/body, male/female) are mutually reinforcing. Where rationality is privileged, the body is rejected as unreliable, especially the fecund female body (McDowell 1997: 34). The apparent incompatibility of heterosexualised femininity and the exercise of organisational power puts women in a damned-if-you-do/damned-if-you-don't position, whereby they are punished for being feminine (unprofessional) and for being professional (unfeminine). A good example of an advertisement addressed to women worried about how to negotiate this dilemma appeared in a poster campaign for Austin Reed clothing in the 1990s. It showed a tall, blonde woman wearing a fairly relaxed trouser suit sitting in a tall office chair. The tag line insists that 'The chairman wouldn't wear it. But his successor almost certainly will!'

It is not just that women have to mimic male dress without looking like men, but also that it is often through clothing that women are able to create a simulacrum of the bounded, defensible body long seen as a necessity of organisational life. As one of their informants told Halford et al. (1997: 247) about her choice of clothing, 'Well, I have my armour that I put on'. Nowadays professional women are dressing more casually (and wearing clothes that show more flesh) but a professional 'look' is still required. Many photographs in the business magazines show women no longer 'held in' by very formal clothing, but still tailored by workouts in the gym.

Trethewey (1999) identifies similar problematic aspects of the presentation of self in her interviews with individual 'professional women' in a relatively conservative southern US state. While female bodies might be called up or sexualised by male colleagues in exactly the way Halford et al. (1997) suggest (for instance, men teasing women when they eat chocolate), they are also a source of antagonism between women as well as a source of anxiety for women as individuals. Her interviewees were particularly conscious of having to manage their size, sexiness and reproductive bodies in ways men did not. Like Tyler, discussed above, Trethewey (1999) makes good use of Foucauldian notions of power to understand women's internalised self-surveillance (Holliday and Thompson 2001; McDowell 1997). She sees women actively criticising each other's body size, because they see being overweight as a sign of being out of control, and therefore a poor advertisement for women's professional competence.

Dealing with the presentation (or, rather, ensuring the erasure) of the reproductive female body is especially important. Showing evidence of menstruation through staining, never acceptable, must be guarded against in the work context at all costs (Trethewey 1999). Longhurst (2001) argues that even the pregnant body is perceived to be out of place in the public sphere, as it evokes fears of fluidity and seepage. Although she does not say so, some of the problems echo the difficulties mothers have in reconciling the way children's bodies seep unpredictably out of the times and spaces set aside for them – evidence of children's sickness, tears and sleepless nights are hidden rather than paraded. Research consistently shows that whereas men in the higher ranks of management are likely to be married with children, among women at the higher levels of management, and many of the professions, women are more likely to be single or divorced and to have fewer children than their male colleagues, often none (Crompton and Harris 1998; Hakim 1996; Wajcman 1998). Although differences exist between occupations, demanding employment is usually still organised around the lifestyle of a male worker without day-to-day caring responsibilities – even if the worker is now female. The routines of professional life make little room for pregnancy or the nursing mother. Although it is true that celebrity pregnancies have made the pregnant state much more visible in the public domain, there is a world of difference between the glamorous, air-brushed body of the cover photograph and the actual experience of managing a three-dimensional pregnancy or nursing a baby in a world set up for other figures.

McDowell's research on the cultural dimensions of gender in City finance (McDowell 1997; McDowell and Court 1994a, 1994b) gives the reader access to the experiences of a more elite group of high-flying finance managers and financial sales personnel. While most share a similar white, middle-class background, including education in leading universities, generational differences in the stylisation of the body are important for both women and men. All the women are highly conscious of the relevance of gender to what they themselves call their 'performance', but compared with the 'feminine but serious' image of the older women, some of the younger women do not attempt to emulate the desexualised, business-like professionalism of their elders. As one of them put it: 'I'll never be a man as well as a man is' (McDowell and Court 1994b: 745), so they adopt feminine decorativeness as a disguise and even an asset. Another said it was 'because you've got to have some fun in life' and disconcerting her male colleagues was part of this. Heterosexual gender performances are also helpful in the uneasy seduction of clients in which both men and women engage. Not only has office dress become less formal, but women realise that 'Every clothes style available to women is marked in some way' (McDowell 1997: 145). To some extent they try to work this to their own advantage.

Perhaps the most interesting aspect of McDowell's account concerns the importance of bodily performance to men's careers in the City, not just women's. We need to be wary of assuming that men automatically measure up to the masculine organisational ideal. The idea of men's bodies as impenetrable or invulnerable is more a defensive social construction than a reflection of natural sexual difference (Bordo 1993; Smart 1996).

Overt interest in the relation between masculinity and work roles is relatively recent, although it has in the past occasionally surfaced. For instance, as the figure of the modern manager gained ground in the US in the 1950s, it was accompanied by anxiety about the implications for the manly virtues, as in Whyte's account of a new ideal type, *Organisation Man* (2002 [1956]). Whyte took for granted that the new executives were all men, but was concerned about the predominance of new values. Men working in the new large-scale corporations had to work as faceless or anonymous members of a co-operative group, as members of the team, accepting a junior place in the hierarchy to begin with and only gradually working their way up the chain of command. They were selected partly through a battery of standardised – and standardising – psychological tests. All this was very different from the constructions of American middle-class manliness that had privileged character and individuality over conformity; self-assertiveness and leadership over blending in; and entrepreneurship and self-employment over employment by others. Whyte clearly feared the rule of mediocre, insipid, conformist men in public life. An unspoken concern was the fear of a decline in men's sexual potency, articulated more overtly in a film that came out in the same year the book was first published, *The Man in the Grey Flannel Suit* (1956, dir. Nunnally Johnson). Here the protagonist, played by Gregory Peck, returns from war only to be emasculated by his routinised existence commuting to work in the 'soft' world of the advertising executive.

Changes in the construction of masculinity are often articulated as changes in the relation between masculinities, conceptualised in the plural, rather than the relation between masculinity and femininity as mutually exclusive binaries (Collinson and Hearn 1994). McDowell distinguishes between two masculinities at work in the City: the slim, sun-tanned princes and the older, pot-bellied patriarchs. As compared to their elders, McDowell's (1997) princes were distinguished by their youthful appearance, energy, activity and virility. Even a hint of recklessness, as in the case of the renegade bond dealer Nick Leeson, did not seem to be a problem. As McDowell puts it, these men 'are seriously sexy, in a self-confident, moneyed way' (1997: 185–8). Their demeanour in part reflects the individualisation and perceived competitiveness of career success. McDowell reports that in their interviews nearly all the younger men, like women, were conscious of the need to pay attention to their self-presentation, in terms of hygiene, fitness and choice of clothing. They point out that many of them spent time and money on working out in the gym.

In contrast, the older men did not feel they had to sell themselves. Such men gain their power from their collective membership of a powerful male elite, illustrated for instance in photographs of the boards of directors of various firms. They are always pictured fully clothed, in suit and tie, standing upright, bodies perhaps cut off at the waist, so that the lower body stratum is denied. Their cultural capital derives from primary socialisation, education and sports in public school and/or Oxbridge; unlike the younger men, they presented no hint of an activity that would 'overheat brain or body'. They are reminiscent of the male Members of Parliament interviewed by Liddle and Michielsens (2000), who found that as compared to women MPs, the upper-middle-class and upper-class men's accounts displayed a sense of natural entitlement to their position. This was never presented as something that they had needed to demonstrate or work towards.

McDowell's 'princes' are a good example of what has been called the 'cultural feminisation' of the labour force, which includes the focus on bodily performance and personal appearance as an integral element of workplace success, for men as well as women (Adkins 2001, 2002). Adkins recognises that men increasingly undertake to stylise and aestheticise their bodily presentation in ways previously experienced by women. As an element in the promotion stakes, the male body too now has to be worked on, through diet and exercise regimes, as a sign of 'a depth of health that goes deep into the flesh' (Holliday and Thompson 2001: 125) and as an index of self-discipline, control and conformity. Thus, in addition to the new valorisation of 'feminine' empathetic management skills, men are increasingly taking up a position as the object of desire, showing a concern with style, fashion and consumption previously associated with women. As Adkins (2001) summarises this argument, gender roles seem to be getting 'scrambled'.

However, Adkins (2001) concludes that, despite the pluralisation or feminisation of masculinities, the male/female binary is still the key axis of organisational body politics. She suggests that men actually gain by being able to perform and appropriate cultural traits formerly associated with women. Performances of emotionality and aesthetics by women are so naturalised that they cannot cash them in as a resource in the career stakes. In contrast, men gain credit for theirs, as an achievement. This gives men a different, more instrumental relation to their embodied identity than women, who are prevented from using theirs to accumulate cultural capital to the same extent. I am less sure that femininity is any more naturalised in a woman than masculinity is in a man. To say that a man 'looks good in a suit' says that he is to the manor born: the suit fits him like a glove. It is rather that emotionality and aesthetics are more rewarded in men than aggression or other stereotypically masculine traits are rewarded in women. Adkins may be right that men have taken on women at their own game, in order to preserve their position in the labour market stakes. If men can play both stereotypically masculine (hard, aggressive) and feminine (empathetic, decorative) roles, the organisation will scarcely need (biological) women at all. But even without this conspiratorial twist, it is easy to see that men's and women's relation to the organisational body is asymmetrical. McDowell too admits that masculinity in a male body is better rewarded than in a female body (1997: 156) and that, perhaps, femininity in an evidently masculine body (ibid.: 182) is more valorised still.

However, before generalising from findings like these, one needs to question whether McDowell's interviewees' consciousness of their gendered and classed embodied performance or Adkins's arguments about the cultural feminisation of work roles mainly reflect perceived career demands in particular sections of professional customer services (such as financial sales, where a successful performance has always contributed to earning commissions) or whether they are characteristic of wider changes in the workplace. Aestheticised styles of the body may be more central to the labour process in jobs such as sales than in those, like surgery, where 'performance' is more clearly dependent on (also embodied) technical skills, even if there is still also an element of showmanship. In other sectors masculine organisational styles may be different or more varied, and shifts in the long-term business cycle are also likely to occasion shifts in leadership styles, as Collinson and Hearn (1994) point out. In manufacturing firms that promote themselves on the basis of technical competence, for instance, a harder, more aggressive style of leadership may be expected, in line with the hardness of the goods they produce (Roper 1994).

An example of embodied masculinities in work that involves much less emphasis on their aestheticisation is Massey's (1996) study of the Cambridge area science sector, which found that men involved in research and product design operated within deeply internalised dualisms. They were characterised by a 'very specific form of masculinity' that privileges rational, abstract thought, seeks to transcend the here-and-now of everyday life, and often denigrates body consciousness as an unworthy waste of (their) time. Her findings echo Traweek's (1988) analysis of American high-energy physicists in California in the 1980s. These scientists almost uniformly refused to see the body or its pleasures as a priority, marrying as very young men, while still in graduate school, so that emotional or sexual neediness would not disrupt their later careers. She says they scarcely noticed what they wore, their clothes having been chosen by their wives. Silicon Valley tycoons, whose success has been jokingly described as 'the revenge of the nerds', also seem to be less affected by the need to aestheticise their public interactions, although technical brilliance may be accompanied by an aggressive masculinity and astronomically long hours that demonstrate the ability to *get things done* (Cooper 2004).

Moreover, changing constructions of the managerial body have to be seen in economic terms, not just as a cultural phenomenon. If highly paid managers like those studied by McDowell see themselves as successfully instrumentalising their body performances as an investment in their careers, from the wider perspective of contemporary capitalism their embodiment is being targeted (as in the case of those lower down the pecking order) to get more work out of them, to realise more value. Holliday and Thompson (2001: 123) argue that corporate bodily discipline is no longer considered an infringement, for 'capital has managed to transform the body of the contemporary, middle-class, urban office worker into the perfect model of self-discipline'. This worker is not only able to work hard and play hard but also has 'the stamina for ten- to fourteen-hour days'. While such a view may exaggerate the efficacy of disciplinary power, it highlights the employer's interest in meeting conventional economic goals, including productivity and output targets, and employers' and office workers' agreement on the attributes of the 'desirable body'.

Thrift (2005) too suggests that since the 1990s, business discourse and practice have been increasingly concerned with increasing motivation by shaping the management body. The latter has been expected to do more, not just to work harder but also to 'spread itself about' that much more (ibid.: 117). As Thrift says, higher productivity, especially for managers, involves changes in the rate of embodied interaction and changes in the ways bodies are arranged in space and time; the use of teamwork as a method of work organisation, for instance, the wearing of more casual, active clothes; and long hours of work, even sleeping under the desk rather than getting home at night – the ideal body is always in movement, rarely standing still. Interestingly, Thrift is under no illusion that this more adaptable managerial body has been feminised, since in his account it is not only explicitly male, but moving too fast for women with domestic responsibilities to keep up.

Conclusions

The research summarised in this and the previous chapter highlights the importance of body politics to the organisation of work, recruitment and training, and the day-to-day experience of employees in modern manufacturing and services. In customer services, including management, there seems to be a new, or at least more explicit, emphasis on bodily discipline and appearance. These changes have particular implications for the social variables – gender, 'race', age, social class, ability, sexuality – that are linked to the sense of embodied selfhood. While equal opportunities discourse suggested that we should disregard these marks of difference, allowing any body to do any job, in reality the reverse seems to be the case. In particular, the instrumentalisation and aestheticisation of the gendered body, rather than its erasure, have become the norm.

The concentration on customer services may exaggerate the contrast between current and past constructions of the working body, comparing the exploitation of the body as a 'material signifier' to the productive body of the industrial worker or workers' gendered performances to the disembodied, desexualised official of classic organisational theory. This usefully highlights the economic importance of the body's emotional capacities, sexuality, gender and aesthetics, since in customer services these are directly related to employers' profits as well as workers' perceptions of career success. We can also see how workers' bodies are used to segment consumer markets, whether in retailing or nightlife, and to add value to 'designer' goods and venues based on their image. We can also see how intertwined are the pressures on workers as workers and as consumers. All this is becoming increasingly integrated into marketing strategies and firms' profits. But although aesthetic qualities are being rendered productive, i.e. given exchange value, *in addition* to other embodied capacities, we should not imagine that the only embodied attributes that matter are those that are being aestheticised.

Researchers who have developed the concept of 'aesthetic labour' have made good use of Bourdieu's concept of habitus in exploring the class-specific dispositions that some high-style venues seek to exploit. However, it may be they underestimate the difficulties involved in adapting a Bourdieusian framework for analysing paid employment. As Lovell (2000) points out, he may overestimate the durability of childhood habitus and underrate the possibilities for 'passing', as adults, as someone else. Clearly if the necessary dispositions have been acquired long before entry into the labour market, little acting or effort is needed to play one's part. But we could say, rather, that what the dispositions acquired in childhood must include, as an aspect of habitus, is more or less ability and willingness *to act*, to distinguish between situations in which different acts are appropriate, and to decide on the amount of effort to put in. As Crossley (2001) suggests, Bourdieu's framework needs to be supplemented by the inclusion of reflexivity as a crucial element of habitus, one that enables social actors to monitor themselves and, in some cases, to engage in habit-busting. It seems that some such step may be necessary if the use of Bourdieu to study occupational habitus is not to result in the neglect of the work that work requires.

Although Crossley does not say so, this kind of reflexivity may not be evenly distributed between different habitus. To take one example, it could be argued that girl children acquire this ability more than most boys, because of their (trained) ability to put themselves in the part of another (Frith 1995). Skeggs's (1997) take on the feminine habitus is especially relevant here, as she posits femininity as something performed by her research subjects, something they do rather than what they are. It would certainly help to explain what seems to be young working-class women's greater access to aestheticised jobs in customer services than their male counterparts (McDowell 2002).

One of the things that makes it difficult to evaluate the changes that seem to be under way is whether the analysis of the organised, 'managed body' allows enough scope for identifying agency and resistance on the part of workers, and of what kinds. In part this is because the legacy of the Foucauldian conception of the docile body makes it hard to conceptualise the worker's agency. Ethnographies like Durand and Hatzfeld (2003) document the ways that industrial workers attempt to maintain their sense of self on the shop floor, but in customer services there seems to be less evidence of the extent of different kinds of resistance or what forms resistance may take. Those who do consider workers' resistance to emotional labour in the customer services sector seem to suggest that workers' attempts to stamp work with their own moral outlook, along with their other coping strategies, actually work to the employer's advantage, in so far as they lead to a better, more concerned level of service (Korczynski 2003; Tyler and Taylor 2001; Wray-Bliss 2001). This may be partly because firms have become expert at recruiting workers with the right pro-customer attitudes (Ashforth and Humphries 1993). Even the cynicism and other 'intra-psychic' forms of resistance noted by Collinson (2003) may not challenge the 'emotional order' of the organisation (Sturdy and Fineman 2001). This is particularly the case in so far as they enable individual workers to distance themselves psychologically without necessarily encouraging more collective efforts directed towards transformation rather than survival (Fleming and Spicer 2004).

Workers' attitudes to the aestheticisation of appearance has been studied even less. It may be that these attitudes are now so deeply embedded in the wider aesthetics of consumer culture that they are taken for granted. We can see in data produced by Leslie (2002) some workers' resentment, but their attitudes towards body discipline are ambiguous, in so far as they share the same picture of the desirable body as the employer. In seminar discussions of this question with students, it seems that it is mainly those who identify as gay or lesbian who are conscious of the normalising nature of sartorial codes and expectations about appearance in the workplace. These individuals develop strategies for dealing with such expectations, such as piercings and tattoos that do not show (Williams (2003) makes a similar point). This suggests that we should be wary of distinguishing too sharply between aesthetic and (hetero)sexual labour, since normative heterosexuality plays such a strong role in normalising, and invisibilising, the effort required by aesthetic labour. The middle aged may find the aestheticisation of work and its stress on a youthful appearance oppressive, but this seems to be evident more in escalating rates of cosmetic surgery 'for professional reasons' rather than open resistance to these expectations.

In the next three chapters I want to consider some other ways of thinking about the body in employment that have been much less frequently addressed in the literature to date. In Chapter 5 I consider issues in work-related health and safety that contribute to the construction of working bodies in both industry and services in ways that have been sidelined by the concentration on aesthetics. I then seek to clarify differences between theoretical perspectives on the body rather more than has been the case in this chapter. While it is not the purpose of this book to choose between them, in Chapter 6 I shall discuss some of the political and other implications of different approaches, using the feminist debate on prostitution and other kinds of sex work to trace their import.

Finally, I shall address in Chapter 7 what I see as a serious blind-spot in the literature on customer services, namely its lack of attention to the interaction of workers' bodies with those of consumers. 'Pure' services are seen as more concerned with performance (Nickson et al. 2001: 172) than with producing an object or processing tangible goods. However, this ignores the tangibility of bodily contact in many consumer services, and the consequent importance of touch in mediating workers' relations with customer, clients and patients. Chapter 7 will provide an opportunity for considering how body work is shaped by the division of labour and the range of relationships within which it is located.

FIVE Vulnerable Bodies: Workplace 'Accidents', Injury and Ill Health

As Claire Williams points out, 'Much of the new scholarship on the body at work tends to ignore writing on occupational health and safety which has always been concerned with the body' (1999: 151). While this is due partly to difficulties in engaging with what Williams calls the 'problematic framework' underpinning much occupational health and safety research in the past, it may also be related to our reluctance to confront the vulnerability of the body and the limits to its plasticity.

Statistical and other studies of workplace-related health and safety are crucial to understanding the relation between work and bodily well-being. But this is only part of the story such studies can tell us, for there are a number of ways in which occupational health and safety (OHS) as a discourse constructs its objects of study, i.e. accidents, illnesses, bodies. These not only reflect but also contribute to the shaping of 'social and political bodies' (Schatzki and Natter 1996b), our point of departure in Chapter 3. Thus while looking at workplace health and safety issues is useful in bringing the materiality of body/work relations to the fore, this is not an argument that we simply need to 'get real'. Recognition of the impact of work on the body depends vitally on the way in which both work and bodies are conceptualised. Moreover, the regulation and management of workplace health and safety is as much influenced by (and in turn influences) the conceptualisations of working bodies identified by academic scholars (for instance Foucault's (1991) 'docile body' or Martin's (1994) 'flexible body') as other management practices. Furthermore, gender ideology has always been central to perceptions about bodily vulnerability.

Rather than attempt to analyse the field of occupational health and safety as a whole, this chapter concentrates on the writings of a number of key critics of OHS discourse and practices, including researchers from within the field itself (Bellaby 1999; Messing 1998b; Quinlan 1999, 1997; Tombs 1999;

Williams 1997, 1993). They recognise that, as Quinlan (1993: 2) says, while work has a physiological dimension, it is fundamentally a social process. This means that in some respects they are in the same position as (other) social theorists, in trying to tease out and conceptualise the connections between power relations, discourses and people's experience of embodiment.

Conceptualising 'accidents' and their incidence

What one might call the discursive management of the relationship between industrialisation and bodily well-being can be already seen by the mid-nineteenth century, when British novelists made the industrial accident a key focus of the Victorian novel. Sapper (1999: 24) suggests that the industrial 'accident' (and its correlate, 'accidental' injury) played a major part in Victorian narratives because it allowed industrial capitalism to come to terms with the fact that industrialisation involved casualties without having to admit its responsibilities in producing them. Novels like *Hard Times* or *North and South*, both first published in 1854, can be read as attempts to resolve uncomfortable truths. According to Sapper, the connection between industrialisation and death or maiming threatened to undermine the positive vision of work as a creative, humanising activity. However, the Victorian novel resolved this contradiction through narratives centred around the saving grace of human idealism, self-sacrifice, leadership or the just punishment of a (single) culpable individual. Even today we allow conceptual slippage between the different connotations of the words 'accident' and 'accidental' to reassure us that because an event was unintended it was also unpredictable or unexpected (Hyde 1997; Sanders 2000; Sapper 1999).

Nowadays some of the most important representations of workplace well-being are the statistics on occupational injury and ill health, so it is not surprising that the figures are much contested. The US Bureau of Labor Statistics reported a dramatic decline in occupational injury and illness in the 1990s, with the *New York Times* citing a reduction of 38 per cent between 1992 and 1998 (Azaroff et al. 2004). In Britain, as in western Europe as a whole, there has been a long-term decline in work-related serious injury and death. The Health and Safety Executive (HSE) claims that the rate of workplace fatal injuries in 2000 was only a quarter of the rate for 1971 (Department of Environment, Transport and the Regions 2000: 3) and the second lowest of the (then) European Union members (HSE c. 2001: 2). (Sweden appears to have the lowest rate of workplace fatal injuries, while Portugal has the highest.) However, since this may be due to the deindustrialisation of contemporary Britain, rather than superior industrial practices or better

101

regulation, we should not pat ourselves on the back too soon. In any case the figures have stopped getting better. A total of 235 people are reported to have died in British workplace accidents in 2004, up 4 per cent on the previous year, and there were 31,000 major accidents, up 9 per cent (Pandya 2005). This rise in the fatality rate was influenced by a massive factory explosion in Scotland (where the Health and Safety Executive had refused to follow up an earlier complaint by a worker) and the deaths of 23 migrant Chinese men and women employed by a local business to pick cockles on the coast of Lancashire, who were swept away by an incoming tide (Lawrence 2005; Pai 2005). Moreover, many people are still dying from cancer caused by past exposures at work; the Heath and Safety Executive puts the number at about 6,000 deaths annually, but admits that there is a high margin of error, with some reckoning the figure could be as high as 12,000 (HSE 2004: 1).

Although the above comparison of fatality rates within the EU is based on rates standardised by Eurostat, in general official statistics on work-related fatalities, injuries and ill health are shaped by different methods of defining, recording and reporting workplace incidents in crucial ways, making comparisons difficult. Definitions of the workplace used to record incidents, for instance, may be so narrow as to exclude a postal worker run over in a public street (Tombs 1999). A particular problem is the underreporting of industrial injuries due to the vulnerability of the workers concerned. Azaroff et al. (2004) argue that the reported decline in non-fatal accidents is steepest in those US industries and regions most affected by restructuring and worsened conditions of work precisely because the most insecure, hard-pressed workers are those least likely to report incidents, seek medical treatment or financial compensation, or put in train the other procedures that would lead to the recording of their injuries. (Fatal accidents have shown a much less precipitous decline, in part because they are less affected by underreporting.) There are many factors that operate singly or together to filter out complaints or applications for compensation and in some cases, as in the American meat-processing sector, factors like industrial relocation, de-unionisation and the employment of migrant workers coalesce (Azaroff et al. 2004; Prasad and Prasad 2003). The more precarious the workers' hold on access to work, the more they are likely to be wary of reporting incidents, for fear of losing their job or losing out on the chance of promotion to easier work. Injuries to workers who lack access to health insurance or access to medical care are less likely to come to doctors' attention; non-unionised workers do not have the help of union officials in fighting a compensation claim; and migrant workers are particularly concerned about possible harassment or deportation by immigration authorities. The inability to build up savings on a minimum wage, plus withdrawal of the welfare net that used to exist for the mothers of young children, also means that the poor have no choice but to keep working when injured or ill.

Nonetheless, sociologists have been able to use official statistics, as well as other data, to draw useful conclusions about the distribution of serious incidents, arguing that their distribution indicates the existence of what Nichols (1997) calls a 'structure of vulnerability'. Nichols (1997), Quinlan (1999), Quinlan et al. (2001) and others argue that the big differences in rates of workplace injury among industrial sectors are a reflection of the structure of different industries, especially the size of enterprises and the extent of self-employment, not just the irresponsibility of particular companies. For instance, the very high rates of fatalities in sectors like construction reflect not only the fact that the injuries incurred are particularly likely to be fatal, but also the economic organisation of the sector. In particular, where subcontracting and self-employment are prevalent constant pressures to reduce labour costs – in addition to swings due to seasonal work – result in uncertain and unpredictable contracts, cost-cutting competitive tendering and outsourcing. These carry particular risks for self-employed workers and small firms forced to minimise costs and 'push themselves hard' in order to make sure that they get work from larger enterprises when it is available. The result is long and erratic working hours, long journeys to work, fatigue, stress, burn-out, injuries, and delay in seeking treatment (Quinlan 1997). In some cases, as one informant told Quinlan, the cost of adequate scaffolding was far more than he could charge for the job.

Increasingly the casualised employment that is related to high rates of injury in construction or agriculture has spread to other sectors, such as cleaning, food processing and care work, bringing with it higher rates of industrial injury and illness (Quinlan et al. 2001). In Britain South Asian, African and Caribbean workers who migrated to Britain in the postwar period of full employment to take the 'dirty', lower-paid jobs rejected by local white workers have long suffered higher rates of occupational injury and death than indigenous white workers, due to their over-representation in the more dangerous jobs (Wrench 1995). Now that heavy industry has been transferred to low-wage economies in the South, even more vulnerable migrants are being employed in work that is difficult to export, allowing their employers to push down wages and minimise on safety so as to compete for contracts from retailers, such as the major supermarkets (Anderson and Rogaly 2004; Lawrence 2005; Phizacklea 2005).

Gender issues in workplace health

Unfortunately, studies of the distribution of serious workplace accidents and fatalities, like Nichols's, may not tell us very much about the injuries, illnesses and impairments suffered by women workers, who are much less likely than men to be killed at work, but who still suffer from injuries and illnesses that have long gone unrecognised. Such studies too readily slip into assuming that 'the normative worker at the heart of safety at work is a man in heavy industry' (Williams 1999: 151). This has in turn influenced the funding of studies of occupational health and safety studies, which as Messing (1998b; Messing et al. 2003) points out have often adjusted women out of the study in order to make their samples of 'workers' more homogeneous.

One of Messing's (Messing et al. 1993) earlier articles on gender and occupational health used the example of prostitutes to emphasise the need to reconsider the definitions, concepts and methods used in research in order to bring women's occupational health problems to light. Whereas the discovery of the incidence of scrotal cancer among male chimney sweeps was a pioneering step in the discovery of occupational disease, the incidence of cervical cancer among female prostitutes is hardly ever mentioned. Female sex workers also suffer from physical violence, sexually transmitted diseases, side effects from hygiene precautions, as well as health problems related to working night shifts (Messing et al. 1993). Although there has recently been more acknowledgement of these and other health problems experienced by sex workers (e.g. Hester and Westmarland 2004), including those experienced by male workers, these are rarely integrated into our understanding of work hazards. This implies that particular conceptions of 'work' and 'working bodies' are still important issues in constructing OHS as a field of study.

Messing et al. (2003) argue that although conventional wisdom assumes that women have fewer 'accidents' because sex segregation keeps them out of the more dangerous jobs, it can also be argued that women have fewer *compensated* injuries because the compensation system developed in relation to the type of accidents characteristic of the jobs in which men predominate. Men have more sudden, traumatic 'accidents' of the kind that take place in the workplace, but women more of the diseases that develop over time (European Agency for Health and Safety at Work 2003). This pattern goes back to at least the nineteenth century, when women workers suffered appalling, disfiguring illnesses due to poisoning from the dust and fumes of mercury, phosphorus, white lead and other substances, vividly described along with other aspects of women's industrial working conditions in Harrison (1996). Exposure to lead in workplaces that women workers called 'white cemeteries' led to colic, constipation, violent diarrhoea, anaemia, fits, delirium, paralysis, blindness and often death (ibid.: 60). Paradoxically, the fact that it was women doing the work may have delayed the recognition of these industrial diseases and their relation to working conditions and chemical substances.

Williams (1999) argues that understanding women's relation to work-related health and safety is bedevilled by 'twin assumptions' that women are not 'workers' and that any work they carry out is 'safe'. This has delayed the diagnosis of the chronic, stress-related illnesses and the musculo-skeletal disorders (MSDs) of the back and upper limbs that now make up the majority of cases of occupational disease (Messing 1998b: 85), because many of these illnesses and disorders are prevalent in occupations in which women predominate. Dembe (1996) notes the American specialist in occupational medicine who insisted throughout the 1950s and 1960s that carpal tunnel syndrome could not be work-related because most of the sufferers were women in light manufacturing or clerical employment who did not do 'strenuous' work. There was also a suspicion that women were suffering from hysterical symptoms or other neuroses, rather than real illnesses.

Messing and others suggest that there are often assumptions about job requirements that only direct observation can dispel, since even when men and women have the same job title, there may be differences in the content and timing of work. For instance, although one might suppose that part-time workers, predominantly women, would suffer from fewer musculo-skeletal disorders than full-time workers, this may not be the case. One observational study of bank workers cited by Messing (1998b) suggested that because women part-timers are employed mainly to work at the counter to cover peak customer demand and are less involved in bank procedures that could be done sitting down at a desk, their rates of MSDs are the same as full-time workers, even though they work fewer hours. Where men and women do the same job, however, there may also be considerable overlap in the problems they face, and indeed taking on board issues originally mooted with reference to women may also lead to improved working conditions for men.

Gender is particularly relevant to understanding stress and other work-related health problems in the service sector. Women are more concentrated in the service sector than men and, relative to their share of the workforce, disproportionally represented in caring, nurturing and service activities (European Agency for Health and Safety at Work 2003). Such jobs include much of the front-line contact with consumers considered in Chapter 4, as well as the 'body work' occupations to be considered in Chapter 7. In Britain there is a high concentration of women in the public sector, especially in health care occupations, where levels of reported stress are rather higher than in the private sector. Forty per cent of the NHS workforce report stress (30 per cent in local government) as compared to 21 per cent of workers in the private sector (Bunting 2004: 184, citing Rose 2000). The high rate of work place-related illness and injury in care work is also found in the US, where according to US Bureau of Labor statistics for 1994, care home workers face the third highest rate of occupational injury and ill health among US industrial sectors (*Health & Safety Practitioner* 1997). High rates of injury and ill health in care and other health professions are related to stress, muscular conditions related to standing and lifting, the use of chemicals and instruments, and illnesses related to working with infectious patients. They may be also related to increased density of work, as nursing is organised around more Taylorised methods. Accidents among carers or childminders working in their own or the employer's home may also play a role in rates of injury among care workers, as the more general correlation between casualised, off-site working conditions and injury rates is also true of care workers (European Agency 2003; Quinlan 1999).

That such high rates of occupational illness are little recognised by the wider public may have something to do with the construction of nurses and other care workers as carers who do not therefore need to be cared-for. Even prospective workers themselves can be misled about what caring as paid work involves, and its potential consequences for their own health. For example, one recent newspaper article mentioned the rarely acknowledged risks of working in complementary therapy. The author herself had so enjoyed massage as a consumer that like others made redundant, or fed up with their jobs, she decided to train in massage herself (Rommi 2005), but at the time of writing was still receiving treatment for her own injuries. 'What the school didn't tell us,' she says, 'was that it is extremely difficult to make a decent living as a therapist (most of whom are self-employed), and of those who manage to do it, many end up with permanent injuries or simply burn out after just a couple of years.'

It is important to remember that the way in which gender is understood has adverse repercussions for men's workplace health and safety as well as women's. As Harrison (1989) points out, gender has always been central to the conceptualisation of bodily vulnerability and how to deal with it. She suggests that a gender double standard has always underpinned the evolution of 'protective legislation', which at first was considered relevant only to women and children. 'Danger' was defined in relation to the class of person, rather than the industrial process (Harrison 1996: 51). The construction of women's vulnerability, Williams (1997) argues, has badly affected the development of OHS practice as a whole, since whereas women were seen as in being need of protection, the contrary image of men as protectors inhibited and continues to affect the articulation of a discourse of protection in relation to men's work. Moreover, because bodies and bodies' need for care and attention has been associated with women and the family, rather than men and the workplace, when men are involved in workplace 'accidents', the sudden visibility of the body (a good example of what Leder (1990) calls the body's 'dys-appearance') is threatening symbolically, as well as in more obvious ways (Williams 1993).

Workplace studies confirm that on the whole men are 'more reluctant than women to say that their jobs leave them vulnerable' (Bellaby 1999: 90), seeing physical work as a 'sign of manliness'. For instance, men in the English potteries seemed to have the attitude that if they could 'master their bodies with their minds . . . they would grow fitter and more resistant to invasion of their bodies by the work-environment and by germs' (ibid.: 91). Although workers complained about draughty indoor work and excessive supervision, the paradox was that the risk of premature death was highest where 'there was an equalitarian peer-group operating free of managerial control' (ibid.: 176). However, Williams's (1993) study of health and safety in the timber industry, noted in Chapter 3, rejects this type of blame-the-victim account in favour of one that recognises the development of a male working-class habitus as something that in part emerges from the experience of coping with the threat, even likelihood, of serious injury at work.

Conceptualising the body in OHS

One of the reasons why it has been so difficult to incorporate OHS into the sociology of work or the sociology of the body is its taken-for-granted reliance on a biomedical construction of the body and a 'primitive conception of the social nature of illness causation' (Williams 1993: 58). With the exception of psychology, Williams says, OHS is dominated by a 'scientific/technicist' understanding of epidemiology and a biomedical view of the body that cannot recognise connections between mind and body in the causation of illness. Because the body is seen as a machine, people's own experiences and understandings of embodied dis-ease are seen as subjective, contaminating evidence of what the expert seeks to study. People are not expected to play a role in their own diagnosis but must accept experts' recommendations for the repair of their bodies.

The clearest examples of the consequences of ways of thinking about the body in OHS discourse concern the diagnosis of the chronic, stress-related illnesses and the musculo-skeletal disorders (MSDs) of the back and upper limbs that now make up the majority of cases of occupational disease (Messing 1998b: 85). Such ailments may not show up on x-rays, may not respond readily to treatment, and are characterised by much more individual variation in susceptibility to serious impairment than, say, falling off a high building. The fact that they are correlated with psychosocial variables has in the past made it difficult for an OHS apparatus dependent on a biomedical model of disease to recognise ailments whose evidence may consist mainly of workers' self-reports rather than visible, 'objective' signs.

In an article first circulated in the early 1990s, Canaan (1999) argued that the refusal of workplace insurance schemes, backed up by the courts, to recognise the incidence of new ailments like RSI rested on the perceived binary between body and mind. Ailments exacerbated by stress or other psychological strains were seen as 'all in the head', if not actually examples of malingering. She argued that the presumption that certifiable impairment can only be demonstrated by objective evidence of pathology in or on the body is related to the centrality of visualisation to the surveillance of working bodies more generally. Although there has now been considerable progress in the recognition of stress as a disabling condition, further recognition depends not only on more large-scale studies correlating particular working conditions and stress, but also the identification of the biological pathways through which mental distress leads to physical conditions (Wainwright and Calnan 2002), rather than self-reports.

Because of the financial implications, standards of proof in OSH are very high and usually require correlations between a single variable and its putative effect in order to be accepted (Messing 1998b). There is also an expectation that the amount or intensity of 'exposure' correlates with the amount or intensity of impairment. This makes it difficult for OSH models to recognise the complex interrelationship between production, work and family (Williams 1993: 58). Taylor et al.'s (2003) study of health hazards in the call centre sector tried to tackle this problem head on, but without gaining much ground with the employers. Taylor et al. (2003) argue for the need to adopt what they term a 'holistic' model of health and safety hazards which, while recognising the existence of 'physical' hazards like the design of work stations, stresses the mutually reinforcing effects of different aspects of the work environment. The three components of the work environment they identify are the proximate environment (e.g. workstation design), the ambient environment (e.g. building temperature and light), and the social environment (e.g. managerial control systems). Call centre workers, they argue, experience these three components in a 'holistic way'. Tight, ever intensifying, targets, the repetitive nature of the work with few breaks, combined with a lack of support from supervisors, not only lead to emotional exhaustion in themselves, but reduce workers' ability to withstand the effects of the other aspects of the environment. However, it is much harder to get employers to accept the 'social environment' as a legitimate health and safety issue that should be included as a proper subject of management–trade union negotiation.

If it is hard to get the organisation of work within the call centre sector accepted as a legitimate health and safety issue, getting recognition of stress occasioned by workers' encounters with customers is also difficult. For instance, Boyd (2002) explores the relationship between emotionally demanding frontline interrelational service sector work and OHS outcomes. Her survey of cabin crew working for three UK airlines is backed up by a literature review that suggests that excessive demands on emotional labour may be associated with a higher risk of stress, anxiety and emotional exhaustion. Boyd gives particular attention to customers' physical and verbal violence, which not only increases stress and anxiety but also represents an occupational health hazard in its own right.

Studies undertaken by British Trades Union Congress (TUC) identify a huge increase in the incidence of customer violence in the UK, with one in five workers subject to an attack every year (TUC 1999, cited by Boyd 2002: 153). An Australian study shows that it is a common phenomenon among taxi drivers, fast food workers, bar workers, nursing and hospital staff and teachers, with females who perform the same job tasks as males more frequently exposed to it. Women are also at risk, according to Messing (1998b: 118), because they are often assigned to jobs in which they are required to calm down annoyed, angry or violent people, such as patients and social welfare clients as well as customers. Workers in the railway and airline industries are severely affected, according to an International Transport Workers' Federation report, with cabin crew members reporting being 'punched, head-butted, kicked on the back, bitten on the cheek, throttled, hit by a bottle' and in one case, stabbed (Boyd 2002: 156).

Again we find that the customer abuse faced by workers arises partly from the way the job is organised, but also that abuse is exacerbated by cost-cutting measures that make violence from the customer more likely. According to Boyd's study of the airline sector, some of the factors that put workers at risk relate to the absence of effective shields/boundaries between customer and worker, including 'the length of time they remain in contact with customers' and the confined space of the aircraft. Other factors reflect employers' profit-maximising business strategies, including their dependence on sales of alcohol as an income stream, advertising that inflates customers' expectations, tight timetabling of flights, leading to hectic turnaround times and more delays and missed connections, and cost-cutting measures that reduce air quality, exacerbating passengers' (and presumably workers') discomfort and anger.

Several studies draw particular attention to the stress occasioned by the blurring of boundaries between work and personal identities and working hours and time off. This implies that it is not only 'conditions of work' that lead to work-related ailments, but the ways in which employers 'lay claim to the worker's sense of self' (Collinson 2003), engendering in them a sense of commitment to the goals and values of the company (Cooper 2004; Kunda 1992). Forseth (2005, 2003) argues that where there are no clear-cut measures of successful work performance, workers are left feeling that they can never do enough for the customer. Based on studies of the Scandinavian airline industry, she argues that the destabilisation of previously fixed organisational boundaries leads to boundless work. 'Adaptable' and 'responsible' workers are not supported by their employers in setting a boundary between themselves as persons and themselves as workers, or between their rights as workers and those of employers and customers. Consequently, their 'flexible bodies' (Martin 1994) end up 'stretched in one direction, then in the opposite,' as one worker told Forseth (2003). Ultimately they establish some kind of boundary only through taking absences due to sickness (see also Tally 2003). The blurring of accepted boundaries also results in vulnerability to sexual harassment, in part because employers' insistence that workers must prioritise customer satisfaction undermines workers' confidence to reject customers' advances (Williams 2003).

Evolving strategies

Examples like those above suggest that the models of causation, work environment and the body that evolved in relation to industrial work need to be modified, but there seems to be little agreement about the best way of doing this. One problem is that, as Williams says, if we remain within the conventional medical model adopted by most OSH practitioners, then the sick and injured worker tends to be constituted as a passive 'object of medical and other kinds of professional intervention and control' (Williams 1993: 58). How we should deal with this is not straightforward, since there are advantages for workers in playing along with this construction as well as problems.

Wainwright and Calnan (2002) take up exactly this problem in considering organised workers' more recent success in having complaints like stress or some MSDs certified by medics as work-induced illnesses, arguing that this only plays into the hands of experts by legitimating their power to define realities. Wainwright and Calnan argue that working conditions are not, on balance, getting so much worse that they would produce an epidemic of sickness due to 'work stress' (or, by implication, other workplace-related disorders such as MSDs). While recognising the existence of research documenting the bodily impact of psychosocial pressures, Calnan and Wainwright say that the real origin of what they term the 'work stress discourse' is political. Changes in legislation and public opinion with regard to strikes, and the discursive representation of workers as members of the corporate team, have made it extremely difficult for workers to express their grievances unless they can medicalise their claims. They suggest that employers have a much harder time refusing to deal with legitimate problems if they are presented as 'causes of physical or mental harm to the worker' (ibid.: 143) certified by doctors than if they are presented as issues of fairness or workers' rights. Wainwright and Calnan are concerned that the popular discourse of 'work stress' (and its support by trade unions) is transforming political issues into medical problems, thereby constructing workers as the passified victims of expert diagnosis and therapy.

While Wainwright and Calnan may be right that complaints about 'work stress' now substitute for other ways of articulating grievances about conditions of work, whether this actually intensifies the passification of workers is questionable. Durand and Hatzfeld's (2003) study of a Peugeot plant in France suggests that workers are able to use the leeway medical certification provides without buying into the ideological baggage it carries.

Durand and Hatzfeld argue that in the context of an increase in the power of employers relative to organised workers, work-related impairments have become a more important and more visible lever through which workers seek to modify the intensity of work. Partly due to the increasing density of gestures and movement required by workstations (see Chapter 3), car assembly workers suffer from a range of MSDs, confirming Wokutch's (1992) finding that lean production entails an increased risk of manual handling/soft tissue injuries (cited by Quinlan 1999: 429). In the Peugeot plant up to 40 per cent of the workers at any one time may be experiencing problems (Durand and Hatzfeld 2003: 193). This is not surprising in jobs that require repetitive, awkward, sometimes forceful movement in restricted spaces, for instance attaching a seal by hammering it with the heel of the hand 5,000 times a day.

The workers at Peugeot have the option of seeking a medical certificate that will restrict their assignment to workstations that do not require the squatting, rotating of the body, standing in a particular way, lifting a heavy load or the repetitive movement of the wrist or elbow that would exacerbate their particular condition. However, applying for a medical certificate usually indicates a worker's conscious attempt to make the most of whatever scope for resistance their situation allows, rather than submission to medical expertise. 'The grant or denial of medical restrictions are at the heart of day-to-day [work] relations' (2003: 180), Durand and Hatzfeld say, and requires careful strategising by workers. In deciding whether to seek certification for their problems, the workers must choose between enhancing their control over which workstation they are allocated, on the one hand, and the risk of being fired as unable to perform their jobs at an acceptable standard on the other. For certain workers 'and for all of them beyond a certain age', Durand and Hatzfeld (2003: 109) say, what is at stake is not just getting a 'good' workstation, but 'the defence of their physical integrity'. Rather than an indication of passification, a successful claim for medical certification demonstrates 'a respect for one's body that the brutality of the line tends to refute' (ibid.: 183).

Durand and Hatzfeld's formulation captures the kind of agency to which Bourdieu frequently refers, namely the ability to carve out a space for the self. This does not always challenge – and may even confirm – relations of domination, in this case the power of medical authorities as well as the employer's. But it also suggests that rather than seeing himself as giving up the control of his body to the employer, the worker actively reminds himself that his subjection is only temporary. However, Durand and Hatzfeld's account of workplace impairment seems to be based mainly on the experience of male workers. There is little consideration of whether women workers in the plant experience their situation similarly or adopt different strategies.

The question is whether or not there are other collective ways of demonstrating the spread of stress- and injury-inducing conditions of work and making these the target of protest. Bunting's (2004) lively journalistic account, based on academic sources and accounts from people working at different levels, points to many ways in which employers get more work out of their staff, not all of which were considered by Wainwright and Calnan (2002): long and/or at unsocial hours; job insecurity; appraisal and assessment systems; staffing levels varied to match changing levels of customer demand, so that staff are always busy; rising expectations regarding customer service; teamwork (and the peer pressure that results); 'de-layering'; and the collapse of the division between work and non-working hours.

Bunting emphasises the restructuring of our sense of time. In poorly paid jobs workers have always had to work long hours to make ends meet, but now the availability of services mean that even managers and professionals work long hours. Management and professional-level job insecurities make people feel they have to be present at every meeting, just to watch their backs. Moreover the use of new technologies is also relevant to increasing workload and work time, making it possible to inspect and measure workers' input and, through mobile phones and laptops, extending working hours into what used to be time off work (Bunting 2004). One of the fashion retail store managers interviewed by Leslie, for instance, said that not only was she making less money than she had done as a filing clerk, but she felt she was 'carrying the weight on my shoulders':

> This is what is frustrating. You see how much money is going through the store . . . You see that you live and breathe the store. You go home and you don't even leave the store because they are calling you on your cell phone . . . You're sweating. (Leslie 2002: 63)

As Gabriel (2003) says, persistent anxiety is a predictable response to working in the glass cage of the modern organisation – not an unforeseen 'accidental' outcome of contemporary capitalism.

Both women and men are affected by the encroachment of working hours on private life and the domestic sphere, but their different responsibilities to support and care for themselves and dependants mean that alterations in the 'work–life' interface may bring different implications (Perrons 2003). Bunting's (2004) interviews seem to indicate that women single parents face particular problems, since they are responsible for both financial maintenance, usually on less than a man's earnings, and for caring for their children. They are less able to forgo income by taking the decision to 'downshift' by taking a less demanding job, for instance, or to grab a few weeks off work by changing jobs. However, we should remember that women's responsibility for others may mean that they are also connected to others, and this may help them deal with stressful conditions more easily than men. This might help to explain the paradox that while women are affected by more of the factors associated with work-related stress, their reported stress, according to the European Agency (2003), is only marginally higher than men's.

The restructuring of time also effects the extent of nightshift working, expected to extend to 25 per cent of the population in the next 15 years, according to Edemariam (2005). She interviewed nightshift car assembly workers, call centre workers, cleaners, police and security workers, cab drivers, and workers and managers in a variety of fields, from gyms to IT. She cites a number of health hazards now being mentioned by some researchers in relation to night working:

- Night working is more damaging to health than smoking 20 cigarettes a day.

- For women of all ages it carries a significant increase in the risk of breast cancer.

- There is an eightfold increase in the risk of developing stomach ulcers.

- Night working pushes the likelihood of coronary heart disease up by 40 per cent.

- Depression and mood swings are 15 times more likely.

There is also an increased likelihood of diabetes and chronic hypertension, while the hazards facing women of child-bearing age include disrupted menstrual cycles, an increased incidence of premature babies and babies with low birth weight, and miscarriage. For women of all ages there is a significant increase in the incidence of breast cancer.

Targeting the (re)organisation of work would go further towards challenging the social causes of workplace-related ill health and injury than the individual strategies adopted by the Peugeot workers. There are very important trade union campaigns on health and safety (the TUC online journal *Risks* and the 'union-friendly' independent magazine *Hazards* are good places for OHS information) and of course the Peugeot workers' right to medical certificates depends in part on earlier trade union campaigns. However,

Bunting (2004) says that the people who write to her, who are mostly professionals and managers, do not usually question why work is getting harder, seeking private solutions for their frustration and quiet despair.

New models?

Asking what has or could be done to protect workers from the harmful effects of work returns us to the questions posed at the beginning of Chapter 3, namely the relation between work systems and the construction of the worker as a docile body. It is easy to see that OHS discourse and practice in relation to industry in the past have contributed to the rationalisation of the body of the industrial worker, since its main aim has been to establish more control over how work is done. Moreover, the measures implemented to exclude what were thought of as 'careless' or wayward workers involved a standardisation of the bodies that were recruited for the assembly line. The question is whether newer formulations that, implicitly, picture a self-regulating, enterprising 'flexible body' (Martin 1994) will offer any better protection.

Many people recognise that the models adopted for regulating working conditions need to be modified, especially since the aspects of working life that lead to ill health or injury are in many cases different from those experienced by the normative male worker of heavy industry, whose conditions of work in any case did not really represent those of much of the labour force. Whereas researchers like Taylor et al. (2003) or Messing et al. (2003) suggest that we develop new measures for regulating health and safety and new models for expanding our conception of the work environment and the nature of work hazards, others propose a different approach, one that returns us to the responsibility of the individual worker for avoiding careless behaviour. Rather than thinking about re-establishing divisions that would help to protect workers against the boundless claims of work or further empowering trades unions to resist them, some commentators argue that it would be better to challenge the assumption that the enforcement of environmental protection is practicable and instead put onus on workers themselves as individuals. Thus not only will they continue to be expected to 'put the strain on themselves', as Taylor (2001) says is now the case in call centres, but they can also be trained to handle (the additional stress of) looking after their own health. This way of seeing work-related health and safety obviously parallels a new emphasis on personal responsibility for one's health and health-related lifestyle choices in the health care system as a whole. However, it suffers from a similar lack of attention to the factors that limit the control people feel they can exercise over their environment.

An example is a recent article about health and safety regulation in Sweden which questions whether work protection through the regulation of the 'work environment' is still relevant (Allvin and Aronson 2003). It argues that as long as the concept of the 'work environment' was applied to industrial labour it had a certain natural logic, but as more and different working conditions have been added, especially those of 'the so-called psychosocial environment' (ibid.: 101), it no longer refers to objective conditions but rather workers' subjective experience of social interaction. Moreover, working conditions are becoming so diverse and flexible that the notion of the working environment is no longer adequate as a framework for statutory rules and regulations (ibid.: 105). In such conditions, 'the individual has to decide for herself when, how often and how much work' (ibid.: 106) to do.

Allvin and Aronson's examples comprise geographically mobile workers who work on their laptops in airports and coffee bars as well as the office, at all hours of the day or night. However, attempts to transfer responsibility for protecting health and safety onto the workers themselves is more widespread. In the UK, for instance, the Health and Safety Commission (HSC 2004; Watterson and O'Neill 2004) has adopted a new strategy that it argues reflects the increasing diversity of work. It includes the rejection of detailed legislative regulation and suggests instead cutbacks in the inspection of premises, where management can be trusted to deal with recognised problems. It could be that the HSC thinks that rather than policing firms employing mainly white-collar workers, they need to devote their contracting resources to the escalating injuries in manual work noted above, but no justification of cutbacks is actually presented. One worries if the workforce is imaged to be divided between, on the one hand, the mobile professionals evoked by Allvin and Aronson (2003) or Thrift (2005), i.e. people with latitude over when and where they work, and, on the other, factory or processing workers still subject to clear-cut industrial hazards. This takes little account of the demands and constraints of the kind of jobs where many women are concentrated. Even though such jobs are located in non-industrial contexts, workload and timetabling remain outside the workers' control.

A striking example of the contradictions inherent in the suggestion that employers' responsibility should be limited to training their workers to monitor their own health and safety can be seen in the following excerpt from a training programme in the National Health Service. The NHS, as we have seen, leads the nation in the proportion of workers who experience stress. The following quotation comes from a website that posted extracts from a talk given at a training session dealing with work-related upper repetitive strain injuries offered to hospital sonographers, i.e. health workers who conduct ultrasound examinations on patients. Since so much of their time is spent using hand and wrist movements to guide a sensor across the patient's body, they apparently suffer from MSDs caused by repetitive motions, as well as stress. While the doctor addressing them admits that 'The exponential increase in the ultrasound workload over the last few years has increased stress levels amongst ALL sonographers' he goes on to comment that:

> We all cope with stress in different ways, some better than others. But consider this[,] if every day sonographers take few breaks, have long queues of irate patients (usually obstetric), then stress levels increase for all. Throw in the odd fetal abnormality, no FH and the worry of a sick family member and stress becomes all consuming, which then exacerbates the pain cycle. BEWARE YOU COULD BE THE NEXT TO SUFFER, learn to manage your body and your workload before permanent damage is done. (Sound Ergonomics 2001)

Along with whatever practical advice such instruction may offer, it also naturalises workers' responsibility for their own work-related health and safety. Since no changes in work organisation, workload or emotional demands are proposed, it is difficult to see that such advice does much more than absolve the employers from responsibility. This sheds yet more light on Wainwright and Calnan's (2002) argument that health and safety discourse, especially the 'work stress discourse', reinforces the construction of workers as victims unable to resist their conditions of work. However, it seems that in conditions where workers have very little control over their work obligations, the proposed alternative construction of workers as responsible and autonomous controllers of their own health can be even more deceptive.

Conclusions

If Thrift's (2005) ironic application of Foucault's depiction of the new space and time dynamics involved in the reconstruction of the body of the factory worker to the post-industrial managerial body (noted towards the end of Chapter 4) is anything to go by, it is no wonder that workers feel very tired and very stressed. How can people protect themselves? Is this even the right way to think about dealing with problems like stress?

As noted in Chapter 4, in critiquing Hochschild's (1983) understanding of the alienating character of emotional labour, Wouters (1989) suggested that workers are able to deploy and distinguish between the 'multiple selves' appropriate to different situations. Indeed, Collinson (2003) identifies a number of different subjectivities, that, he argues, are adopted as survival practices by individuals working in 'surveillance-based' organisations. These include 'conformist selves' that superficially accept the identity preoccupations expressed by careerism, building a wall between 'public' and 'private' selves, by distancing themselves physically, through absenteeism or psychologically, by 'splitting self'. 'Dramaturgical selves' become skilled manipulators of self-performance, adept at choreographing their own practices to evade monitoring. 'Resistant selves' manage to deal with their discontent by maintaining a sense of themselves as cynical dissenters within the bosom of corporate culture. While no doubt people do adopt these kinds of strategies, the problem is that although creating such multiple selves may allow us to experience a heightened sense of agency, each of us has only one body and it feels the pinch. The integration of health and safety issues into the mainstream of sociological research is vitally necessary if we are to keep in mind the organic as well as the symbolic level of work experience.

SIX Will Any Body Do? Conceptualising the 'Prostitute Body'

No book on the body in work would be complete without considering the obvious importance of sex work as an aspect of embodied work. The common-sense understanding of prostitution, stripping, lap dancing, pornographic performance and other kinds of commercial sex work is that they are perhaps the most embodied form of work. As O'Neill says, the identity of the sex worker is seen to be wrapped up much more closely in her bodily functions than is the case for other workers: most of the key signs of prostitution – fish-net stockings, mini-skirt, red-gash of a mouth, skin-tight clothes – flirt with the revelation of the body (O'Neill 2001: 95, 136). In fact, as Holliday and Thompson (2001) imply, the prostitute body is seen as the inverse of the sovereign body at the heart of organisation: open to view on the street, rather than hidden in an office; penetrated and leaky, as against closed and dry.

Yet when people say that sex work centres on the sexed female body, they actually mean by 'the body' very different things. Feminist contributions to debates about prostitution and other kinds of sex work have been so fiercely analytical, extensive and diverse that they make an ideal vehicle for exploring not just sex work as a topic in its own right, but what is at stake in competing understandings of the body and the theory-laden constructions of the body that underpin critique or defence, in this case of prostitution as an institution. Whereas in Chapters 3, 4 and 5 we were concerned mainly with understandings of the relation between body and society, feminist debate on sex work draws particular attention, in addition, to different conceptualisations of the relation between body and self, which as we saw in Chapter 1 is one of the key foci in both feminist and mainstream sociologies of the body. Part of this exploration must also include, of course, research on how sex workers themselves manage their identities and activities through body management strategies.

Prostitution and other kinds of sex work are generally agreed to be growing as an important, but relatively hidden, contribution to economic activity. Based on a recent study, the media has been reporting that in Britain about 80,000 people, four-fifths of them women, earn their living through prostitution (Home Office 2004; Smith et al. 2004). One of the reasons the British Government recently decided to obtain views on changing the laws on prostitution was a perceived rise of 50 per cent in the number of working prostitutes in the five years to 2004, with some £770 million changing hands (Smith et al. 2004). The British Government says it is especially worried about the number of prostitutes coming from abroad, linking prostitution to issues like people trafficking and illegal immigration, while others worry about the spread of the sex trade out of London and other major cities into smaller towns and suburban neighbourhoods (Toynbee 2003b). Other kinds of sex work are also growing. For instance, the upmarket lap dancing clubs that recently entered the Britain entertainment scene are said to generate over £300 million in turnover (Jones et al. 2003: 215). Of course that is still small beer compared to the US, where one US newspaper reported that 'Americans now spend more money on strip clubs than at Broadway, off-Broadway, regional, and non-profit theatres; at the opera, the ballet and jazz and classical music performances combined' (Liepe-Levinson 2002: 3).

Nor can we see prostitution and sex work in isolation. As West and Austrin (2002) point out, many feminist researchers have seen connections between sex work and occupational and/or organisational identities more generally. For instance, we saw how Adkins (1995) and others concerned with customer services highlight employers' insistence that women provide gendered sexual labour as part of their jobs, flattering male customers with the pleasure of feminine attention and sexuality along with their other tasks (Hancock and Tyler 2000b; Tyler and Abbott 1998). More recently a few theorists have taken a quite different tack. For instance, interested in the possibilities of challenging the deadening weight of organisational constraints and controls over the expression of sexual power and pleasure, Brewis and Linstead (2000) favour 're-eroticising' organisation and have looked to sex work to tease out the interplay of money, sex and power, which they argue does not necessarily always disadvantage women. Still other theorists, for example Anderson and O'Connell Davidson (2002) or West and Austrin (2006), identify other parallels between sex work and other kinds of paid work, including sometimes the other kinds of 'body work' that will be explored mainly in Chapter 7. Such considerations put a different gloss on sex work as an issue than the worries of criminologists or community health workers, which fuel the concerns of many policy analysts.

Sex work has been the focus of such acrimonious debate among feminist commentators trying to specify, as Pateman (1988) put it, 'What is wrong with prostitution?' that it is impossible to begin with an agreed set of definitions. Most of those who accept prostitution as a legitimate form of work challenge the stigma carried by the word 'prostitute' by adopting neologisms like 'sex work' and 'sex workers' instead. In contrast, those who seek the abolition of prostitution, not merely its regulation, oppose the normalisation of prostitution that terms like 'sex work' and 'sex worker' imply. These latter include two distinct groups: firstly traditional, often Christian, moralists and secondly, radical feminist critics. The former group tends to blame prostitutes for deviating from the high standards women should maintain, thereby tempting men into debauchery and commercialising a use of the female body that should be confined to holy matrimony. Frequently they link prostitution with the spread of disease or the break-up of families (Smart 1985).

In contrast, many feminists see themselves as taking the issue out of the realm of sexual morality (or crime) and posing it in terms of gendered power relations. Some see prostitution as a central plank of patriarchal power, something that not just involves, but legitimates and organises the sexual abuse of women by men (Barry 1995; Giobbe 1990; Jeffreys 1997). For instance, Jeffries (1997) prefers to call prostitutes 'prostituted women' to indicate their victimisation by men, and avoids calling the prostitute user a 'client', presumably because it implies a legitimate business relationship. She employs instead gender-specific terms like 'john' or 'punter'. Other feminists may be happy to speak of sex workers and clients, although a term like 'prostitute user', suggested by Julia O'Connell Davidson (1998), while having the merits of gender-neutrality, also assumes that paid-for sex involves a relationship that is different from that which pertains between professionals, like lawyers or advertising executives, and their clients.

Since accepting one or other definition at the outset could not but foreclose some of the key issues, I have used both the terms 'prostitute' and 'sex worker'. However, because my discussion includes, as far as possible, lap dancing, erotic dancing and so on, I tend to use the term 'sex work' to refer to a wide range of paid work involving sexual performance and contact and 'prostitution' for a narrower range of transactions.

The substantive issues involved in conceptualisng the prostitute body involve much more than definitional differences, echoing longstanding debate in Western philosophy and political economy about the relationship between the self, the body and labour. As O'Connell Davidson (2002: 85) points out, John Locke's foundational text of liberal thought dictated that:

> every man has a property in his own person. This nobody has any right to but himself. The labour of his body and the work of his hands, we may say, are properly his. (Second Treatise on Civil Government 1690)

Yet at the same time as Locke recognised the bodily capacity to labour as a legitimate commodity, he also saw the body as having a different relation to the self than any other sort of property. While we may have drifted away from Locke's belief in the human body's uniquely God-given character, nonetheless its special relation to the constitution of the self is still at the heart of many controversies, including not only prostitution and other kinds of sex work but also the sale of body parts, gametes and gestational 'services' (Dickenson 1997; Pateman 1988; Scheper-Hughes 2002, 2001, 2000).

This chapter identifies six distinct ways of conceptualising the construction of the prostitute body within feminist writing on prostitution, and I will examine each in turn. While they are not mutually exclusive, they are more than a device for organising the discussion. The ways in which the body is conceptualised in feminist research, not just on sex work but more generally, is deeply embedded in political stances, wider theoretical presuppositions and rhetorical strategies, and has important implications for social policy. As is no doubt clear already, the chapter focuses on constructions of the sexed bodies of female prostitutes, although it would be interesting to see how it might have to be altered if extended to include men.

The body as text

We owe the focus on the body in debates on prostitution to Foucauldian feminists, who identified the 'prostitute body' as a key discursive construction in the history of sexuality. This view has the advantage of recognising that neither sex nor the body is ever unmediated, since both are always discursively constructed. In this view the prostitute body is appropriated by neither the client nor men in general, but by a discourse that inscribes her body as 'Other' (Bell 1994; Mort 1987; Spongberg 1997). This view has become a lynchpin in the defence of prostitution as an institution, insisting that since its meaning is dependent on contingent, local discourses, we cannot say that there is anything intrinsically wrong with it.

It is useful to begin with this approach because it so usefully provides historical depth. A wealth of documentary research has produced a clear picture of the prostitute body as a historical construction, a vehicle for the expression of typically Victorian anxieties (Bell 1994; Bland 1992; Mort 1987; Nead 1988; Spongberg 1997; Walkowitz 1980; Wood 1982). The location of the sin of prostitution in the body of the prostitute, rather than that of the client, owed much to the ways the Victorians linked health and moral hygiene. The prostitute was seen as guilty of spreading venereal disease to soldiers and other men, not vice versa, because her disease reflected and confirmed her debased moral character. The prostitute's dangerous sexual autonomy, her willingness to tempt men rather than dampen down their urges, was contrary to bourgeois expectations of natural feminine decorum and dependence, whereas male prostitute users were only doing what came naturally – for a man (indeed, the British Army felt it necessary to provide adequate sexual outlets). It should be stressed that written on the prostitute body was not only unruly sexual desire, sex as a disruptive force, but also, in Britain, fears of rebellion, revolution and non-conformity (Nead 1988; Smart 1992, 1989, 1985).

The regulation of prostitution in Britain through draconian nineteenth-century legislation put in place particular constructions of the prostitute body (Walkowitz 1980). The Contagious Diseases Act of 1864, modified in 1866 and 1869, enabled women defined as prostitutes to be inspected for signs of venereal disease, forcibly if necessary, through internal vaginal examination by doctors. It also provided for their incarceration for at least 3 months in special 'lock hospitals' to prevent them spreading the disease while they were being treated (with wholly ineffectual remedies, as we now know). The latter Acts said that women once identified in this way had to register and make themselves available for inspection every two weeks. In England these regulations covered mainly garrison towns, where troops were barracked, although in the last Act there was an attempt to deploy them more widely, something that was partly responsible for setting off the Repeal movement. Although agitations by the Ladies National Association and its allies succeeded in getting the Acts suspended and subsequently repealed, as Walkowitz (1980) argued, the legislation had put into place a particular understanding of prostitutes as a distinct, readily identifiable category. Indeed, they were assumed to be so visibly marked by difference that police constables on their beat would have no trouble identifying them as prostitutes requiring apprehension and inspection. Whereas prostitution had been a temporary redress for young women at times of economic hardship, they now became locked into a criminal career and a defining social identity.

In the British colonies, anxieties about the contagion inherent in the bodies of prostitutes were intensified by fears about racial difference, implying the need for even greater control than at home. Parliament made provision for the inspection of women working in the brothels that serviced British troops in India and elsewhere in the British Empire, not just within Britain. For instance, the Cantonment Act 1864 regulated the sex trade within military stations in India as part of the regulation of commercial activities in military towns. (A cantonment is a military camp or military station where troops are barracked.) The Indian Contagious Diseases Act 1868 made provision for the supervision, registration and inspection of prostitute women in major Indian cities and seaports. According to Levine (1994), syphilis in India was seen as a different, more virulent and corrupting strain than the one prevalent in Britain, and was frequently compared to leprosy. The wider scope of the regulations covering India than at home, Levine argues, posed the Indian prostitute body as a greater threat. Moreover, the debate over the passage of the two Acts covering India, Levine argues, lacked the 'rhetoric of redemption and moralism' that accompanied passage of the CD Acts covering Britain, implying that foreign prostitutes were beyond reform.

The legal construction of prostitutes was accompanied by other expert discourses, especially in medicine. For instance, Dr Parent-Duchatelet, having previously studied the sewers of Paris, turned his attention to statistical measures regarding several thousand Parisian prostitutes in the early nineteenth century, who were also seen as a source of pollution. He itemised the supposed physiognomy and physiological features of the prostitute body, covering not only genital malformations but also the quality of the voices, shape of the eyebrows, and hair and eye colour as well as family inheritance (Bell 1994: 45–6). By the end of the century, sexologists like Havelock Ellis were arguing that women who became prostitutes represented a congenital, degenerate type of female criminality.

The pathologising of the prostitute had shifted somewhat by the 1950s, focusing on psychological rather than physical deformities. For instance, the Wolfenden Committee Report (1957) concluded that prostitute women, by putting themselves outside the norms of the community, demonstrated either antisocial values or psychological weaknesses and could legitimately be denied civil rights (Smart 1985). The Report was compiled in the context of anxieties not totally unlike those of the nineteenth century, including racist fears (loss of Empire and, by now, fears about migration) and postwar concerns about family instability. Smart (1985) suggests that in the 1980s magistrates who rejected an outright punitive discourse in favour of welfarist or other help for prostitutes were still mainly concerned with the harm prostitutes caused the community.

In current debates in Britain on regulation of prostitution, the view of prostitutes as a public nuisance still dominates, especially in kerb-crawling debates, where prostitutes' 'bodies and lifestyle' are seen as threatening (Kantola and Squires 2004b; see also Phoenix 1999; Kantola and Squires 2004a). In Birmingham prostitutes were described by community organisers seeking to clear their neighbourhood of streetworkers as 'scum', as 'the human scavengers polluting our streets' (Kantola and Squires 2004b: 82, citing an article in the *Birmingham Evening Mail* of 27 July 1997). It is not surprising, therefore, that the murder of prostitutes rarely attracts as much concern as the killing of 'respectable women', while worries about HIV infection among prostitutes are related more to fears about its spread into the 'wider population' than sex workers' own health (O'Kane 2002). Strip clubs, lap dancing establishments and sex shops are also seen as a nuisance, in part because the groups of men they attract harass the (respectable) women of the neighbourhood (Ferguson 2004).

However, there are some problems with the emphasis on discourse and representations as the site of oppression. Some interpretations tend to mistake the harsh imposition of civic inequality, intrusive medical inspection and physical incarceration for (mere) discourse. Walkowitz (1980) and Nead (1988), however, while influenced by Foucauldian discursive analysis, were pointing to the inscription of the prostitute's body, and the shaping of her life chances, by the social relations of class, gender and Empire. In some accounts, like Shannon Bell's (1994), the prostitute's embodied experience disappears: the humiliating internal inspection by what the nineteenth-century repealer Josephine Butler called the doctor's 'steel penis', incarceration in lock hospitals, and exclusion from the body politic to which Walkowitz (1980) and others drew attention, recede in favour of merely textual representations. The prostitute's historically specific experiences of felt embodiment are either ignored or reduced to what Bell calls 'behavioural consistencies at the level of the body' (Bell 1994: 11). Instead, Bell sees only the body's surface imprinted by history, ignoring, as she acknowledges, the shaping of the material body. This is very much a liberal appropriation of Foucault, implying that changes in discourse will be sufficient to change prostitutes from (discursively constructed) shamed victims into self-managing businesswomen in control of their destiny. Arguably much needed legal changes, especially the decriminalisation of prostitution, would result in a less stigmatising construction of prostitutes. But we also have to question, as O'Connell Davidson (1998) implies, the presumption that it is only legal or medical discourse that 'Others' them. O'Connell Davidson suggests, as we will discuss later, that the users' embodied interaction with the sex worker may confirm and reproduce her Otherness along with their own sense of sovereignty.

There is also an inconsistency at the heart of the textualised prostitute body in that while the prostitute body is seen to be constructed discursively, the client's body and sexual desires are deemed natural. Bell (1994: 84), for instance, rejects MacKinnon's (1987: 49) idea of sexual desire as strictly a social construct emerging from social relations, an odd position for such an otherwise consistently constructionist commentator to hold. Like many liberal theorists, she justifies fighting what she defines as repressive measures through claims about the natural and inevitable character of sexual desire. Similarly, McNair sees sex as 'the exchange of body fluids', a biological function similar to others: 'we eat, we excrete, we fuck, we sleep' (2002: 1). While it is more usual to explain the client's desire in terms of the biologically inevitable and unstoppable nature of male desire, recent attempts to invalidate feminist critiques make the same claims for female sexuality, arguing, like McNair, that the commercialisation of sex is democratising, opening up access to sexual pleasure on the basis of cash rather than gender or other dimensions of status.

The construction of the prostitute body as text is particularly salient in debates on pornography, because the body seen by the viewer in photographs, the cinema, or computer monitor is necessarily a screen(ed) body. The crucial concept in McNair's (2002, 1996) accounts of the sexualisation of visual culture is the notion of 'mediated sex', which is how he characterises pornography, as distinct from telephone sex, striptease clubs and sexual aids. He says that he took this characterisation of pornography from Andrea Dworkin (McNair 2002: 41), although without referencing a particular source, on the grounds that whereas in prostitution the woman has to sell herself, with the risk of violence and infection, in pornography the use of the woman is mediated by the camera. But while Dworkin presumably referred to the fact that pornographic images were produced by taking pictures or films of real bodies having sex, in McNair the physical interaction between bodies that takes place in the making of most pornography is literally never mentioned. This is a view of the body so defined through fantasy that it disappears as embodied experience; in other words, a textual body seen through the eye of a consumer free to assign meaning to the images they see and to choose between them.

The essentialised body

Although early radical feminist writing on prostitution scarcely mentions the body (for example, Barry 1984, first published c.1979), more recent attempts to rebut arguments defending prostitution offer a distinctive construction of the meaning of the body and its relation to the self. The most characteristic aspect of the radical feminist approach to embodiment is the refusal to take an interest only in the body's discursively constructed surface, which, as seen above, remains a problem in Foucauldian approaches. In contrast, radical feminists see prostitution as something that takes place 'in and on our bodies' (Barry 1995: 280), one reason, perhaps, why commentators influenced by radical feminism, for instance Pateman (1988), restrict their definition of prostitution to activities involving sexual penetration. Neither prostitution nor pornography can be relegated to a realm of representation or disembodied fantasy (MacKinnon 1994).

Radical feminist critics typically describe the experience of prostitution in exceptionally graphic terms, as a way of demonstrating the 'profound experiences of the body involved in the retailing of intimacy' (Jeffreys 1997).

What Scarry (1985) calls the reality-conferring function of the body is explicit in the account of Glasgow streetwalkers that Jeffreys (1987: 349) cites. The researchers comment that

> This was the first occasion that the reality of what being a prostitute entails had been made starkly apparent – alone, on your knees, with a client's penis in your mouth. It is difficult to say why, but it was incredibly shocking to see that reality. (McKeganey and Barnard 1996: 11)

Jeffreys gives equally graphic examples of the effects of prostitution on women's sense of self, citing for instance the prostitute who has come to feel 'as if she is moving through life inside a boil or clothed head to toe in a rash' (Hoigard and Finstad 1992: 108). Defence mechanisms are ineffective against such torture: another woman says that she uses tampons all the time, even when she is not menstruating, and that 'because I'm afraid of stinking I never sit to close to people, I wash my ears ten times a day because I'm afraid guck is running out of them' (Hoigard and Finstad 1992: 92, cited by Jeffreys 1997: 271).

Prostitution results in such profound self-hate, radical feminists (want to) believe, that it could never be undertaken willingly, so the distinction between forced prostitution and prostitution undertaken by choice is a false one. The picture we have is of a body–self that has been so injured that it cannot recognise its true interests. Barry (1995) sees the body of the prostitute as 'de-selved' and turned into a body-object. Although this notion is meant to address the disassociation between self and body imposed by prostitution, it also carries the implication that what prostitutes say about themselves can be discounted, since the prostituted woman is no longer a subject who can speak for herself. Rather, the injured body of the prostitute speaks for her: it is injury and pain that define the prostitute body. Other interpretations of prostitution, even prostitutes' own, are mere defence mechanisms. Only once the woman has escaped from prostitution do we hear her true voice.

Commentaries based on graphic images of what Doezema (2001) calls the 'wounded body' are hard to argue against, as we fear the implication that objections would deny the reality of sex workers' pain. Yet other feminists question whether this essentialist view of the body represents an adequate way forward, since it seems to counterpoise the filthiness of prostitution against women's purity. Pitts (2003), for instance, argues that radical feminist writing presumes an essential, untouched 'pristine body' that pre-exists its corruption by male culture. As Haaken (1996) puts it in another context, for radical feminists 'everything bad' comes from 'outside'. There are obvious comparisons here with the purely natural body beneath the trappings of 'beauty culture' we saw in the short story by Brown (1991), discussed in Chapter 1.

This view of the natural purity of women's bodies has enabled radical feminists to forge a problematic alliance with traditional moralists, with whom radical feminists share a preoccupation with protecting, saving and therefore rescuing the innocent victim (Kantola and Squires 2004b). Even if radical feminists do not condemn the guilty sinner in the way traditionalists would, they share an outlook in which women are constantly being 'duped, tricked or lured' into prostitution by people-traffickers. This in turn enables them to hold onto the idea of women as essentially innocent.

A related problem in these writings on prostitution (and pornography), noted also by Scoular (2004) and Oerton and Phoenix (2001), is that sexuality is presented as a singular and unique form of embodied interaction, a view with parallels in nineteenth-century moral purity thinking. Jeffreys (1997), for instance, explicitly refuses to recognise any continuities between prostitution and other kinds of (dirty, humiliating, intimate) work or to take on board the (also dirty, humiliating and sometimes intimate) kinds of work that women, and too often children, might well have to turn to in order to support themselves. Not only does their position seriously underestimate the relative rewards of prostitution as an active choice, whatever the cost, but there is an almost wilful refusal to acknowledge, as Montgomery (1998: 148) puts it in the case of child sex workers in Thailand, that

> the children did not have a choice as to whether they were exploited or not or between prostitution and work-free childhood. If they were not prostitutes they would still have been impoverished and probably forced into the illegal labor market in a sweat shop or as a scavenger.

Recognising this would make it clear that in many countries providing realistic alternatives to prostitution is linked to almost intractable wider socio-economic constraints, and not just issues about women's rights.

The disabling assumption that women cannot assess or explain their own interests is the most disturbing aspect of this approach, and it is no wonder that spokespeople for working prostitutes' organisations attack it (Doezema 2001; West and Austrin 2002). It insists on binary oppositions, with no middle ground. Women are constructed by prostitution as objects appropriated by men, if they are involved in the trade, or, once they have been rescued, active in combating it. There is no room here for the working prostitute as an active subject, however constrained. As O'Connell Davidson comments, abolitionist feminists imagine that by 'requiring a woman to temporarily fix herself as an object, prostitution permanently, completely and literally extinguishes her as a subject' (O'Connell Davidson 2002: 92).

The ways in which radical feminists conceptualise the prostitute body also carry over into new areas of research, for instance on other kinds of sex work. For example, research by Kelly Holsopple (n.d.), an ex-stripper previously associated with the radical feminist organisation WHISPER, analyses stripping (including table dancing, lap dancing and other kinds of club work that involve even more bodily contact with customers) as a form of sexual violence more similar to prostitution than dancing. Like prostitution the work involves the perpetration and (again, graphically described) intrusive, often violent acts by customers and staff who 'smell so sour, they breathe very heavy and kind of wheeze when women are near' (Holsopple n.d.: 14). Moreover the club owners and managers impose petty but intrusive rules over the workers, including 'when they may use the bathroom and how many can be in the dressing room at a time' (ibid.: 4). They are also fined for myriad infractions, like using telephones without permission, touching the stage mirror, taking off their shoes, being sick, not cleaning the dressing room, and using baby oil on stage. Graphic descriptions counter the picture of stripping as harmless fun, a glamorous alternative to ordinary jobs. Holsopple says that girls going into it think they will 'have fun and get paid for it' but have no idea they will have to 'fight men's hands, and dicks, and tongues' (ibid.: 13).

Much of the more recent writing and campaigning is directed towards the issue of trafficking. As Scoular says, 'the injured body of the third world prostitute in trafficking discourse . . . acts as a powerful metaphor' (Scoular 2004: 351) for advancing feminist interests. The rejection of a meaningful distinction between women's forced and voluntary participation in migration for the purpose of prostitution has become central to the agenda of the Coalition against Trafficking in Women (CATW). US legislation on trafficking, as well as the UN Protocol on Trafficking, both reflect their view that the consent of the victim is irrelevant to the definition of sex trafficking (Stetson 2004), although the US legislation specifies harsh penalties only if coercion or children are involved. In Britain radical feminists present a more nuanced analysis distinguishing between assisted migration, smuggling and trafficking and some recognise differences between voluntary migration, involuntary trafficking and debt bondage (Kelly 2003; Kelly and Regan 2000). However, Kelly argues that the terms under which women first migrated are only part of the story, because women may migrate intending to work in the sex industry, but find themselves having to work under abhorrent conditions and, due to debt and fear of immigration officials, become trapped in it. Although Kelly (2003: 140) provides examples of extreme coercion ('because they are real'), she implies that such emotive 'trump cards' can cloud more complicated arguments.

The commodified body

A third view of the body sees it as a form of property, a legitimate object of trade that the subject is, or should be, free to use as she (or he) wishes. This argument is central to the sex work lobby's advocacy of the decriminalisation and normalisation of prostitution as similar to other kinds of paid employment. Chapkis's (1997) *Live Sex Acts* has been especially influential in defending prostitution on these grounds. However, it has been one of the main critics of this view, Pateman (1988), who has been the more influential in debate on women's employment more generally.

Defining prostitution and other kinds of sex work as the 'performance of erotic labour', Chapkis's argument is directed mainly against radical feminists, who as we saw above, assume that the commodification of the body devalues the self and turns it into an object, depriving the prostitute of 'respect, honour and dignity' (Barry 1984: 268). In contrast, Chapkis sees the alienation of 'erotic labour' as no different in principle from that involved in other kinds of paid work, analogous to the emotional labour undertaken by many other workers, and largely overlapping with it. As in many accounts of emotional work discussed in Chapter 4, however, Hochschild's (1983) original emphasis on emotional labour as a form of embodied labour disappears from view.

Chapkis's defence of prostitution stresses ways that sex workers, like others whose work involves paid emotional labour, are able to distinguish the self from the roles they play at work. There are several problems with the way Chapkis equates sexual and emotional labour, however. First, Chapkis totally ignores Hochschild's critical edge; although Hochschild agrees that the commercialisation of feeling need not lead to the destruction of the self, she stresses that 'there is a cost to emotional work; it affects the degree to which we listen to feelings and sometimes our very capacity to feel' (Hochschild 1983: 21). Moreover, as will be discussed further in Chapter 7, Hochschild's views on the commercialisation of intimacy have become even more critical, increasingly stressing the interconnections between the commodification of intimacy and global inequality (Hochschild 2003, 2001). Chapkis also tends to assume that similarities between sexual and (other kinds of) emotional labour justify the equation of sex work with highly valued occupations such as psychotherapist or child care worker. Although Chapkis notes that the effect of performing erotic labour parallels emotional labour in being affected by 'exogenous factors' like organisation, occupational structure and cultural values, as well as conditions of work (speed-ups, increased duties, supervision), she avoids considering which factors and conditions are likely to be most typical of sex work. In practice a comparison of sex work with lower-status occupations may be more realistic, especially those that involve stigmatised bodily states and wastes and involve a high degree of routinisation and, in many cases, the denial of emotional involvement.

Chapkis's definition of prostitution as the performance of erotic labour seems to echo the notion of performativity as developed by Judith Butler (1991, 1990), although Chapkis does not make this link explicit. Another commentator on sex work, Liepe-Levinson (2002), though, does use Butler in presenting the 'strip show' as a transgressive performance that challenges several aspects of gender normativity, including feminine modesty and, in the case of male strippers like the Chippendales, the repositioning of men as the objects rather than the controllers of the gaze (see also Smith 2002). The key question here is whether the content (or context) of erotic performance typically problematises gender scripts in the way Liepe-Levinson implies. Although Butler sees the stylisation of the body taking place within a highly rigid regulatory framework governed by normative heterosexuality, she is most interested in performances that challenge the normative stylisation of the body. And although the performance of a drag queen may problematise the link between gender and 'sex', as Bishop and Robinson (1998: 229–6) say, most strip show performances replay conventional gender scripts. Moreover, in so far as the customer usually seeks in the performer's personal attention a confirmation of their own masculinity or femininity, not simply a theatrical display (Wood 2000), then gender roles are also reproduced.

Responses within feminist debate to the commodification of the body entailed by sex work are very varied. A particularly influential feminist critique of the body as a commodity was developed by the political theorist Carole Pateman (1988). Pateman refused the separation of body and self, labour and subject, implied by the idea that the prostitute sells (or in Chapkis's terms, performs) 'sexual services'. Firstly, Pateman argues, although we conventionally distinguish waged labour from slavery, nonetheless the embodied self is always the object of the wage labour contract, but one obscured by the 'political fiction' that labour power is a form of property separable from the embodied person. Actually, she says,

> The employment contract gives the employer right of command over the use of the worker's labour, that is to say, over the self, person and body of the worker during the period set down in the employment contract. Similarly the services of the prostitute cannot be provided unless she is present: property in the person, unlike material property, cannot be separated from its owner. (Pateman 1988: 203)

There are a number of problems with Pateman's account (including her conception of power, which I discuss later). Like the radical feminists noted above, Pateman tends towards essentialising 'mystical notions' (Liepe-Levinson 2002: 109) of the relationship between female sexuality and self, seeing sexuality as uniquely personified:

> [T]he self is not completely subsumed in its sexuality, but identity is inseparable from the sexual construction of the self. 'Womanhood' is confirmed in sexual activity, and when a prostitute contracts out the use of her body she is thus selling herself in a very real sense. (Ibid.: 207)

Another problem is Pateman's assumption that the aims of punters who use the prostitute's body are entirely different from those of conventional employers who deploy workers' bodies in order to create outputs or 'profits'. Pateman argues that the involvement of the body in prostitution is different from its use in other kinds of work, because in other kinds of work the employer has no intrinsic interest in the body of the worker, being concerned only with how its output affects profitability. It is not true that employers normally have no interest in the bodies of their workers, which as we saw in Chapter 3 are perceived to influence productivity and profits. But it is certainly true that Pateman's stress on the embodied, 'selved' character of the worker draws attention to the uses of the sexed body in commodified interactions.

In the debate on prostitution some commentators do not reject the commodification of the body involved in prostitution, as does Pateman, but still analyse this construction far more critically than Chapkis. For instance, Phoenix (1999) shows that the UK sex workers she interviewed adopt the discourse of the body as property in the person as a flexible idiom within which to articulate varied, changeable feelings about working as a prostitute. While Pateman assumes that conceiving of a person's body as mere property is disabling, in a society where, as Dickenson (1997) points out, being a subject is defined by property-holding, seeing one's body as property (or in Bourdieu's terms as embodied capital) may operate as a support to self-esteem, especially in a society in which women have had characteristically fewer rights in their person than men. For instance, a woman might say that 'The first time I turned a trick was the first time I felt in control of my sexuality' (Pheterson c. 1996: 54), a comment echoed more powerfully by the 14-year old Brazilian girl who told Scheper-Hughes, 'Nanci, the first time I was paid to "put out" I knew what it meant to be a person and to be the owner [dona] of myself' (Scheper-Hughes 2001: 51). According to Phoenix (1999), women working as prostitutes also use the notion of their bodies as a form of property to distinguish between the control over their bodies they feel ownership *should* confer, and their feeling of hopelessness if they lose this control to a pimp.

Another approach is to widen the framework of analysis beyond the relation between prostitute and punter, on which both Chapkis and Pateman concentrate. Truong Thanh-Dam's (1990) approach suggests that accepting the commodification of female sexuality as an object of analysis, rather than rejecting it as a political fiction, is not incompatible with the critique of prostitution as an institution, so long as we focus on the wider social conditions that produce sexual labour as a commodity, rather than assuming that it results from the decisions of individual women to prostitute, as does Chapkis. This also means rejecting Pateman's interpretation of the power relations of prostitution in terms of a dyadic model of intense personal control, in favour of a focus on multi-faceted structural processes (Fraser 1993). Pateman's assumption that those who use the prostitute's body are not interested in the creation of outputs or 'profits' characteristic of conventional waged labour does not do justice to the subordination of client–prostitute relations to increasingly globalised sex industries, such as sex tourism.

Truong argues that while sexuality is a natural, biological capacity, sexual labour is not a natural resource. The transformation of sexuality into sexual labour, a commodity, is produced by the globalisation of capitalist relations and contributes to the profits of local and international capital. Although the body is universally a carrier of 'physical assets' used to produce pleasure, the construction of sexual labour as a 'category of labour derived from the utilization of the body – its sexual elements – as an instrument of labour' (Truong 1990: 91) takes place only under specific historical and social conditions. In Thailand, for instance, the origins of the sex tourism industry lie in the construction of Bangkok as a playground for American servicemen stationed in Vietnam on leave. The sexual labour force was produced through the dislocation, through migration and militarisation, of 'natural' relations of social reproduction within households. The production of consumer demand (from male soldiers and migrants no longer living in conjugal households) and available labour (from women no longer able to produce a livelihood from household industries and farming) form the preconditions for the entry of capital into the organisation of reproductive activities as a source of profit – not just sexual activities but other 'body work' services. Eventually those who control and manage the sex tourist industry can drive forward its development only through actively recruiting the rapidly depleted age and sex specific (sexual) labour force as the basis of their profitability, using coercion and violence if other forms of recruitment fail (Bishop and Robinson 1998; O'Connell Davidson 1998; Truong 2001).

While it may tend to naturalise the drives that send people halfway round the world for sexual experiences, Truong's account provides an essential plank in understanding the economic drive behind the expansion of the sex industries and sex tourism as a source of profit, now the subject of much research (Clift and Carter 2000; Kempadoo and Doezema 1998; Kempadoo 1999). It is also relevant to the expansion of other body work services in parts of the Third World, such as the spas and yoga schools in Asia or Mexico (see Chapter 7). Truong (2001) also illuminates the role of international criminal gangs in the migration of women from their own localities to work in the sex industries in richer countries, shifting the emphasis away from the question of whether women choose to work as prostitutes or are trafficked against their will, and placing it instead on the organisation of the sex trade and its contribution to the international economy.

The social body

Nick Crossley's (2001) conception of the social body brings to the foreground the corporeal aspects of social agency and highlights, following Bourdieu, the embeddedness of embodied subjectivity in social interactions. Building on the insights of the phenomenology of Merleau-Ponty, he argues that one's body is one's point of view on the world; it is turned outward to the world 'in a sort of circuit with the social world' (Merleau-Ponty cited by Crossley 2001: 4). The subjective sense of self is formed not by looking inward, but relationally and comparatively, through social interactions (Crossley 2001: 143). Crossley also highlights the centrality of the Hegelian notion of the desire for recognition to social interactions and social relations.

This notion of the social body provides a useful way of characterising the understanding of the prostitute body emerging from the writings of Julia O'Connell Davidson (2002, 1998, 1997, 1995a, 1995b), Jacqueline Sanchez-Taylor (2001, 2000) and other colleagues (Anderson and O'Connell Davidson 2004). Although they do not cite Bourdieu (or Crossley) as a key influence, they draw from some of the same sources, and like Bourdieu relate misrecognition and the infliction of what Bourdieu calls 'symbolic violence' to positions in social hierarchies. They also reject a view that sees the prostitute body constructed only in and by discourse; rather it is social relations and social interaction that are 'written on the body' (Sanchez-Taylor 2000), not discourse, and that structure embodied experience. Nor do they presume a universal female body defined by its potential penetrability. In fact, for O'Connell Davidson and Sanchez-Taylor the prostitute body is defined less by its sex or gender, as in radical feminism, than by its positioning in power relations.

O'Connell Davidson's definition of prostitution is meant to draw attention to prostitution as a power relation, not just an economic one, and highlights at the outset its implications for the flesh-and-blood body. The social transaction that defines prostitution, she argues, gives the user the (temporary) right to

> command the prostitute to make bodily orifices available to him, to smile, dance or dress up for him, to whip, spank, massage or masturbate him, to submit to being urinated upon, shackled or beaten by him, or otherwise submit to his wishes and desires. (O'Connell Davidson 1998: 9–10)

For O'Connell Davidson the use of such graphic imagery, which she shares with radical feminists, is not so much indicative of a personal repugnance at the 'ickiness' of what prostitutes may be asked to do (which Chapkis (1997) claims lies behind many objections to prostitution). Rather, it is a way of demonstrating the extent to which the prostitute is required to relinquish, to a variable extent, control over her bodily boundaries, dignity and personal safety, which are socially constructed as both an index and cornerstone of individual sovereignty. The implication is that the things the sex worker may be asked to do are not 'wrong' because they tarnish sex (nor even because they involve sex) but because they so graphically reflect and affect on the one hand the prostitute's relative inability to define her bodily boundaries, and, on the other, the client's use of prostitutes as a way of evading 'the complex web of rules, meanings, obligations and conventions which govern non-commercial sexuality' (O'Connell Davidson 1998: 188). Sociality and community presuppose that we 'experience others as experiencing others' (Crossley 2001: 144), yet it is precisely this lack of regard for the prostitute as subject with their own history and desires that characterises prostitute use. The user seeks a person who is not a person, a 'person who is physically alive but socially dead' (O'Connell Davidson 1998: 134).

Thinking about prostitution in terms of the social body also makes it possible to incorporate boys and men as sex workers within the same framework. From the beginning O'Connell Davidson rejected the assumption of many feminists that the power of the prostitute user was based on his sex. The power of the male client – and here she echoes Marx – rests in his pocket 'not in his Y fronts' (O'Connell Davidson 1995a: 8), although obviously his greater economic power is related to gender. Heterosexual Western women now also carry (relative) power, in their purse if not their pocket. Indeed, by visiting the Caribbean or other regions, Western women can obtain the attentions of male lovers, usually disguising the relationship by financially supporting their lovers informally in the long or short term, rather than paying for sex outright. The women are able to use their greater economic resources and/or racialised identities to 'reaffirm their sense of "womanliness" by being sexually desired by men', to feel that they 'exist as sexual objects' and 'to limit their risks of being rejected or humiliated' (Sanchez-Taylor 2000: 46, 47).

Clearly, in this formulation the desires of both men and women as prostitute users are socially defined, rather than reflecting simple physiological needs. Erotic life is seen to be 'grounded in the ideas we use to categorize, interpret, and give meaning to human experience', 'not some fundamental, timeless, or general human desire for sex' (O'Connell Davidson 2002: 90). In this sense the racialisation of the body of the sex worker is more than incidental to the desires driving the sex tourist. While the legacy of slavery and colonialism has marked racialised bodies as lascivious and even savage (Cranny-Francis 1995; McClintock 1995; Nagel 2003), O'Connell Davidson and Sanchez-Taylor (1999) argue that it is not simply that 'exotic' bodies are seen as particularly desirable, but rather that sex tourists' projection of racist fantasies, combined with the typically more diffuse transactions characteristic of sex tourism, enables them to mask the monetary nature of the transaction and delude themselves with fantasies about their own sexuality. The racialisation of the sex worker enables male prostitute users to experience themselves as sexually powerful. Men who would never admit to the neediness implied by using a prostitute at home are furnished, through sex tourism, with the illusion of full 'sovereignty over their own minds, bodies and selves'. As one British tourist in Thailand explained:

> Over there, you don't have to worry about going out and getting someone, because you know any time, day or night, you can have anyone you want within seconds. You feel so powerful, you feel you're in control of your sex life. (O'Connell Davidson 1997: 176)

Women tourists' delusions are not the same as men's but their positioning vis-à-vis local men enables them to obtain recognition of their femininity, which they feel men deny them at home. Tourism provides them a stage on which they can 'affirm their femininity' through the ability to obtain the attentions of a local man (Sanchez-Taylor 2001: 760).

Although prostitute users gain recognition of themselves as fully sexual beings, however, the experience of the sex worker is one of misrecognition. O'Connell Davidson shares with radical feminist views on prostitution a common phenomenological frame which sees the body as integral to the self. She argues that 'To contract out sexual use of the body requires the woman to sever the integrity of body and self, something that carries grave psychological consequences' (O'Connell Davidson 2002: 87), but she draws different political conclusions. This is partly due to the way she conceptualises the power relations of client and prostitute, which she sees in less totalising terms. Sex workers vary in their capacity to defend their sense of sovereignty, depending on their social status, organisation of the sex trade, perception of their rights and biographical history. Key variables in the organisation of prostitution are the legal framework, including policing; the involvement of third parties, such as pimps; the formality or diffuseness of the transaction; and the time span it covers.

The implications for policy are thus different from those propounded by Pateman or radical feminists, in so far as O'Connell Davidson and colleagues target the wider social relations that position the 'prostitute body' rather than attempt to prohibit its use. O'Connell Davidson supports the decriminalisation of prostitution, but she does not defend it as an institution. Trying to gain rights for sex workers by validating the work is a mistake, she argues; rather, policy should be based on the idea that 'a person's human, civil, and labour rights, and their rights to respect and social value as a human being' are not contingent on whether or not they perform labour that is socially valued (2002: 93). Although she is pessimistic about the potential for transformatory collective political action by prostitutes, her emphasis on the undermining of personal sovereignty involved in much prostitution suggests the possibility of identifying criteria on which to evaluate changes in the criminal justice system. For instance, recent attempts to stop prostitution by further criminalising both the prostitute and the client can have detrimental consequences, limiting the sex worker's ability to refuse distasteful or unsafe acts.

In principle, O'Connell Davidson's analysis is not confined to sexual use, for it also applies to other kinds of work that depend upon the misrecognition of the Other. It makes it possible to consider similarities between prostitution and paid domestic labour, for instance, wherein the employer explicitly seeks 'a person who is not a person' to do work the employer considers too dirty or humiliating to put their own hands to (Anderson 2000; Parreñas 2001), work in which connections between disgust, dirt and the transgression of bodily boundaries are also present. There are also similarities with the coerced or compensated 'donation' of kidneys and other body organs by those in financial need, or by those in a position of personal dependence, on the grounds that it will 'save a life', even if it means 'cannibalising' the insides of others' bodies (Scheper-Hughes 2001).

It is worth stressing that although this view sees something in common between sex work and other kinds of work, Sheila Jeffreys (2003) is quite wrong to conflate it with those who seek to legitimate sex tourism. Although patriarchy is not seen as primary, the social relations of prostitution are still conceptualised as power relations and not, as is the case for apologists for sex tourism, those of mutual exchange.

The body-without-organs

The body-without-organs (BWO) is a shorthand in postmodern scholarship for an understanding of embodiment based on the work of Deleuze and Guattari, admirably summarised by Fox (1999). In relation to prostitution this view has been developed mainly in a recent book by Brewis and Linstead (2000). Like the first of our approaches, it builds on a Foucauldian understanding of the body as constructed in discourse, but goes much further in challenging the construction of the body as an object. Whereas modernist views see people maintaining their bodily and psychological boundaries in defence of their individual sovereignty, autonomy and identity – both Hochschild and O'Connell Davidson are examples – poststructuralists challenge the value liberals put on autonomy and the model of a body as a container of the self (Battersby 1997). Those influenced by Deleuze and Guattari, in particular, see this as self-defeating, in so far as the bounded body is an object-body, closed off by its skin. Moreover, linking sovereignty to one's sense of control over bodily boundaries, such as suggested by O'Connell Davidson, seems to Brewis and Linstead the wrong basis for a theory reaching towards liberation. Instead, for them progressive thought moves across the body and outside it, disappearing its reality as a body with organs. Partly because fantasy and desire play a large role in challenging the modernist body with organs, prostitution is seen as a suitable example for exploring this theoretical development. The question is whether, intriguing as it is, this approach really provides enough grip on the experience of sex workers in contemporary global society or the possibilities that are open to most of them.

According to Brewis and Linstead (2000), the pleasures and play of body contact potentially exceed and even transform the discourses and social relations that contain it. From this point of view, one might even see in the graphic descriptions of the prostituted body presented by some radical feminist critics an underlying fear of giving way to the leakiness of the body. For Brewis and Linstead desire is an autonomous force that defies social determination. Yet, if sexual relations always potentially carry with them the possibility of spontaneity, desire and joy (which is no doubt true), whether the potentialities should define prostitution as an institution seems rather wishful. Indeed, Brewis and Linstead can raise it as a possibility only because they maintain a focus on what they call their 'core countries', the US, Britain and Australia, and pay almost no attention to either sex tourism or the position of migrants to Europe or the US. As Bishop and Robinson say, Western sexual theory that valorises experiment, performance and transgression fits very awkwardly over relations between Thai sex workers and foreign men (1998: 229). Yet Brewis and Linstead push it for all its worth in order to present the social relations of prostitution as indeterminate in structure or outcome.

Postmodernist intellectuals may revalue the leaky body, but it would seem that, as Brewis and Linstead (2000) themselves recognise elsewhere in their book, those sex workers who have, or deal with, the most open, leakiest bodies are those least able to protect themselves from violence or disease. Indeed, prostitutes with relative power and control, like O'Connell Davidson's (1995) 'Desiree', are more concerned to limit access. Most reports from sex workers suggest that, rather than transgressing boundaries, they seek to maintain them. For instance, Liepe-Levinson (2002) suggests that strippers typically 'zone' regions of their bodies between pubic availability and private enjoyment. Other sex workers seek to transform relations with clients into known relations of marriage or kinship (Hoigard and Finstad 1992).

Brewis and Linstead's (2000) account (see also Brewis 2000) is part of a larger intellectual project in which they examine both sex work and sex at work, seeing both as challenging the supposed binary between sex and work.

They highlight the potential of sexuality for transforming social relations, including relationships within organisation. Like Foucault they see the intersection between power and sexuality as inevitable, and their relation as mobile and productive rather than fixed in gender terms. This is why they give a lot of importance to showing that sex workers can and do enjoy the sex involved in their work, as this would indicate that sexual pleasure need not (and indeed could not) be extricated from power relations or pecuniary considerations. Moreover, it provides women with opportunities to exercise power; sexuality has the potential for transforming and re-energising organisation, at least once it is untethered from organisational instrumentality.

It is worth pointing out that Brewis and Linstead's (2000) chapter on the 'materiality' of sex work well recognises the material constraints emanating from the organisation of prostitution, noting factors not dissimilar to those listed by O'Connell Davidson (1998). Moreover, Brewis and Linstead's sensitivity to sex workers' agency means their account of sex workers' management of their identities through the organisation of their bodies in time and space is especially rich in detail. Having trawled a huge amount of published research on sex work, they provide much evidence of sex workers actively shaping their experience of prostitution (see below). But the omission from the Conclusions to their book of the material constraints analysed in the earlier chapter suggest how hard it is to take on board the constraints sex workers face (and which draw most of them into the trade) in the context of the intellectual currents Brewis and Linstead want to pursue.

The agential body

Finally, we need to consider one further construction of the prostitute body that appears in the feminist debate. Whereas radical feminist commentators quote the accounts of sex workers who describe how they respond to what has been done *to* them, the main way in which the lived body becomes visible in accounts defending prostitution is through depicting 'acts of negotiation, resistance and subversion that belie the worker's designation as passive object' (Chapkis 1997: 20). Although, as we saw above, radical feminists also present a picture of the lived body from the inside out, of how prostitutes experience themselves and their environment through their bodies, in the context of such a politicised debate defenders of prostitution need to draw on radically different accounts that stress what Williams and Bendelow (1998: 208) conceptualise as the active and mindful body. As Wood says, sex workers try to resist objectification by using their bodies to defend a sense of themselves as 'interactive subjects' (Wood 2000: 6).

Focusing on the micropolitics of sex work is a crucial level in understanding the power relations of sex work. It forms an important counterweight to the undifferentiated view of power that, as O'Connell Davidson (1998) concludes, has been one of the weaknesses of the polarisation of debate on prostitution. She argues that both sides of the debate tend to view power in totalising terms, seeing prostitutes rendered completely powerless by those who abuse them, on the one hand, or as having broken free from constraining normative prescriptions on their use of their bodies on the other. As Foucault suggests, power relations are not structured as a zero-sum contest, in which if one party holds power the other holds none. O'Connell Davidson stresses people's capacity to deploy power even when they are subject to power, as well as individual, biographical differences in people's ability to identify and utilise opportunities to exercise power in the situations in which they find themselves. While very much closer to radical feminism than Foucauldian analysis, more nuanced accounts like Kelly's (2003) also recognise that victimisation does not exclude individual agency.

Many of the sex workers whose accounts validate the existence of the agential body are or were working as exotic dancers or strippers, and they emphasise very different aspects of their bodily experience than Kelly Holsopple (n.d.), discussed above. They show us how as sex workers their bodies are produced as well as consumed (to adapt a phrase introduced by Brewis and Linstead 2000: 270). Whereas radical feminists like Barry see the prostitute body as 'de-selved', these strippers show us that the body is 'selved' or re-selved through the labour of self-presentation. Their strategies of body management include putting on a kind of body armour, not unlike the woman executive putting on a power suit. In a long and illuminating exposition, Frank, who performed on the outdoor patio of a strip club, explains that on stage, despite her nudity, she is not really revealing herself, but creating an appearance:

Naked? No. I am a performer, as fully clothed as anyone here, even without my bikini, if only through my painstaking ministrations to the 'costume' of my bare body.

She describes her scrupulous attention in detail:

You can't miss a stray hair on an ankle or thigh. Pubic hair must be carefully tended – you cannot be completely clean-shaven and must, for legal purposes, have at least an inch of trimmed fuzz in the front, but most of the women remove the rest. Razor burn looks awful . . . Bruises and veins show up mercilessly, as do scars. Makeup can cover them inside, but out here, unless you are endlessly vigilant, the makeup will streak or be just a shade away from your natural skin color . . . Eye makeup also needs to be perfect. Chipped toe nail polish, gray hairs, and fine lines around the eyes – every detail must be tended diligently. (Frank 2002: 172, 173)

Frank's almost obsessively described diligence, along with the way she uses her sunglasses, putting them on to hide from the sun, taking them off to reveal her eyes to the audience, is part of the way she constructs boundaries between her self and her audience. Her particular attention to her skin is perhaps especially significant, given the complexity of skin as both barrier to the world and a point of interface with it (Ahmed 1998). But the skin is, inevitably, both armour and part of the feeling self:

> The sun is setting over the high fence that surrounds the pool area. The last rays fall on my skin, reaching around the sides of my body with a pleasant warmth. My back, my butt, are cool and I am aware of the movement of my hair on my skin. (Frank 2002: 174)

Many strippers' accounts show that their interaction with punters fosters a feeling of empowerment. Pasko suggests that stripping for tips is structured around a confidence game in which gaining the customer's confidence, educating him in tipping behaviour, and managing his ultimate disappointment all involve 'an assumption of power over the victim' (Pasko 2002: 52). Wood also says that strippers' experience of commanding the attention of the men in the club gives them a feeling of being 'sexually or erotically powerful' (Wood 2000: 26). As Frank (2002) says, they also gain a sense of personal power through their bodily deployment of 'costume, makeup, body adornment, facial expression, and ways of moving' (Liepe-Levinson 2002; Wood 2002). Ironically, controlling the audience can be part of the job, because the dancer is usually made responsible for policing the bodies of the audience to prevent infractions of ordinances restricting the touching of dancers' bodies (Pasko 2002).

However, the agency exercised in interactions with customers needs to be contextualised by its embeddedness in male-defined, normative heterosexuality revolving around attentiveness to male egos. As one informant told Wood (2000: 12), the girls who 'do really well' are not necessarily the ones with the better body, but those who are 'better with humoring the customers, and eye contact and stuff'. As Pasko concludes with respect to stripping, customers 'possess a pervasive power: the sex-object role dancers must assume and perform is designed and managed by men and their desires' (Pasko 2002: 50). Even Frank admits that, although dancing on stage (to music she has chosen) makes her feel subjectively powerful, the customer has the power to 'appropriate and redefine' her act as a performance he commands (Frank 2002: 201). Wood (2000) neatly captures the restrictions within which strippers' undoubted agency operates when she notes that strippers can and do drop their smiles by turning away from the audience – but only under the pretext of showing off their backsides.

Are such analyses of sex workers' agency (and its limits) equally relevant to understanding the experience of women working as prostitutes? Some prostitutes, like dancers, stress the extent to which they exercise control over access to their bodies. O'Neill (2001) mentions the refusal to kiss customers, faking penetrative sex, speeding up the trick, and stealing money before any sex occurs as some of the ways prostitutes exercise power over the punter. Many of the women consciously adopt temporal and spatial strategies to differentiate between work and private life, public and private body. They create and follow rituals around going to work and coming off the job, for instance having a last cup of tea before going to work (Brewis and Linstead 2000: 215), while work clothes, which symbolise sexual availability, may be consciously hidden away in the wardrobe, out of sight. And like the stripper, the prostitute's 'techniques of the self' also help her to transform the 'prostitute' into the 'sex worker'.

Brewis and Linstead (2000) and O'Connell Davidson (1995a) also highlight prostitutes' development of skills in time management and bodily control that enable them to limit the time spent in encounters with clients. 'Desiree', an entrepreneurial prostitute with considerable autonomy over her business and choice of clientele, says that she exercises her pelvic floor muscles to make sure that clients 'come and therefore go' quickly (O'Connell Davidson 1995a). Brewis and Linstead, with their usual attention to the symbolic importance of many sex worker strategies, point out that strict time-keeping not only enables the worker to see more clients, but also helps to distinguish the transaction from sex in personal life (Brewis and Linstead 2000: 202). Using condoms with clients but not lovers is another way prostitutes symbolically distinguish between different kinds of sex (ibid.: 214).

However, depending on the surrounding social relations and important differences in the organisation of the trade, there may be more limits to the experience of agency in prostitution than in dancing, and more constraints in some kinds of prostitution than others. It seems obvious that reports of body management techniques are more likely to come from women whose working conditions allow more latitude in negotiating bodily and role boundaries. As O'Connell Davidson stresses, sex workers vary greatly in their capacity to exercise discretion over the acceptance of custom or their ability to defend bodily boundaries. The variable capacity to deploy power is heavily dependent on the type of work, and access to types of work that carry more opportunities to exercise discretion is in turn heavily dependent on 'race', class and other aspects of social hierarchy (Phoenix 1999; McClintock 1992). For example, ten years ago an Amsterdam prostitute could report that by using her street mirror, she could see men coming 'before they see me', and that refusing anyone was 'my right and my security' (Pheterson c. 1996). However, today there are several reports that the indebtedness of undocumented migrant women in the Netherlands and elsewhere, who may have been smuggled or trafficked, means that they are unable to turn down requests for anal sex and other 'specialist services' that prostitutes were not expected to have to do a few years ago (Toynbee 2003b).

Moreover, the effects of coping strategies may affect people's embodied agency (and in Bourdieu's terms, embodied capital) in the long term. The use of drugs or drink as a coping strategy is particularly problematic. Drugs and alcohol may be used to dull the pain and fuel the bravado and their use is very prevalent among street workers (Hester and Westmarland 2004; O'Neill 2001; Phoenix 1999). As one Scottish prostitute told McKeganey and Barnard (1996: 91):

> If I've no had a hit, you jus' want it over an' done with. If you've had a hit, you can stand and work nae bother, it does nae bother you, you know what I mean.

Although drugs or alcohol can help workers to stay awake, or to 'numb physical and emotional pain' (Giobbe 1990: 68) they can become part of a vicious cycle, leaving workers less able to protect themselves, more likely to let down their guard or accept 'funny' customers, and make it much harder to build a higher-status career on the earnings from sex work or to improve their situation as sex workers. Because the body is biographically constructed, it incorporates signs of its history. Street prostitutes are said to find it difficult to move into 'indoor' work in massage parlours because of the chaotic lifestyle and drug use associated with street work (Toynbee 2003b; West 2000). Some strippers may also find that because of individual biographies shaped by class and racial inequalities, they lack the embodied cultural capital necessary for obtaining work in the better-paid clubs (Frank 2002).

However, it seems that even narratives that defend prostitution provide only occasional glimpses of the individual prostitute's embodied agency, especially as compared to strippers' accounts. This may be because detailed depictions of prostitutes' interactions with customers are thought even less appropriate for analytical writing, but it may be also because people whose identities are defined by their (stigmatised) bodies develop strategies for self-definition that focus on some other aspect of self. Not focusing on the body may be a coping strategy in itself. Bishop and Robinson point out that prostitutes working in the Thai sex industry rarely speak about their embodied experience in work at all: pain and humiliation are at best indicated indirectly, when a worker explains that she 'had to go to the doctor' or 'maybe he like to fuck too much' (Bishop and Robinson 1998: 229).

Conclusions

Each of the ways of conceptualising the body outlined here is useful in shedding light on the organisation of sex work and sex workers' experiences but each has limitations. Considering the body as text is essential in showing how the prostitute's body was and is targeted as the problem by legal and medical discourses. But 'while the body is a text', as Scheper-Hughes (2002: 2) says, 'it is always a great deal more than that'. As Vikki Bell (1999) points out, albeit in another context, the anti-essentialist 'flight from the materiality of the body' that can accompany an emphasis on the body as a discursive construction has political implications. The 'futural abstractions' and promises of liberal discourse – what Shusterman calls 'an unhealthy idealism that identifies human beings-in-the world with linguistic activity' (Shusterman 1997: 173) – are politically suspect, especially in so far as they ignore questions of felt embodiment.

In the case of prostitution, overemphasising the role of discourse in the construction of the prostitute and the problems she faces inevitably underestimates the effects of prostitution on the material body of the worker, including the long-term effects of her own strategies, such as drug use, as well as being processed through the legal system. Decriminalisation of prostitution is necessary to reduce stigmatisation, and might make it easier for women to access help without leaving the trade. However, it would do nothing to change the social inequalities that, in many cases, lead women to opt for sex work in the first place. One also wonders whether the dematerialisation of the prostitute body popular in studies of pornography as fantasy overweigh the experience of the consumers' use of the images, as against the sex workers whose bodies are used in their making.

The essentialist view of the body central to radical feminist analyses of prostitution and other uses of the female body goes too far in the other direction. Although there are strengths in their recognition of the organic moorings of subjective experience, as Bell (1999) suggests, too close an attachment to the body can also be politically problematic. For instance, claims of 'common blood' as the basis of identity can be exclusionary and racist. Others have argued that total immersion in 'woman' as a category is a form of imprisonment (de Beauvoir 1972; Riley 1988; Smart 1996). But the main problem with this approach is the construction of the embodied prostitute as victim, a discourse that is now very influential in both US and UK social policy. For example, the recent discussion of prostitution in the Home Office's (2004) *Paying the Price* adopts this discourse in order to strengthen its determination to control prostitution, which it sees mainly as a danger to the community, by stressing its danger to the prostitute's self. The construction of the prostitute as an innocent, wounded body, in combination with moralist discourse, implies that prostitutes can be treated sympathetically only if they can be positioned as victims of social or psychological maladjustment, trauma or force. Such a discourse does nothing to challenge hostility to women who work in the trade, implying only that hapless victims should not be tarred with it. Because the Home Office does not want to be seen as supporting prostitution, the victim discourse is no doubt a convenient one for it to adopt, but means that help will be available only for women leaving the trade, not for those who continue to work.

The debate about the commodification of the body brings ethical issues to the foreground. Whereas Pateman insists, *pace* Terry Eagleton's (1993) nice distinction (quoted in Chapter 1), that the body is something that I am rather than something that I have, clearly the body *is* also something that I have/ own and which according to some accounts can be legitimately traded. The latter view has been influential in the decriminalisation of brothel-keeping in Europe (Kantola and Squires 2004b; Outshoorn 2001) as well many accounts of sex tourism (Clift and Carter 2000; Kempadoo and Doezema 1998). Clearly bodies can be and are 'traded', so the point of contention between the two accounts is a moral/ethical one: an ethical one for individuals (ought I to do this?) and a moral issue for socio-legal policy (should 'trading' in bodies be made illegal?). Both views have wide circulation, and the clash between them is at the heart of disputes over prostitution. However, there are more socio-logical questions that can be asked, and the comparison with emotional labour is useful in so far as it draws attention to the effects, positive and negative, on the self. Truong Thamh-Dam's (1990) emphasis on the wider social conditions and commodification as the object of analysis is very impor-tant here, and returns us to the embeddedness of sex work in the global political economy, as highlighted by the discussion of Harvey (1998, 1989) in Chapter 1.

The postmodernist construction of the body-without-organs seems to me to have too little purchase on the experience of the majority of sex workers, and is problematic in so far as it is not clear if or how the material constraints on sex workers that its proponents recognise can be integrated into its theo-retical framework. Whether or not sex workers enjoy (any of) the sex that is part of their work does not seem to me the issue; in any kind of job it is better if there is some work satisfaction, but it is not clear that sexual engage-ment is, from the sex worker's point of point of view, the defining charac-teristic of prostitution, never mind work more generally. However, this approach is very successful in sensitising us to the controlling impetus present in some constructions of prostitution, as in the Home Office (2004) report noted above, which seems governed more by fears about social disor-der than ethical issues. At the same time as the Consultative Paper regrets that innocent victims are 'paying the price', the tone of the Home Office paper suggests that its authors feel themselves stymied by the existence of people who unaccountably do not take control of their chaotic lifestyles or refractory bodies, and allow themselves to be led by them into dependencies.

In this sense the postmodern approach can help in developing a political response to 'care plans' and 'case work' and other attempts to discipline lifestyles that aim to produce more tractable bodies.

Drawing attention to the body's agency seems to me essential to any approach to the body. The interpretation of how sex workers produce their working bodies as a means of resisting objectification, rather than merely colluding with it, is especially important, as is documenting strategies that at the micro-level expand personal space and control, against all the odds. Even if such strategies do not lead to collective or transformatory resistance, they attribute to sex workers an ability to re-selve their bodies that would seem to be a stronger starting point for transformatory action, individually or collectively, than the construction of the prostitute embedded in victim discourse.

The 'social body', a construct that is implicit in the writings of Julia O'Connell Davidson and Jackie Sanchez-Taylor, seems to be the most promising of these approaches. It acknowledges the social construction of the prostitute body, without reducing its determination to discourse. It recognises that the body is constructed relationally and interactively, and this goes for the prostitute user's as much as the prostitute's, in the sense that the prostitute–client transaction is constitutive of the power relations in which they are enmeshed, not only an outcome of wider economic and social inequalities. It recognises differences in how prostitution is organised and regulated, differences that affect the sex worker's experience in important, not trivial ways. It may not fully explain why the commodification of sex, particularly, permits the purchaser to exempt themselves from the complex web of rules, obligations and conventions which govern non-commercial transactions, since as West and Austrin (2002) point out, this may happen in other kinds of commercial transactions too. However, this seems to be an advantage in some respects, as it provides a starting point for thinking about the similarities between the misrecognition that characterises prostitute use, the purchase of organs from live donors, and other forms of body work. It is to the latter that we turn in the next chapter.

SEVEN Body Work as Social Relationship and as Labour

In much of this book we have been concerned with constructions of workers' bodies and the implications for their experience as embodied workers. This chapter focuses on another aspect of embodiment in work, namely workers' relationships with clients, patients and customers in which the work involves intimate bodily contact. This brings workers' interaction with the bodies of clients, patients and customers into the picture in a way that the concept of emotional labour (Hochschild 1983) has tended to sideline. It builds on the analysis in Chapter 6 of the micropolitics of sex work, but considered now as just one example of paid body work.

As we saw in Chapter 4, in the sociology of employment the term 'body work' has been used mainly for the work that people are expected to do on or to their own bodies. Originally suggested by Shilling (1993) in discussing Goffman's ideas about the face work and other work involved in the presentation of self in social interactions, it has been increasingly deployed to refer to the work that people are required to undertake on themselves in order to meet the expectations of employers or peers (Halford et al. 1997; Hancock et al. 2000; Kerfoot 2000; Williams 1998). I would argue that this is too narrow a focus, obscuring many of the most important features of body work in contemporary society. The idea of body work as involving an interaction with the bodies of others, such as patients, is captured in some research in the sociology of health and healing, especially nursing, and in some of the sociological literature on care work (for example, Atkinson 1995; Glassner 1995; Jervis 2001; Lawton 1998; Lupton 1996; Murcott 2002; Shakespeare 2003; Twigg 2004, 2000a, 2000b; Van Dongen and Elema 2001), but it has not yet been developed systematically or applied to employment relations more generally.

Feminist scholars are undecided about how to understand the commodification of intimate work with people and their bodies. Should we use the same models that sociologists have developed to analyse the production of things, in industry, and the less intimate customer services we considered in Chapter 4? Whereas some apply wider categories to body work almost without comment, such as the use of the distinction between Fordism and post-Fordism in relation to employment as health care practitioners (Walby and Greenwell 1994), others, like Hochschild (2003, 1983) see the work of care and intimacy as involving distinctive human values and relationships, while at the same time exploring the contradictions their commodification involves.

This chapter extends my earlier interest (Wolkowitz 2002) in widening the concept of body work as an analytical tool that would help to highlight these contradictions. It draws attention to the experience of those whose paid work involves the care, pleasure, adornment, discipline and cure of others' bodies. While the term 'body work' risks being confused with 'bodywork', widely used, especially in the US, to refer to 'hands-on therapies geared to health, healing and relaxation' (Oerton 2004), it has the advantage of stressing that these new therapies (and the constructions of the body associated with them) comprise only a small proportion – and perhaps the cleaner, more glamorous part – of body work as a form of employment.

Paid body work: An overview

In contrast to Foucauldian approaches that have explored the relationship between power and the body mainly through its textualisation of the body by expert knowledges (seen for instance in the first of the approaches to prostitution discussed in Chapter 6), 'body work' is used in this chapter to conceptualise employment that takes the body as its immediate site of labour, involving intimate, messy contact with the (frequently supine or naked) body, its orifices or products through touch or close proximity. Paid body work is a component of a wide range of occupations, including beauticians, hairdressers and barbers; care assistants; coaches and fitness instructors; dentists and dental hygienists; doctors (specialists, GPs and pathologists); maids, nannies and other child care workers; masseurs and other spa workers; midwives, nurses, orderlies and home visitors; occupational and speech therapists; opticians; paramedics and other emergency workers; podiatrists; physiotherapists; practitioners of complementary therapies; radiographers (including mammogram service workers) and radiologists; sex workers; tattooists and body piercers; undertakers, mortuary workers and forensic anthropologists; Weightwatchers leaders; and yoga instructors, as well as salespeople whose jobs involve measuring or touching customers as a matter of course (cosmetics, corsetry or shoe sales, for instance).

Some occupations are included because, although they do not usually require frequent or intimate touch, they deal with body fluids and wastes. An example would be hospital ward cleaners, whose work is organised around and in relation to human bodies. For instance, Hart (1991) reports that in the hospital she studied, the cleaners' distinction between what they called 'top work' (dusting, cleaning table trays) and the more polluting 'bottom work' (cleaning floors and bed pans) was based on an imaginary line bisecting the patient's body, while Messing (1998) notes the contribution of hospital cleaners to patients' recovery.

There is also a case to be made for the inclusion of occupations whose explicit purpose is the discipline of bodies, although the control they impose usually takes place at arm's length. Examples would include police officers and prison wardens in charge of the 'warehousing of bodies' (Sudbury 2002), as well as those workers, thankfully a relatively small category, responsible for executions and torture, but I have not tried to deal with such occupations in this book.

The current sociological neglect of paid work on others' bodies goes counter to its importance as an economic activity since, as discussed below, 'body work' occupations are among the fastest growing in both Britain and the US. Its invisibility as a category seems to be due, rather, to seeing the commodification of the body (Featherstone et al. 1991; Giddens 1991) as an issue about consumption, thereby following consumer discourse in obscuring the social relations within which goods (and by extension, services) are produced (Billig 1999; McRobbie 1997; Wright 2004). Workers' own discourse may also be responsible for blurring our understanding of body work as a source of livelihood. As Glassner (1995) says, many of what he calls body (re)makers in health and cosmetic practice were first drawn to their occupation because of their experience as consumers, and they may still carry that perspective as part of their practitioner identity (see also Sharma 1992; Stinson 2001). Moreover, workers sometimes find it strategic to make a case for more resources by linking their demands to consumers' interests in better services, rather than arguing their case in terms of their interests as paid workers (Munro 1999). Still other factors limiting the visibility of body contact in employment may be the preponderance of women in body work occupations of the kind listed above, many of them low-paid or tinged with sexual connotations, and the fact that much of the work is undertaken largely away from the public eye.

However, the main reason for the invisibility of body work in research on employment is that the distinctiveness of social relations of work in the service sector, especially customer services, has been theorised mainly through the notion of emotional labour, defined by Hochschild (1983) as the labour involved in inducing or suppressing feeling in oneself or others. As discussed in Chapter 3, the evolution of this concept, as Witz et al. (2003) have argued, has led to the conceptual 'retirement' of the body in theorising service sector employment. The identification of emotional labour as a distinct input, separate from the performance of physical tasks, as in James's (1992) influential analysis of caring work, has inadvertently replicated Cartesian mind – body dualism. By identifying emotional work as a separate component of care, the understanding of physical care of the body is concomitantly narrowed, as Leder (1990) would put it, and identified with mindlessness or mechanical activity. Moreover, the distinction between 'caring for' and 'caring about' (Yeates 2004a) may fail to pay enough attention to their possible overlap or variations in the relationship between them.

Important attempts to challenge the mindlessness of (what I am calling) body work have been made by corporeal feminism and others. Paralleling in some respects the exploration of a gender-specific 'ethic of care' proposed by Carol Gilligan and other feminist analysts (Gilligan 1982; Tronto 1993), corporeal feminists not only challenge the stigma attached to 'dirty work' (Hughes 1984) by valorising bodies' abjection and 'leakiness', they privilege the mutual connectedness that can be engendered through caring and touch (Grosz 1994, 1989; Shildrick and Price 1998). The influence of Deleuze and Guattari, in particular, is associated with the potential 'de-territorialisation' of the body, a term connoting nomadic escape from/resistance to the disciplinary ministrations of modern medicine and caring (Fox 1999). However, conceptualisations of the unreciprocated gift of care, which is sometimes suggested as an alternative to instrumentally organised caring, seems to bypass rather than confront the social relations and status distinctions within which much body work is currently embedded.

An alternative approach would be more explicit in recognising the centrality of body work to economic life, including changes in the organisation of services that give rise to, as well as reflect, new understandings of the body. The centrality of body work to post industrial national and global economies is seen particularly clearly in the burgeoning literature on the relation between migration and care work (for example Anderson 2000; Ehrenreich and Hochschild 2003a; Hochschild 2001; Kempadoo and Doezema 1998; Kofman and Raghuram, forthcoming; Phizacklea 1996; Pratt 1998; Yeates 2004a, 2004b). Much of the body work labour force in the more affluent countries now comes from abroad, relying especially heavily on the migration of (often racialised) labour from poorer countries. Studies of the importance of migration to the formation of the labour force in, for example, medicine and nursing, household and institutional caring, and sex work are crucial in demonstrating what Hochschild (2003a) calls the 'wrenching global inequalities' at the heart of paid body work.

Yeates's wide definition of care work as the tasks and activities undertaken to 'promote the personal health and welfare of people who cannot, or

149

who are not inclined to, perform those activities themselves' (2004a: 371) comes closer to my notion of body work than the even broader category of reproductive labour (Glenn 1996), which includes work, like gardening and catering, that does not involve bodily contact (and which, not coincidentally, employs many more men). Neither is usually used to refer to personal service workers, like hairdressers or spa workers, but this neglects the increasing overlap between categories. Although one can agree that some kinds of work are, objectively speaking, more necessary to human reproduction or survival than others, especially for people who cannot look after themselves, the increasing focus on 'wellness' as a health goal, the expansion of cosmetic medical procedures and the overlap between beauty and complementary therapies are blurring the conventional division between health care and personal services.

Although it is by no means easy to estimate the extent or incidence of body work employment in Britain or the other OECD countries, everybody seems to recognise that it is growing overall. Indeed, Warhurst and Thompson (1998) ironically forecast an employment future focusing on 'care and constraint', include corrections officers and security personnel as well as health care practitioners, because such jobs cannot be exported to low-wage economies abroad. As they say, given such trends, it is odd that anyone thinks jobs in the contemporary economy no longer require hands. But so much body work is undertaken in private homes, such as paid domestic service, in criminalised locales, such as sex work, or is otherwise unrecorded by official statistics that figures on the size of the sector are at best estimates.

One of the factors in the growth of paid body work is demographic change. Folbre (2001: 55) estimates that the growing care sector encompasses 20 per cent of US jobs (Hochschild 2003a: 20), with personal attendants the fastest growing job category in the US (Farr and Ludden 1999, cited by Rivas 2003: 292). Another example is the expanding market for beauty work and spa treatments. The value of the professional beauty industry in the UK was estimated at £366 million, up 6 per cent on the previous year (Black and Sharma 2001: 103; see also Black 2004, 2002). In fact, following the census in 2001, hairdressing was identified as the fastest growing occupation in the UK (Nolan 2004; Cohen 2005). The spa industry, although still relatively small, was estimated at £5 million to £7 million by Mintel (2005), but figures provided by the beauty sector suggest more rapid growth, with the chair of the British Spa Business Association claiming 15 per cent annual growth in recent years (Frost 2005). However, there are also contradictory trends that may limit the numbers involved in some kinds of body work, as demonstrated by cuts in the numbers of cleaning and catering staff in hospitals in Britain in the 1990s (Carvel 2005; Munro 1999). There may also be limits to its total cumulative growth, in so far as demand for different body work services is age-specific. For instance, older people may be big consumers of health care and reproductive care work, but lack the income to purchase the 'pampering' services used preponderantly by people in employment, especially women (Mintel 2005, 1999a, 1999b, 1998).

In the rest of this chapter I discuss four key aspects of body work that link workers to the wider labour market, shape their relationship with clients, customers and patients and affect their experience as workers. These are: definitions of the body; the body work divisions of labour; distinctions between spatial sites; and the micropolitics of workplace interactions.

Definitions of the body

Body work occupations appear to be shaped in the first place by definitions of the body which empower or constrain workers in relation to it. Taking a broad historical or cross-cultural perspective would show radical differences, as well as similarities, in the concepts of the body structuring different kinds of body work, depending on the social relation within which they are located. The transition from relations defined by forms of personal servility (slavery, domestic service, women's conjugal obligations as wives or their religious duty as nuns) to waged labour relations mediated by the market has important implications for the definitions of the body that guide and emerge from body work occupations. Even within the narrower scope of Western medical history, we see a broad shift in conceptions of the body that have accompanied changes in the relationships between doctors and sick persons since the eighteenth century. As Jewson (1976) pointed out, whereas the practitioner competing for the patronage of a small coterie of fee-paying patients built rapport based on recognising the individual client's 'psychosomatic totality', hospital medicine produces a more object-oriented perspective (Annandale 1998).

Research on definitions of the body in medicine is of course legion in the sociology of health and healing, where the biomedical conception of the body and medics' responsibility for health outcomes has been under attack from different directions. For one thing, recent attempts to make people take more responsibility for their own health are reputedly shifting the focus 'from the body itself to the intersubjective space that surrounds the client' (Vasselu 1998: 19). The more usual challenge is associated with alternative medicine and new discourses in nursing, in which holistic models of the mind–body precept are often contrasted to the biomedical conception of the body as a purely physical object divided into distinct symptoms and parts. For instance, Lawler (1997, 1991) recommends conceptualising the body in nursing as a 'lived body', one invested with positive meanings because contextualised within caring, giving relationships. Moreover, Parker (1997) suggests that the concept of 'living flesh' both demands and is based on certain kinds of touch. Such conceptualisations may be out of touch, however, in so far as they ignore the materiality of body work practice. Indeed, some have accused 'New Age' nursing theory of etherealising the body by removing 'the dirt and mess of bodily life' (Dunlop 1986: 664). Oerton, too, suggests that the 'bodymaps' of many alternative practitioners sometimes seem to 'offer a dissolution of the corporeal body . . . as demonstrated in the use of such concepts as the "subtle body" or the "astral body"' (Oerton 1998: 4).

However, many such definitions, whether holistic or biomedical, have been derived from interpretations of prescriptive texts. We do not as yet have as much data on the largely implicit concepts of the body that circulate in actual workplaces, based on sociological observations of the interactions of workers of various kinds with their patients, clients or customers. Lawler recognises that her use of the concept of the 'lived body' to understand nursing's relation to the body is based on a study of 'expert nurses', not nurses' practice more generally (Lawler 1991: 29). However, new inroads are being made through closely observed studies of nursing, caring and beauty work. Wong Woon Hau's (2004) detailed study of nursing wards in Singapore, for instance, suggests that the use of the word 'beds' as metonym for patients indicates the extent to which managerial accounting considerations have colonised the health care professions. Lee-Trewick's (1997) ethnography found care workers taking as the focus of work the efficient production of 'lounge standard bodies' fit for display in the public areas of the nursing home. Foner (1994) follows Gubrium (1975) in recognising that many care workers implicitly conceptualise their interaction with patients as 'bed and body work'.

Research on beauty work also suggests that workers generate implicit conceptions of the body that enhance or explain their own roles. For instance, Sharma and Black's (1999; see also Black and Sharma 2001; Black 2004, 2002) observations in Britain suggest that beauticians' practice is underwritten by a notion of the 'deficit body', one not so much lacking in beauty or style as deficient in the self-love and confidence that workers see themselves helping to restore. However, this may attribute too much uniformity to relationships between beauty workers and their clients.

Kang's (2003) study of New York City 'nail care' salons deploys a concept of 'body labour' that parallels the concept of body work developed in this and earlier work (Wolkowitz 2002). Her ethnography of three salons owned and staffed by Korean immigrants draws attention to how far workers' focus extends beyond 'the managed hand' of the client, depending on the gender, class and racialised positioning of both customers and workers. Only the upmarket salon serving a white, middle-class clientele tried, like the salons studied by Sharma and Black (2001), to pamper the whole person and not just manicure clients' nails. The service provided by the two salons in less elite neighbourhoods was different. The cheaper provided simple manicures and perfunctory interactions with its racially mixed clientele; the other provided sophisticated designs for African-American and Caribbean customers who enjoyed using their hands for artistic self-expression. Like the other studies noted above, Kang directs attention to the actual social relations and employment conditions under which different concepts of the body are developed and sustained.

Divisions of labour

Looking at body work as a whole encourages us to examine the social processes involved in 'bundling' work tasks into occupational niches (Hughes 1984). Higher-status occupations tend to see themselves dealing with a bounded body, partly through mapping it as a system, leaving lower-status ones to deal with what is rejected, left over, spills out and pollutes (Douglas 1966; Hughes 1984). Littlewood (1991) even suggests that the higher-ranked medical specialisms generally deal with the head and heart, while specialisms like gastro-enterology and urino-genital medicine have a lower status.

In body work the more general segmentation of the labour market by class, sex and 'race' is deeply intertwined with attitudes towards (parts of) the body. These distinctions may be as important as the more usual divisions between manual and non-manual labour. For instance, care work is overwhelmingly female, and male practitioners are either positioned as exceptions, like doctors (Hughes 2002), or constructed as homosexual, as in the sexual stereotyping of male flight attendants or male nurses. Workers' positioning as classed, gendered and racialised subjects intersects with the differential status of forms of care that puts direct care-givers further down the hierarchy than those who identify the need for care or plan its provision (Hughes 2002; Twigg 2000a).

The hierarchical character of the division of labour also reflects, and contributes to, relationships between types of practitioners and the people whose bodies form their site of work. Abel and Nelson (1990, cited by Foner 1994: 152) argue that where higher-status groups provide care for lower-status groups, it shades into social control, something most apparent in the case of medical and professionalised nursing care. On the other hand, where clients, patients or customers have a higher social status than those who care for them, workers may be subject to humiliation or abuse. The corollary, I suggest, is that higher-status groups are more attracted to occupations that are seen as controlling, rather than as caring for or servicing others' bodies, and may have an interest as workers in perpetuating these hierarchical distinctions in how the work is constructed. Moreover, the gender and other identities in which we have invested limit the flexibility of our identifications with and as bodies, and our willingness to adopt reciprocity and interchangeability in body work roles.

The highly gendered (and sexualised) character of body work occupations is seen most clearly in the history of health care occupations, where the construction of medicine as a professional occupation suitable for middle-class men could take place only if prolonged interaction with the patient's body was limited and hived off, along with the tasks of 'mopping up', to female nurses (Davies 2002). However, within (the largely female) nursing sector there are also divisions of status which reflect different relations to the body, sometimes conceptualised as the difference between 'technical' and 'basic' nursing, the first involving 'cleaner' tasks and the latter involving meeting the gross, even polluting, physical needs of the patient, including the 'dirtier jobs' (Grimshaw 1999; Jervis 2001; Lawler 1991; Van Dongen and Elema 2001). This hierarchical distinction has been exacerbated by managerial cost-cutting strategies that seek to surround a 'core' of highly paid 'knowledge nurses' with a 'periphery' of cheaper care assistants (Witz 1994: 40, cited by Annandale 1998: 245).

Jervis (2001) argues that nurses' attempts to shed the 'dirty work' associated with contact with bodily wastes has intensified the symbolic pollution of care workers lower down the occupational hierarchy. Her ethnographic data on an inner-city care home in midwestern US include examples of care workers' feelings of disgust towards the substances they have to deal with, and their shame that they are stained by them. They do not seem to be able to shed the stigma that the job carries (Goffman 1963), nor have they successfully developed the status-conferring strategies for maintaining positive self-esteem noted by Ashforth and Kreiner (1999) or Bolton (2005), instead referring to themselves as 'butt wipes' (Jervis 2001: 89). One worker reported that when riding home on the bus, she worried that she 'smelled like piss', and other workers mentioned undertaking what were essentially rites of purification upon getting home from work, similar to those undertaken by some sex workers (see Chapter 6).

The body work division of labour is also highly racialised, including the distinctions between levels of nursing noted above. As Glenn argues with reference to the US, it is not simply that continuing discrimination has left black and other 'subordinate-race' women and men overrepresented in lower-ranking jobs in the economy as a whole, but that historically black women have been overrepresented in reproductive labour and, within nursing, at the lower end of the hierarchy (Glenn 1996; see also Anderson 2000; Bhavnani 1994; Foner 1994; Jervis 2001; Munro 2001; Woody 1992). As an African-American woman interviewed for the film *The Life and Times of Rosie the Riveter* (1982) said about being forced to return to domestic service after the Second World War, 'They save those jobs for us.' It is only relatively recently that African-American women have been able to move into management and supervisory roles in the care sector (Woody 1992).

While the concept of skill may be saturated with gender, as Phillips and Taylor (1986) argued, the presumption of a binary distinction between emotional and physical aspects of body work is too often saturated with 'race', obscuring the emotional content of what are sometimes defined as merely manual jobs. Rollins (1985) pointed out, for instance, that while white women employed in private homes in the US are called au pairs or nannies – a caring role – African-American women were usually called maids, even when the content of their jobs is basically the same. Other kinds of intimate work have also been deeply affected by a variety of racist ideas about bodily contact, including personal services like barbering and hairdressing (Boyd 1996; Peiss 1998), while sex tourism and sex work are organised around longstanding stereotypes about white and 'other' sexualities (Kempadoo 1999; McClintock 1992).

More recently, 'doing the dirty work' in contemporary Western societies has become the responsibility of migrant women (Anderson 2000). Many are actively recruited as waged domestic labour in preference to local workers, because they can be given work considered too polluting to give a compatriot. Anderson argues that

the relationship between hatred of women (misogyny), hatred of the body (somatophobia) and hatred of racialised groups (racism) is played out in the use of racialised female labour to do the work of servicing the body, and in the treatment of domestic workers by their employers. (Anderson 2000: 142)

As Anderson says, the worker is employed to carry dirt's stigma, as well as to labour, and is metaphorically racialised by her association with dirt. As we saw in Chapter 2, in the Victorian era the servant's body, like the prostitute's, was envisioned as a kind of conduit, a sewer responsible for carrying wastes between the middle-class domestic realm and the public street. It was the servant's labour that kept the bodies (and the unpaid body work) of middle-class families out of the public sphere. Moreover it was the servant identification as the 'nether regions' of the social body that allowed the Victorian middle-class lady to signify its heart, purity and tenderness (Davidoff 1983; McClintock 1995; Wolkowitz 2001).

We also need to consider the contribution of paid body work to intra-household and inter-class divisions of labour. Nowadays an expanding labour force of paid carers, cleaners and beauty workers inside and outside the

MY DOMESTIC ARMY

(From the housekeeper to crystal therapist: the 15 people this businesswoman needs to make her life run smoothly)

Figure 7.1 'My Domestic Army' by Diana Appleyard, *Daily Mail*, 6 March 2001. Photograph by Mark Lawrence. Reprinted with the permission of Solo Syndication.

home allows people at the top of the career hierarchy to protect and project polished professional bodies apparently untouched by the messy necessities of life. Historically most men have been able to disavow reproductive work by passing it on to wives and others, and now some women too can afford to meet expectations regarding the successful organisational body by throwing off the leaky 'maternal body' of domestic life. Newspapers are fascinated by women who manage to employ a 'domestic army' of new servants, which also frees ample time for firming up one's own body in the gym. In an article by Diana Appleyard (2001), for instance, Sue Alexander Clark explains why 'I need 15 helpers', including housekeeper and childminder at home, as well as make-up artist, reflexologist, homeopath, nutritionist, manicurist, and other individuals who, she says, form her 'back-up team' (see Figure 7.1). A similar article by O'Hagan (2002) about 'Jo Vickers', who employs a nanny, a cook and 'a couple of PAs', reports that Britons now spend £43 billion a year to 'get someone else to do the job, including childminders, nannies, cleaners, gardeners, [and] masseurs'. While few households can afford the same level of expenditure on personal services as the women identified in these articles think they require, the managerial and professional careers of both men and women frequently depend on the employment of nannies for children and carers for elderly relatives, often as an alterative to reorganising the gender division of labour between family members (Gregson and Lowe 1994). The employment of an individual nanny to work within the home rather than sending children to crèches also enables a professional/managerial household to reproduce their embodied cultural capital because the child can be cared for within the habitus of their own home, and the carer can take children to their piano lessons and other activities (Anderson 2000). The employment of domestic servants was always available for the very wealthy, but has now percolated further down the social scale.

Perrons (2003) is one of few commentators to notice this dependence of professional and managerial employment in the 'new economy' on paid domestic workers, who are disproportionately women and ethnic minorities. Indeed, such services are sometimes funded by companies for their key employees. In order to get away with the long hours of work they require of their staff, large companies are 'providing concierge services and "lifestyle fixers" for their top employees, including meals, shopping and dry cleaning, as well as organising childcare and home maintenance' (Perrons 2003: 134–5). Their motivation is self-interest, because provision of such services increases the productivity of their senior staff.

In the US paid domestic cleaning is big business, and the polarisation of earnings means that many households can afford to employ cleaners. According to Ehrenreich, although the majority of cleaners are still freelance, independent workers, the biggest growth is among the large company franchises whose turnover has been growing by up to 25 per cent a year (Ehrenreich 2003: 94; see also Ehrenreich 2001). Her research identifies some of the (relative) advantages and costs for the workers of the different arrangements under which they are employed. She also tries to decipher some of the effects on social relationships of the growing employment of paid housekeeping and the purchase of other commodities made by underpaid workers under oppressive conditions. Ehrenreich argues that it is not simply a matter of low wages and poor working conditions, important as it is to change these, but that expanding employment of paid cleaners in the home legitimises social hierarchy, since it is usually only done under the assumption that the employer has 'something better' to do with her (or his) time, as do their children, who a generation ago would have helped with the chores. She adds that to 'be cleaned up after' is to achieve 'a certain magical weightlessness and immateriality' (ibid.: 102), i.e. putting into place particular constructions and experiences of employers' bodies as well as of the bodies of their domestic workers.

Sites of labour

The division of labour in body work can also be mapped in terms of spatial divisions, both local and transnational. These spatial divisions both reflect and contribute to the meaning of different kinds of body work and the recruitment of workers.

Body work is more characteristic of some kinds of places than others, including homes, hospitals, clinics and hospices, for instance, as well as gyms, salons or spas grouping together a number of specialisms. The division between spaces that are conceptualised as private and those located in the public domain is especially important. One reason body work is so readily ignored is because it is usually less public than other service sector activities and less frequently observed by outsiders. Even when conducted in hospitals or other public institutions, intimate procedures are normally undertaken 'behind the screen' (Lawler 1991), and even at the hairdressers certain treatments tend to be located furthest from the front door and reception area. Indeed, the sociological neglect of the relationship between emotional labour and body work arises partly because the latter can rarely be observed without invading the privacy of client or patient. Even an innovative study like Alan Arthur's (2004), which observed home care workers' interactions in the homes of the people they cared for, limited its account of the relational aspects of care work to workers' conversations with clients, without including the bathing or other body work they undertook. Yet as Twigg (2000a) demonstrates, bathing is one of the key interactions in which an emotionally sensitive carer negotiates her relationship with those she cares for. Indeed, as Van Dongen and Elema (2001: 159) remind us, 'the moments of intimate body contact are also the moments of social contact'. One suspects that the privacy within which much body work takes place is one reason why nursing research – often undertaken by researchers with experience of working as nurses – has been to the fore in considering the embeddedness of emotion in body work, especially touch (Jervis 2001; Lawler 1991, 1997; Shakespeare 2003; Van Dongen and Elema 2001).

The division between public and private spheres is particularly important because of its relation to the competing rationalities that govern the conduct of caring (Waerness 1984). For instance, unpaid caring in the home is spread throughout the day (and night); not only is it well suited to the timing of care needs in the morning and bedtime, outside normal working hours, and the unpredictable needs of dependent individuals, but it also takes place within family relationships and may be organised around individual personality and preferences. In contrast, institutional care involves a division of labour governed by standardised norms that fragments caring into instrumentally defined tasks. Hence concepts of care – what counts as care and what it includes – 'are actually specific to, and [constructed] within, either the private or the public domain' (Thomas 1993: 649, cited by Hughes 2002: 107). When this is forgotten, the division between emotional and physical care tasks, originally the product of the rationalising impetus of institutional care, is naturalised and taken as a given, rather like the division between mental and manual labour.

However, as we saw above, it is no longer possible to link the private sphere of the home with unpaid, family care, and the public sphere with paid employment. Nor does the distinction between public services and private, profit-oriented care organisations carry the weight it once did. In Britain and elsewhere the mixed economy in care, much extended since policy debates in the 1980s, has led to the contracting-out of services in hospitals and other public institutions, the employment of private agencies to provide home helps (except for the most specialised services) and the dominance of managerial cost-accounting in the planning of service delivery (Ungerson 2000). This has led to even more fragmentation of care tasks, lowered terms and conditions of work, and in many cases to lowered levels of work satisfaction for workers. Giving the severely disabled the cash to employ carers themselves is one of the few moves towards consumer choice that may actually empower the direct consumer, as against organisations acting on their behalf. However, even this is only true for those in a position to obtain and evaluate information on which to make decisions, or who have family or friends who can take on this work. While it may improve consumers' sense of control over their environment (and over their own bodies), it is not clear whether it necessarily increases satisfaction for workers.

The sites at which paid body work is undertaken are connected through an increasingly transnationalised division of labour, but one that differs from the forms this takes in other sectors. Because its focus is the direct care of the human body, the transnational networks within which personal care work is embedded are different from those that link the production, distribution and consumption of things, and also different from services where, for instance, electronic communication makes distance work feasible. Body work is normally deployed in the locality of the consumer, although consumers also move to access service, for instance health tourism, sex tourism or retirement to 'sunbelt' colonies that provide a ready market for reproductive services. Although in the UK some patients are sent abroad for non-emergency surgery and there are possibilities for diagnosing conditions through long-distance electronic transmission of scans and other images, this makes hardly a dent in overall care requirements.

While both free and forced migration have long been sources of reproductive labour, including for instance domestic work and nursing, we can also include body work services outside the home (Ha 2002; Kang 2003). Salon work provides particular opportunities for women migrants as both entrepreneurs and workers, something that goes back to the original founding of some of the big American cosmetic empires by European women immigrants like Helena Rubenstein (Peiss 1998), but their experience has not yet been the subject of much research. Federman et al. (2004) report that the number of manicurists in California practically doubled between 1987 and 2002, with the increase made up almost entirely by Vietnamese immigrants. They argue that the market for manicures increased because the Vietnamese entrepreneurs created new kinds of outlets that increased consumer demand, especially the walk-in shop where no appointment is necessary.

Much more is known about the experience of female women migrants working as carers, whose number has increased not only in Europe and the US but in parts of East and South Asia (see, for example, Adams and Dickey 2000; Cheng 2004; Lan 2003). Hochschild's (2003a, 2003b) notion of 'global care chains' conceptualises the links between people that are formed when care and love become commodities – the 'new gold' – imported from poor countries into private homes in more affluent societies. Women are migrating from countries where they cannot support their children as they would like to more affluent societies where they work as carers, taking up the slack in dual-career private households. In this migration, they leave the 'care deficit' that is in turn created in their own homes to be filled not only by adult relatives and older children but also by the employment of local women as domestic workers, or of women from even poorer countries.

There has been a certain amount of debate as to whether Hochschild's concept of 'global care chain' adequately conceptualises the transnationalisation of reproductive labour. Yeates (2004a, 2004b) and Kofman and Raghuram (forthcoming) argue that because it was originally constructed around a single occupational category, namely nannies working in private homes, it obscures the extensive overseas recruitment of highly skilled women and men, for instance doctors and nurses. Admittedly, some of the latter end up having to join other migrants in working as care assistants in institutions located within the formal sector (Carvel 2004; Cottell 2005; see especially Yeates 2004b for a useful history of nurse migration). Bringing these groups into the picture shows that it is not only the 'care deficit' within households that provides openings for migrants, but also the demand for (other kinds of body) labour in public health and care services.

Of course, there are many connections between the recruitment of migrants to institutional and domiciliary care work and into other low-paid jobs. Migrants provide much of the cleaning labour force in firms' premises, educational institutions, stores and other public buildings, along with jobs in the food industry processing or packing fresh produce or producing ready-made meals and sandwiches, all goods and services intended for immediate consumption. Such work cannot be easily exported to countries where people are desperate for work at any wage (Lawrence 2005; Pai 2004b; Phizacklea 2005). Instead, employment agencies and gangmasters have carved themselves out a position as crucial intermediaries in supplying migrant labour to agriculture, food processing and office cleaning, as well as to hospital and care home services at all levels. They monopolise points of entry and access to these jobs, sometimes keep out locals who would be in a stronger position to agitate for better conditions, and help to push wages down still further. So while the preference for employing migrants in occupations taking bodies as their immediate site of labour depends in part on naturalising migrant women's ability to care, based on racialised 'imagined differences' between the employers and their servants (Cheng 2004; Hochschild 2001; Parreñas 2001), such ideologies need to be seen in relation to the broader compass of patterns in the exploitation of migrant labour.

Workplace interactions

The micropolitics of bodily interaction is conditioned not only by all of the wider disparities and ideologies already mentioned, but also by legal regulation, professional codes of practice and other factors that shape employment and employment practices in different body work occupations. Because the human body is a unique focus of work, its treatment is hemmed in by all sorts of detailed stipulations. Such strictures may be as important as employment law in governing workplace interactions and include, for instance, regulations governing the licensing of medics and other health care practitioners, child-minding, daycare centres and nursing homes; criminal law covering prostitution; and local ordinances about how much of the body strippers can reveal or customers be allowed to touch. Even hairdressers and beauticians face a battery of regulation. In addition, customs and practices of different occupations, managerial philosophies and payment systems all have implications for embodied interactions.

Because most body work mirrors other service sector employment in being structured by the three-cornered relation between the employer, the employee and the customer/client/patient (Macdonald and Sirianni 1996), the potential conflicts of interest among 'stakeholders' are extremely complex. This includes most obviously medicine and nursing, where professional demarcations and the organisation of care are under constant review. In both the US and Britain rationalisation and standardisation in health care

161

provision is said to have pushed aside distinctive professional cultures and reduced work satisfaction (Bone 2000; Walby and Greenwell 1994), in some cases altering relationships to patients and their bodies.

Paid caring is another area in which the organisation of work can have contradictory implications for workers and the cared-for. Some see workers facing an increasingly contradictory situation in which the marketisation of care services, which is seen as empowering clients or patients as consumers, leads to the routinisation of care, the deskilling of many workers, and lowered work satisfaction for workers (Harrington et al. 2001; Smith 1999). Comparisons between institutional care and care of the impaired in their own homes persistently suggest that people requiring help with the daily living enjoy greater autonomy and privacy if they live in their own homes, but that the more individualised care they hope for can be at the cost of workers' employment rights (Foner 1994; Glenn 1996; Twigg 2000a). Hard-pressed employees may themselves seek to offer individualised care, whether they work in an institution or private homes, but where time constraints bite, they may find themselves unable to respect patients' bodily autonomy or privacy, leading to intense frustration for both parties. Even in home care, for instance, care organised by employment agencies working to tight margins set either by the terms of their contracts with public authorities or reflecting their own profit-maximising strategies, means that sometimes the timetables of home nursing and care workers are so strict that they can end up leaving their clients in extreme discomfort. Under such conditions it is no wonder that people often turn to one-to-one care for their relations if they can possibly afford it.

Workers also experience conflicts between standards of best practice and caring for their own dependants, although as Harrington et al. (2001) report, workers are often reluctant to talk about conflicts between their obligations to clients and patients and their own family obligations. Work–family balance in health care (and other care occupations) is a particularly important issue. As Smith (1999) says, especially at the casualised end of nursing and care work, the absence of sick pay or holiday entitlement means that workers are financially unable, or do not feel entitled, to take the time they need to meet their family's needs. However, some of the conflicts are inherent in the nature of care. The relatively inflexible timing of some care tasks, in the morning and bedtime, may conflict with meeting the care needs of the families of a largely female workforce (Ungerson 2000).

The conflicts between care responsibilities facing workers who have migrated from overseas are particularly extreme, since they have to 'care at a distance' for their own families while giving their daily attention to their charges. If they are employed in private homes, the ways they resolve the contradictions are deeply woven into the way they see and do their jobs. The construction of the domestic worker as a member of the family can be partly a 'management strategy' adopted by the employing household, but it is also one deployed by workers in their own interest, something noted by almost all studies of paid care work. For instance, Parreñas (2001: 153) argues that one of the ways migrant domestic carers working in the US downplay their servitude and mitigate their sense of downward mobility is by embracing intimacy, which is at the same time a source of authority for employers.

This does not mean that the relations between employees, workers and consumers are always intrinsically conflictual, but they are always complex. The continuing critical staff shortage in midwifery in Britain is a particularly good example. For some years NHS policy has tried to be more sensitive to the needs of women giving birth. According to Sandal (1999), NHS hospitals tried to achieve this by making one midwife responsible for a woman throughout her labour. However, this had such dire implications for the predictability of midwives' working hours (and thus their relationships with and care of their own children) that it made recruitment and retention of midwives increasingly difficult. Since then, in fact, staff shortages have prevented health authorities from implementing the maternal care strategies they had intended. Providing the individualised care many women want is not inherently incompatible with midwives' interests, and many of the latter also want the opportunity to establish longer-term, individualised relationships with clients, but this requires a more radical reorganisation of midwifery services than the NHS has been willing to countenance. In the meantime, some midwives unable to offer the kind of care they want, either go into private practice or leave the profession entirely (Hunter 2004).

But although the relationship between worker and client, patient or customer is conducted within the wider parameters and constraints I have outlined in this chapter, as Foucault stresses, working on bodies may give rise to relations of power and control, not just reflect them. The micropolitics of bodily care provides a minefield of opportunities for the carer and the cared-for to exercise power, even if their position in wider hierarchies cuts against it.

Despite the relative weakness of body workers in some situations, or the potential for connectedness and even merging that may be present, one suspects that there is an inevitable drift towards the territorialisation and objectification of bodies by those who administer to them. The doctor, nurse or salon worker is empowered not only through the symbolic authority of her or his 'white coat' (Van Dongen and Elema 2001) but also through their bodily positioning in the interactional order of care. Even when the worked-on body is not physically weakened through disability, old age or the humiliation of double incontinence, it is frequently anaesthetised, supine or naked, or rendered immobile by gown or facial mud pack, making it difficult for the patient, customer or client to just get up and leave. Of course, some 'consumers' have at least the choice not to return, but for patients who have insufficient power to dictate the minimum level of control over interactions that all people need or want, 'exiting' is too often a last resort.

Workers' control often operates through touch, as well as other mechanisms of which Foucault gave little account. Touch is said by Van Dongen and Elema (2001: 149) to be part of the 'silent culture' of nursing. Although touch is often implied rather than explicit in training ('press the stethoscope firmly' being a typical textbook instruction), it is central to care, related to age, gender, power and social relationships and influencing emotional response in important ways. Different kinds of touch construct patients, and are experienced by them, differently. Van Dongen and Elema (2001) highlight both the objectification and subjectification of the patient that takes place through touch, and Salmon (2002) testifies to this through personal experience as a neurology patient. For instance, the hoists and latex gloves that protect the worker may operate at the cost of rapport engendered by direct touch (Shakespeare 2003: 51).

The dispersal of a medicalising touch is equally relevant to those paid workers, for instance beauticians and other salon workers, who by comparing themselves to doctors or nurses attempt to efface the sexual connotations of their body work (Sharma and Black 1999). In fact, Sharma and Black imply that the mediation of relationships in such work is shifting from a feminised touch, which links salon work to circles of sharing among women kin, or shared beauty work among women friends (as documented by Furman 1997; Gimlin 1996; Peiss 1998), to a unisex (and in this context, status-conferring) holistic approach that mirrors the discourse of alternative therapy, one that carries, as Stacey (1997) suggests, its own characteristic forms of surveillance and control.

Workers also develop means of controlling their interactions with clients, patients and customers through their greater experience or through emotional succour – mechanisms to which Foucault paid little attention. For example, O'Connell Davidson (1996) identifies ways in which a prostitute's greater experience may enable her to stage-manage the sexual encounter and timetable the client's orgasm; Lawler (1991) highlights the ways in which nurses gain access to patients' bodies; and Lee-Trewick (1996) the emotional support institutional care workers offer (only) those patients willing to accept their dependence gracefully.

Moreover, many of the differences in the ways workers explicitly or implicitly conceptualise bodies can be traced partly to differences in their material experiences of interacting with the bodies which form the site of work, not just the social environment in which they take place. For example, Foner (1994) implies that washing and toileting paralysed people can be to experience them, phenomenologically, as immobile objects, while Parreñas (2001: 159) notes that some carers prefer to look after the elderly rather than children because it is easier to care for an 'immobile person'. One suspects that some of the differences in the treatment of the 'patient body' and the 'client body' arise because of the 'organic moorings' (Williams and Bendelow 1998: 60) of social status, rather than being due only to contextual factors. These include some of the demographic inequalities that Chambliss (1996) suggests intensify nurses' objectification of their patients – for instance, nurses' relative youth and their superior 'racial' positioning, education, income and health status.

Differences between alternative and conventional health practitioners' concepts of the body could also be argued to reflect their material relationships to the bodies they treat, as much as to guide them. If alternative health practitioners find it easier to continue 'looking for the gold in everyone' or 'Saluting the Buddha in the person' (Oerton 1998: 6), this may be attributed not only to their ideological predispositions, or the receipt of fees as the basis of payment, but also because such independent practitioners are more likely to be dealing with clean, cared-for, continent bodies. How far holistic concepts of the body are sustainable only under such conditions, and how readily they are transferable to the treatment of the kinds of ailments or surgical operations dealt with by conventional hospitals, are important questions. Alternative practitioners' preference for non-invasive forms of treatment may make it less likely that they will feel the need to distance themselves from the polluting body fluids (or unavoidable infliction of pain) which routine nursing involves.

Menzies-Lyth's (1988) understanding of depersonalising nursing practices as defences against the unconscious anxiety that nursing work evokes is very relevant here, even if the turn to primary nursing (Annandale 1998) – in which each nurse is supposed to take responsibility for a set of patients, rather than there being set tasks for many – has tried to alter practice to some extent. As Menzies-Lyth (1988: 46) says, the objective character of nurses' work includes contact with people who are 'physically ill or injured, often seriously'. Confronted with uncertain recovery, suffering and death, their work involves tasks which, by ordinary standards, are 'distasteful, disgusting and frightening'. Moreover, 'intimate physical contact with patients arouses strong libidinal and erotic wishes and impulses that can be difficult to control' (ibid.: 46). Madjar (1997) found in her study of a hospital burns unit that nurses whose work involved painful procedures had developed a more depersonalising attitude towards patients than other nurses, including a denial of their patients' subjective reality. While Madjar sees these nurses' coping strategy as dehumanising nurses and patients alike, her evidence suggests that many relationships in the workplace are shaped by the specific character of the embodied encounter.

However, we should recognise that the worker's subjective experience of working with or on others' bodies may lead her to feel more powerful than is warranted by her structural position. Bartky (1990) argues that a woman responsible for 'feeding egos and tending wounds' in her personal relations, though 'ethically and epistemologically disempowered by the care she gives', often experiences the outflowing of care she gives as a 'mighty power'. As Bartky says:

> [T]he power a woman feels in herself to heal and sustain . . . is, once again, concrete and very near. It is like a field of force emanating from within herself, a great river flowing outward from her person. (Bartky 1990: 115–16)

This feeling of empowerment through care may also extend to women's roles in paid caring, and may be one of the reasons why many migrant workers apparently often deal with their oppression by working harder, 'lavishing their affluent charges with the love and care they wish they could provide their own children' (Hochschild 2003: 22). O'Neill, who points out the relevance of Bartky's insight, applies it to the sense of power exotic dancers say they experience, in so far as their work usually involves successfully commanding audience attention (O'Neill 2001: 143).

Yet if the micropolitics of body work goes some way towards positioning workers advantageously in relation to the customer, patient or client, there are other aspects that clearly disempower them. Women workers may experience extreme vulnerability in intimate bodily encounters, in particular the violence commonly faced by sex workers but also, not infrequently, by nurses and complementary therapists (Kingma 2001; Lawler 1991; Oerton and Phoenix 2001). Much more widespread is the symbolic violence that denies body workers social recognition. This may be due primarily to the wider power relations that structure the employment, especially when these are racialised. For example, Rollins (1996), an African-American sociologist who worked as a cleaner during her ethnographic research, found that her presence in employing households was literally erased. Family members discussed the most intimate matters over her head, as if she were not present, and locked the front door when they went out, as if the house were empty. But the constructed invisibility of the worker can also be an extension of the invisibility of reproductive labour more generally. Even people struggling to keep their own homes clean know that housekeeping done well 'doesn't show', and that the results of effort disappear as quickly as the dirt and clutter build up again.

Some degree of social invisibility is almost inevitable for workers employed in private homes, since not only is their work performed away from the public eye, but they may also have limited access to the public sphere, especially if they are recent migrants. They may be further constrained by their employers to limit their use of personal space, for instance being confined to their own rooms outside working hours (Cheng 2004; Parreñas 2001). But invisibility is not simply the result of poor employment practices. Rivas's (2003) analysis of care work suggests that in order to maintain (a sense of) independence, severely disabled individuals who receive assistance in daily living often deny their dependence on their paid carers. In fact, especially for teenagers or young adults, receiving care from a paid worker may be experienced as independence, as compared to the perceived dependence involved in relying on family members for the same tasks. Rivas suggests that the social invisibility of middle-aged immigrant women 'allows them to more easily achieve the invisibility the job requires' (Rivas 2003: 74), allowing the disabled person to feel that 'I am doing this'. While this construction of care work partly reflects, as Rivas notes, ideals of self-reliance privileged in American culture, the use of a paid carer to reduce the sense of shame associated with receiving help with bodily functions may be more general. When a carer says that 'I'm like an extension of his body' (ibid.: 77), we can see that by allowing their labour to remain 'invisible', the carer allows the cared-for to experience a sense of sovereignty over his or her own body.

What Rivas sees as the carer's 'transfer of the authorship of one's efforts to another person' (ibid.: 77) may also extend to other kinds of work, both within and outside the home. For instance, women who employ domestic workers to clean their houses still feel pride when their home looks shiny clean. It seems that when tasks are closely linked to the moral economy of the household, claiming responsibility for the fruits of the labour, if not their actual performance, is a frequent, if take-for-granted phenomenon. Gimlin's (2002) data on hairdressing and exercise classes also highlight how the expertise and/or labour of service workers is rationalised (away). She suggests that clients at the hair salon she studied frequently discredited the expertise of the working-class stylists, while beauticians say that they see themselves 'bringing out the best' in their clients (Sharma and Black 1999). Indeed, workers who lead exercise classes (and presumably also personal trainers) or Weightwatchers groups (Stinson 2001) are caught in a cleft stick, in so far as they may try to enhance their client's sense of achievement by attributing success to the client's efforts rather than their own.

Of course, in some cases the worker's effort is not invisibilised, but their care is explained (away) through gendered and/or racialising constructions that obscure the pecuniary relationship between worker and client. The appeal of the advertisement for L'Oreal hair colour ('Because you're worth it!') is presumably that it permits women to rationalise spending money on themselves, as against the more socially acceptable alternative of sacrifice for others (Whitehead 1984), but it is also a refrain in advertisements for spas and other pampering enterprises. Kang (2003: 835) found such attitudes typical mainly of customers in her upmarket salon, patronised by white, professional women. Her findings suggest that the workers, of Korean origin, could only earn their tips through pampering the clients in ways that validated the latter's sense of superiority. Pampering included not just social contact, such as friendliness, but physical activities, including massage, cleanliness and the adoption of a 'sensitive touch'. Some data from interviews with spa workers in Indonesia suggest that their clients, women who travel abroad for spa holidays, frequently naturalise the sweet, caring nature of spa workers through racial stereotyping (Ben Lo, personal communication). In these intimate kinds of work, the role of sovereign customer also confirms the body of the client as a superior bearer of value, as Bourdieu might have put it, through the worker's apparent willingness to undertake the 'dirty' work that detoxes and purifies it.

Conclusions

As we saw in Chapter 4, the healthy, fit and attractive body is not only a sign of class privilege but may be becoming increasingly central to achieving career aspirations or reproducing professional and managerial status. Yet sometimes the discussions of the body work of self-presentation forget that much of the labour involved in the (re)making of bodies is not done by individuals on themselves, even though they get credited with the cultural capital it produces. This includes not only cosmetic support for one's appearance, but also the reproductive labour required by workers' dependants as well as their own bodies.

This chapter suggests that for a full picture of embodiment in the workplace, we need to go beyond existing research on the production of embodied self-identity as a form of classed cultural capital and consider systematically the making and remaking of bodies as the focus of economic activity. Moreover, for many people their interaction with the materiality of others' bodies forms an importance aspect of the experience of work. With the sociology of the body providing many avenues for phenomenological understanding of the lived body 'from the inside', as Grosz (1994) put it, it becomes that much more important to understand how people experience others' bodies, from the outside, in routinised workplace encounters, mediated by the cash nexus, and located within wider social inequalities. At the same time, in many occupations the relationship to the other's body is also constitutive of workplace relations and can define the worker's own body in terms of their job.

Several other conclusions can be drawn from the material considered here. First, in considering occupations that involve body work, such as paid caring, we should be wary of accepting as descriptions phrases such as 'immaterial services' (Puwar and Crowley 2004: 1) or of drawing a sharp distinction between tangible and intangible products (Yeates 2004a: 376). As economic products 'care', 'diagnosis' or 'pampering' may be more intangible than cars or fruit, but body work usually still involves manual work, including, to a varying degree, contact with the materiality of others' bodies and transformation of their physical state. There is a problem here, though, in making this aspect of the work visible, not only because it often takes place in private, but because occupational groups themselves tend to obscure it; distancing themselves (or, if that is not possible, distancing their image) from polluting contact with organic dirt is part of the way occupations rise up in the body work pecking order. But even if people at the top of the body work division of labour minimise the amount of body work they say their occupations involve, we should be wary of validating inputs like emotional labour by distinguishing them from physical labour, at the cost of discrediting the input of workers whose labour commands less status.

Second, there is clearly an unresolved tension between two perspectives that implicitly structure the discussion in this chapter, and a tendency to bounce between them. On the one hand, workers whose contact with consumers involves touch, nudity, even death, are exposed to potentially powerful and unsettling experiences, and even when it becomes routinised it still carries the potential for sensate interaction, identification, desire and merging. We should be wary therefore of accepting methods for characterising or quantifying care (for instance Yeates 2004a) that count only so-called physical tasks. Body work often entails (and may even presume) that employees guided by an ethic of care are willing to work 'beyond contract' (Ungerson 2000). On the other hand, we must not assume that the relationships between bodies are fixed or universal, since these relationships vary between objectification and subjectification in ways that are connected not only to workers' values, professional codes or training, but also to the kinds of social inequalities and aspects of work examined in this chapter. The research on sex tourism by O'Connell Davidson and Sanchez-Taylor (1999) shows how easy it is for consumers to delude themselves about the pecuniary motives underlying workers' attentiveness, especially when worker obligations are particularly diffuse.

The conflicts between ways of thinking about body work and the ways in which it is organised and regulated cross-cut many areas of social and economic policy. The most obvious example is the discourse of globalisation that assumes the natural and inevitable primacy of the market (Young 2004). The General Agreement on Trade and Services (GATS) requires states to open up specific services to competition, including foreign providers. These developments are likely to go a lot further under the Bolkenstein directive currently being debated in the EU (Rowland 2005) which, by redefining public services as 'services of general interest', seek to treat health care and social work like any other economic activity.

An example of more local interest is the recently publicised crisis in Britain over the spread of antibiotic-resistant MRSA in hospitals, which can lead to serious illness or death. The newspaper discussions about the need to improve hygiene in hospitals have targeted a number of factors that relate the conditions under which MRSA spreads to the rationalisation of care and cost-cutting; for instance the contracting out of cleaning services has reduced staffing levels by up to 45 per cent, according to Unison (Carvel 2005), targets for patient throughput relocate patients from ward to ward (Neuberger 2005), and medical and nursing staff do not always take (or have) the time to wash their hands between patients (Batty 2005). The fact that this crisis has occasioned so much surprise confirms my perception that the relation between 'dirty work' and patient wellbeing is usually ignored, partly because it is convenient or apparently 'cost-effective' to do so, but also because it lacks social recognition. This is besides a failure to recognise that Taylorising the treatment of human bodies carries its own costs.

In this chapter it has not been possible to do more than deal relatively superficially with the enormous literature in the different fields touched on, such as changes in the organisation of health care or the transnationalisation of care work. But it should be enough to suggest that we can more fully understand particular occupations and settings if we keep their location within the broader category of body work in view.

EIGHT Concluding Remarks

My starting point in teaching and writing on the body/work relation is that it is 'good to think with' (Douglas 1966), helping to draw our attention to particular aspects of both the body and employment and to raise new questions about the relation between them. Just looking at this morning's newspaper as I began to draft these Conclusions, several stories leapt off the page. Stephen Moss (2005: 3) reported on his conversations with men working as nightclub bouncers, including their comments on Moss's own attempt to try out the work as part of researching his article. His workmates that evening told him that 'You have to show them who's in charge . . . You have the right build, but you don't have the look . . . You have the wrong kind of smile.' Apparently Moss's stance was also a problem, his weight not evenly balanced between his feet, and he is told to hold his hands so as to make his belly look flatter. He also had the wrong colour shirt, which should have been black rather than blue, but at least his hair was closely cropped. Then there is Joan Bakewell (2005), a British journalist and television presenter who comments in her column 'Just 70' on the difficulty of maintaining one's 'staying power' as you get older:

> The truth is that our bodies begin to let us down. No matter how keen we are to keep going, the joints play up, the muscles sag . . . It falls particularly hard on those whose careers depend on being on their feet. Hairdressers and surgeons develop varicose veins; teachers take to administration as much to get the weight off their feet as the children off their backs . . . (Bakewell 2005: 7)

Turning to the television listings for the evening (*Guardian* 2005), we find they include an episode of *All New Cosmetic Surgery*, a programme of graphic horror that had been running all week, and, just to remind us that worries about the body are not completely new, a broadcast of the film *Mary Shelley's Frankenstein* (1994), based loosely on the novel first published in 1818.

Such stories are a good way to begin thinking about the body/work relation, but clearly they cannot tell us one best way to think about it. Even these brief examples suggest that the body in work has to be seen from a range of perspectives. For instance, Bakewell reminds us that experiences of work are deeply intertwined with our embodied conditions of existence. Her way of thinking about the body's inherent limitations has unfortunately become rather unfashionable in sociology, including the sociology of the body. While the physical strains of work, or the relation between ageing and productivity, feature in occupational health and safety, where they tend to be dealt with in terms of discrete ailments and conditions rather than subjective experiences, they have not been integrated into the sociology of employment as a whole. Yet they should form an important counterpoint to the plasticity of the body highlighted by postmodernist approaches.

Moss's account of bouncers' self-conscious stylisation of their bodily appearance and demeanour comes much closer to the concerns of the sociologies of the body and of work to date. It can be read as a picture of the deployment of the body as a 'material signifier' sending particular messages to club customers, but it also alludes indirectly to the bouncer's dependence on a prior habitus, a learned gestural economy that is wider than the bouncer's work role. Moss's article, along with existing academic research on bouncers (Monaghan 2002a, 2002b) or boxers (Wacquant 2002), also rejects the idea of the body as a passive carrier of cultural capital or a target for re-formation, instead seeing it as active in defining and physically sustaining the habitus that the job requires.

The succession of TV programmes on cosmetic surgery, of which *All New Cosmetic Surgery* insists it is the latest, draws attention to the role of representational practices in constructions of the body, presenting the body as an infinitely malleable object of a scrutiny that goes deep below the skin. Such programmes also confirm the possibility of transformation, of being 'made-over', and play on the tension between actively choosing to change one's face or body and passively lying under the surgeon's knife. The public's consuming interest in such programmes also suggests an obsession with the boundaries of body, a fascination with the fragility of the divide between its inside and outside. The media, I have argued elsewhere, provide many such examples of material through which many of the anxieties of our age are played out, including those stemming from workplace relations (Wolkowitz 2004). The televising of Mary Shelley's famous fictionalisation of her fears about the creative process is an important example of the use of the body as a metaphor. Such examples remind us that grasping embodiment in work has to be seen within the context of many other representations of the body and experiences of embodiment within which our work lives are located.

Although such examples emphasise that the body is so multifaceted in its symbolic and experiential aspects that there will never be a 'best way' through which to approach it, nonetheless this book suggests that if we want to move forward in integrating employment into our understanding of the body, and appreciating embodied experience as an aspect of paid work, some directions may be more immediately productive than others. Writing in 2003, Terry Eagleton comments that the 'labouring body' is almost absent from the explosion of writing on the body in social and cultural theory, having been replaced by the 'coupling body' and other erotic constructs. Since the turning away, theoretically, from Marxism and to poststructuralism and postmodernism and the collapse of the communist 'Second World', the question of radical and emancipatory social transformation has given way to attempts to map shifts in contemporary global capitalism, on the one hand, and the exploration of people's ability to craft their own identities, subjectivities and selves on the other. With many important exceptions, the tendency is to locate 'the body' within the second of these realms of discussion, which reduces social change to questions of individual agency, leaving the former out of the reckoning. But I hope that the focus of this book on the working body as deployed and experienced in contemporary Western capitalist economies may help to bring them together.

Like many sociologists, I came to the body through Foucault's writings but have come to think that we need to move forward in other ways. This is mainly because we need to give more attention to the changing institutional environments within which bodies are positioned and to our relation as embodied social actors to social inequalities of many kinds. This is particularly necessary in thinking about the body and employment because of the increasing polarisation in employment opportunities, remuneration and security that has taken place over the past 30 years. While a concluding chapter may not be the place to conduct an extended discussion of high theory, we can indicate several points where the use of Bourdieu's conceptual framework, especially his concept of habitus, could help to move empirical research forward.

McNay (1999) argues that Foucault presents us with a dichotomous choice, as between the external power exercised in the construction of the passified body of his early writings and the scope for autonomy provided by the practices of the self imagined in his later work. She argues that we may make more progress through the development of Bourdieu's social theory, which focuses on what we can term the social body, one 'made up of meanings and values, gestures, postures, physical bearing, speech and language' (Skeggs 2004: 21). To date this approach has been adopted in the sociology of work mainly with respect to the recruitment of the 'aesthetic labour' required of workers in 'designer' retail and hospitality outlets (as discussed in Chapter 4). However, it is potentially of greater relevance, linking the individual worker, through their body, to their position, biographically, in the wider social structure; or, in Bourdieu's terms, the social field. It may also be useful in understanding the effects on the social body of different kinds of employment (and unemployment), for instance the stamp of authority developed by leading executives as they grow into their roles. Just as employment has implications for inequalities in health and fitness, so too bodily demeanour can be seen as one of its outputs. The Bourdieusian concept of habitus is particularly important because rather than separating off the biological body as outside the sociological purview, and focusing only on its inscribed surface, it can help to show how social inequality registers in the competencies of the body through the bodily activity of social actors.

By way of conclusion, therefore, I want to return to some of the themes articulated in this book, beginning with those identified in Chapter 1, and see where we have been able to add to our knowledge base through material discussed in later chapters, pointing where feasible to the further contribution recourse to Bourdieusian and other concepts might make.

In considering the sociology of employment it was argued that it had mainly treated the body as an absent presence, only recently making it the direct focus of attention. As discussed in Chapter 4, the history of research on emotions in work is particularly instructive in this regard. When Hochschild (1983) first introduced the concept of emotional labour, she saw it as involving the effort required to manage bodily sensation, affects and display. Now though it is rarely seen in this light, the emphasis being rather on emotion as a form of intelligence and cognition. In contrast, research identified with the sociology of the body claims emotion as an aspect of embodiment, seeing it as forming a bridge transcending the mind–body binary. This kind of example begins to suggest that bringing together the concerns of the sociology of work and the sociology of the body is no easy matter.

The first of the themes in the sociology of the body we considered was the relation between the body and society. This book has tried to show that focusing on the body is an effective way of linking changes in employment relations, labour processes and the experiences of individual workers. First of all, the changing requirements of capitalist labour processes reconstruct, modify and use (up) different aspects of the body. As we saw in Chapter 3, sociologists have rightly taken on board Foucault's analysis of the way a particular work system, such as the factory system, makes the docility of the working body to a degree inevitable. Moreover, as Harvey says, Foucault can rightly supplement Marx in showing how 'older capacities of the human body are reinvented, [and] new capacities revealed' (Harvey 1998: 406).

However, we need to stress also the body-knowledge learned 'on the job' through practice. This may involve gaining experience of the proper use of tools, the adequate perception of the quality of materials, the management of physical strength, and the learning and maintenance of manual dexterity. We should also include here, as Williams (1997, 1993) suggests, the development of coping strategies that enable workers to deal with physical dangers, in some cases, or the stamina to stand or sit in fixed poses doing repetitive work in others. Although such bodily capacities often may have been acknowledged, they were not necessarily seen as forms of embodied cultural capital, nor was workers' dependence on their network of co-workers, family and friends – their social capital – recognised. So although the body as a vehicle of labour was recognised, it was not recognised, as a social body, but naturalised, perhaps as 'brute strength' or nimble fingers, as the merely 'physical'. Indeed, one reason for the relatively disembodied character of so much sociology of employment in the past may have been that instead of challenging these constructions of the 'physical body', the sociology of employment tended to avoid the corporeal, on the grounds that it represents what is natural, possibly base or feminine, and therefore having little place in accounts of the social relations of production and organisation.

As we saw in Chapter 4, there are a number of different ways in which the body and the social figure in conceptualisations of service sector employment. The importance of 'social inputs' (see Casey 1995) can be highlighted through a contrast to bodily effort, and this is also true of some ways of thinking about emotional labour (Bolton and Boyd 2003; Boyd 2002). Others have argued that women's 'gender performances' are so naturalised that they get no credit for them (Adkins 2002, 2001; Tyler and Abbott 1998), although I have argued that the same may be true for men, for instance in the way they embody leadership styles. Other theorists have used Bourdieu's concept of habitus to identify the embodiment of the aesthetic and other attributes employers look for as an explicit job requirement (Witz et al. 2003). Such attributes are now the focus of much of the training offered through job clubs for unemployed people.

The research by Witz et al. (2003) suggests that we need also to be aware of how the deployment of these naturalised, embodied social inputs, and what they involve, has changed. Of course, gender and racial ideologies play a big role in naturalising aspects of bodily capacities. However, we also need to consider the role of the capitalist labour process, which does not just construct and use up bodily capacities but 'decides' which capacities are to be recognised and recompensed and which normalised, i.e. using gender, racial and (less explicitly) class as justifications. Someone like Judith Butler might say that it is precisely such ideologies that hide aspects of the effort that workers put into performing everyday work roles in the required fashion. However, we have to be careful that the notion of habitus is not deployed in the same fashion, i.e. to obscure the effort work requires. And indeed this recognition may be taking place. People are more conscious of the grooming and surveillance of habitus and it is brought more explicitly into consciousness, demanding a degree of reflexivity that Bourdieu had perhaps not sufficiently recognised. The 'worked up' habitus of fields of labour has, in this sense, become more mindful. It is increasingly difficult to run on autopilot.

It might also be argued that in Bourdieusian terms, employment represents a kind of symbolic violence to the complexity of workers' experience of embodiment in the way it discounts the interweaving of feeling, intelligence, sexuality, skill and outward appearance and fragments them into purchasable commodities. For this reason, although I think that the identification of emotional, sexual and aesthetic labour in research on organisations represents a step forward in putting the embodiment of service sector employment, and especially customer services, on the map, it unfortunately also mirrors rather than challenges the fragmentation of the body by the labour process. Detailed phenomenological accounts of embodiment in interrelational customer services work, were they available, would perhaps point to the integration and mutually determining interplay of embodied experiences that employers perhaps disregard, including the increasing mindfulness of physical activity and the physical exhaustion that 'mental' and 'emotional' labour can entail.

Competition for jobs and promotion has important implications for the self–body relationship, which is another aspect of the sociology of the body identified in Chapter 1. I suggested that that while we can appreciate the rich view of subjectivity provided by the anti-dualist perspectives that challenge the Cartesian mind–body, self–body binaries, they have avoided considering the embeddedness of these and other dualisms in the structures and experiences of paid employment, where discursive binaries are backed up by the pecuniary and other incentives and sanctions of the workplace. The commodification and deployment of the body as something one *has* rather than something that one *is* has become almost a *sine qua non* of consumer capitalism and the marketisation of the self. But as important are the ways in which people divide themselves as a means of resistance or coping within the workplace. For instance, Durand and Hatzfeld's (2003) study of a Peugeot plant, discussed in Chapter 3, sees a 'double relation' to the self as integral to waged employment, but argues that the splitting of the self car workers experience is intensified by their having to give up full control over their bodily movement while working to the tighter and tighter cycles required by the assembly line. Within the working day and working week, car assembly workers move back and forth between subject states. As operatives they 'lend "body and soul"' to their work, and

> to that extent they have assented to being dispossessed of themselves. From this ensues a split between the state of the subject when active but 'loaned out' and in the state of self-recovery. (Ibid.: 113)

This latter state is more characteristic during lunch and tea breaks and in workers' time off. The locker room, it will be remembered from Chapter 3, is a space in which they reclaim their 'selves' as they change their clothes.

A double, even multiple, relation to the self is also characteristic of other kinds of paid work. Many of the strategies deployed by workers in attempting to cope with the insecure identities that the flexibilisation of employment has engendered, as identified by Collinson (2003), involve dividing the self or drawing boundaries between the self and its environment. He suggests that employees in 'subordinated work' may seek to survive through conforming to work demands on the one hand, but on the other, distancing themselves from the job, physically through absenteeism or psychologically through 'splitting self' or in other ways. Collinson suggests that workers of many kinds also use the body as a resource, along with ethnicity, religion, possessions, gender, age, and so on in crafting multiple identities (2003: 534), learning to play the corporate game cynically, through their construction of 'dramaturgical' and 'resistant' selves. Such strategies confirm the body as primarily a carrier of cultural capital that has exchange value, rather than seeing it as integral to pleasurable experience, stimulating exercise or whatever for their own sake.

Such examples suggest that workers develop a relation to their bodies as resources as part of the active construction of the habitus needed to survive in particular occupations or corporate cultures. This suggests that rather than focusing on whether the subject-body is imagined as integral or divided, we have to consider the ways in which such constructions operate as strategies in, and as a response to, institutional power. Indeed, as we saw in Chapter 4 and Chapter 5, workers who are discouraged from asserting boundaries between their work selves and their private selves can end up on long-term sick leave as the only way in which they can reinstate some kind of (temporary) boundary (Forseth 2005; Forseth and Gullikstad 2005). For instance, the Scottish call centre studied by Taylor et al. (2003) not only had high rates of absence due to sickness but very high turnover rates of over 9 per cent per week, amounting to 37 per cent annually. Not only does this suggest that the maintenance of two or more selves in the same body may not be so easy in the long run, it also emphasises the need to incorporate workplace health and safety within the sociology of the body and employment.

The strategic aspects involved in the construction of the body–self was particularly evident in the discussion of the emergence of what Wainwright and Calnan (2002) term the 'work stress discourse', which points to differences between workers in their willingness to 'call up' the body as a visible component of self-identity or their attempt to silence bodily discomfort. Stress and other bodily impairments have become one of the few ways in which workers can legitimately counter or limit the workloads and deadlines set by employers (Chapter 5). Wainwright and Calnan argue that by articulating work dissatisfactions in the form of stress, workers may be extending their docility by subjecting their futures to the findings of biomedicine, especially the medical practitioners who legitimate sick leave or alterations to work requirements. However, we could argue instead that workers are *embodying* their dissatisfaction, although given the power of doctors to pronounce on our bodies, this unfortunately also means medicalising it. I do not mean to imply that Wainwright and Calnan dismiss the 'real' effects of mental stress on physiological functions, which they do not, but they fail to recognise how powerful embodying dissatisfaction is, precisely because of the body's reality-conferring functions. Although we might want to question whether distress should need to be legitimated by medics, it seems to be the case that we should see calling up the body as a strategy, adopted sometimes by employers or co-workers (through sexual harassment, for instance) but also by some workers in support of their own interests. As we saw in Chapter 6, many of the critics of prostitution as an institution also call up the body strategically, partly because of its unique relation to the self and partly because it evokes longstanding human values. Other critics, and some sex workers, strategically play down the involvement of the body in favour of other constructions of their work.

The third theme outlined in Chapter 1 was the relation between embodiment and gender. The contribution of feminist scholarship to the ongoing emergence of an embodied sociology of employment has been enormous. One might even argue that in considering the body in employment, feminists have had the advantage over other researchers, since their interest in the implications of bodily difference has been so central to feminist theory (Andermahr et al. 2000). Moreover, it is possible to argue, more hypothetically, that as theorists women have been less inhibited than men by the traditional Western disdain for the flesh, or by prohibitions against appearing to be too interested in other people's bodies. Feminist scholarship has been crucial in revealing the gendered character of the organisational body and tracing the changing body/politics of organisation life that workers negotiate through their presentation of self, their movement through space, their verbal 'calling up' or silencing of the body and sexuality. It has also done much to illuminate the use of gendered bodies as resources by employers as well as workers themselves.

As we saw in analysing feminist debates on prostitution and other kinds of sex work in Chapter 6, feminists adopt a range of quite distinct ways of conceptualising the body and are arguably well aware that the conceptions that underwrite their various approaches have different political implications. Moreover, one of the purposes of that chapter was to highlight the reflexivity of concepts of the body in everyday life, trying to show how sex workers too, as well as their advocates, have recourse to a range of different implicit and explicit concepts of the body and the body–self relation through which to condemn prostitution on the one hand, or to maintain their self-esteem and defend or obtain civil rights on the other. These are combined with corporeal practices through which sex workers try to defend their bodily boundaries and/or invest their bodies with agency.

Some of the ways sex workers negotiate the relation between body and self we have seen replicated in other areas of work, including especially the 'splitting' that Collinson (2003) and Durand and Hatzfeld (2003) refer to, and the use of dress, make-up and so on in the construction of corporate identities. However, sex workers clearly vary in their ability to exercise these kinds of individual agency, just as more conventional workers do, and their agency is rarely directed towards transforming the social relations of prostitution. Indeed, when prostitutes' collectives' campaigns have been successful in obtaining new regulations that protect some sex workers, this may be at the cost of further entrenching the differentiation between workers who qualify and those who are excluded (West and Austrin 2005), again a finding not dissimilar to what we know about the history of labour movements more generally.

Finally, Chapter 1 considered what I called the 'political economy of the body' as articulated by Harvey (1998), Lowe (1995) and Ebert (1996, 1993). One of Harvey's points is that looking to the performativity of the body as a potential site of resistance is problematic, since this is to return to a body already shaped by the very processes against which it rebels. His comment is directed, implicitly, against theorists like Judith Butler, who argue that because of the embodied nature of 'speech acts', they always exceed the processes that shape them. In his 1998 article, Harvey is particularly concerned with locating the (re)construction of the body within Marx's understanding of the insertion of the human body into the circuits of capital accumulation. But of course this parallels the circularity of the relationship between individual and society which, in different ways, has been the bread and butter of sociological theory since Durkheim (Crossley 2001). This circularity is one of the reasons why it is hard to get a 'fix' on the body/work relation. It may be that the only way to deal with it is to recognise a range of reflexive relations through which the body is constructed and to make these, rather than the body itself, our focus. These include aspects of the relation between body and society, body and self, and the body and gender already mentioned, but we can deepen the picture further.

Although the body/work relation is manifestly one of the circular, reflexive relations through which both the body and work are repeatedly (re)constituted, it is not very easy to specify its import. Within sociology, Skeggs's (2005, 2004a, 2004b) recent research on constructions of the self also highlights the embeddedness of embodiment in relations of social inequality. She stresses that postmodern constructions of the body, such as the aesthetic or prosthetic body, actually address extensions of the capacities and value of the body that accrue mainly to the middle class. Using Bourdieu she indicates important possibilities for theorising the social body that go far beyond surface inscription. However, as she herself notes, these do not give very much importance to employment, since waged labour is no longer the only or even the main arena in which the body functions as a resource in the reproduction of class. As O'Neill (1985: 100) puts it, the 'massive exploitation' that takes hold of the body is no longer confined to the exploitation of labour input; rather capital now employs 'every technique of the body in a unified field of production and consumption'. The identity work of corporate cultural change policies is in some respects but an extension of the construction of identities through consumption. Whereas at one time capital took hold of the body most vitally during the 'working day', now that interpersonal relations and identity formation outside work are so highly subject to the surveillance and control by an external and internal gaze this is surely no longer the case. The circular construction of the body seems to include and stitch together both paid work and consumption in ever widening and tightening circles. Indeed, since the workplace now includes not just the factory and office but also the school, hospital, hotel, leisure park and private home, it is increasingly difficult to identify a separate 'world of work' that is spatially separate from the rest of life (Glucksmann 2004). We can but hope that the 'flexible self' as the preferred self of corporate capitalism is also a 'leaky' self that can exploit some of the contradictions that capitalism requires and generates.

One of the most important aspects of Harvey's analysis from my point of view is his willingness to include in his political economy the representational practices through which bodies are portrayed, and through which we give them various meanings. We also have to recognise that the human body is itself a sign that is frequently deployed rhetorically in representations of various kinds. Although as we saw in Chapter 2, representations of bodies have long been important to defining the character of work (noble or heroic;

dangerous or safe; disembodied or sexual), nowadays representations of working bodies play an increasing role. Aestheticised images of working bodies play a significant part in the realm of consumption (such as the bare-chested worker in the well-known Pepsi advertisement, or the unemployed working-class strippers in *The Full Monty*), and are to be found even in movements that attempt to counter some of the worst affects of global capitalism, such as the Fair Trade movement, whose representations of the bodies of coffee workers in their advertisements have been analysed by Wright (2004). But increasingly, as we saw in Chapter 4, aestheticised images of work are used in training workers, photographs being used, according to Warhurst et al. (2004) not just in training workers in what to do but in how work should look. Indeed, in some cases human bodies are themselves being turned into representations as part of their work, becoming what Tyler and Abbott (1998) term 'material signifiers', appropriated by organisations to signal brand ethos or to demonstrate the wearability or allure of the clothes of the fashion retailer. As Macdonald and Sirianni (1996) emphasise in their joint contribution to the collection of articles they edited on the service sector, the gender and race displayed by bodies play an especially significant role in signalling to consumers what they can expect in an interaction. For this reason I think we should be wary of going too far in separating gender and the body as foci of analysis, although we cannot collapse one into the other either. Just as bodies only become 'culturally intelligible' if coherently gendered, so gender (and race) may need bodies to function as intelligible signs.

The strongest way to make visible the circularities involved in the construction of the body in work – and perhaps to identify where some of the contradictions might be found – seems to me to pursue intersubjectivity as a key reflexive relation in the constitution of embodied selfhood in work relations. Without considering here the various understandings of intersubjectivity in phenomenology (but see Crossley 1996), we may still argue that intersubjectivity is the ultimate reflexive relation in so far as the person comes to feel that she is the author of her acts by being with another person who recognises her acts, her feelings, her intentions and her independence (Benjamin 1988: 21). It epitomises a reflexive relation in so far as it includes not only the other's 'confirming response', but also how we find ourselves in that response. As discussed in Chapter 6, O'Connell Davidson and Sanchez-Taylor have been theorising the wrongs of prostitution through the mis-recognition it requires. They argue that the prostitute–user relation requires and legitimates ideologies that construct the Other as socially dead, as a non-subject. This formulation, I argued, recognises that the 'prostitute body' is inseparable from the social relations of inequality on which such a social construction ordinarily rests.

Although O'Connell Davidson and Sanchez-Taylor do not draw on Bourdieu's conceptual framework, their approach is not dissimilar in so far as they stress that inter-corporeal relations can best be understood sociologically, as configured by and within social inequalities. Bourdieu drew heavily on Merleau-Ponty and Sartre, who were also concerned with issues of recognition, and was also influenced by Franz Fanon's understanding of the centrality of recognition and misrecognition in the construction of race. Bourdieu locates recognition as structured into a hierarchy of domination, in which symbolic violence of the most fundamental kind is practised. O'Connell Davidson and Sanchez-Taylor's analyses of sex work are particularly important in so far as they are developing a critical account of the relation between work and the body that does not depend on a notion of the body's pre-given essence.

Chapter 7 continued the emphasis on intersubjectivity by focusing on the relationships between many other workers and their customers, clients and patients where the interaction also requires a high degree of bodily contact, intimacy or stigmatised 'body work'. It also attempted to understand these relationships within the context of the inequalities within which they are often established. These inequalities may pertain to the hierarchies that govern the ranking of different occupations, the wider social relations of gender, race and class with which these intersect, and the inequalities inevitable in the relations between practitioners and ill, immobile or otherwise incapacitated individuals. Like the particular example of sex work, workplace relationships that involve touch, or stages of undress, or the relation between different bodily postures (think of the dentist and their patient) make the embodiment of social actors and social interaction much more overt than in many other kinds of employment and its negotiation more conscious. Such relations are too rarely dealt with in the sociology of employment, although they are increasingly the subject of research in the sociology of health and healing and there have been other moves in this direction, as discussed in Chapter 7.

How can we move forward so far as research on the body/work relation is concerned? How ambitious should we be? One of the slightly worrying conclusions of this book is that if 'bodies R us', then our existence as embodied beings has to be integrated into the study of all employment, not treated as a separate field. One would want all researchers in the field of employment to pay more attention to the embodiment of their informants, even when it is not explicitly targeted by the employer or mentioned by the informant as such. I suspect that this invitation is not going to be taken up in a big way, in part because serious consideration of the sensibility of the worker as an embodied subject risks unsettling the abstractions used to investigate paid work, including some of the more rationalistic assumptions about how identities are formed. We would also be forced to recognise limits to the plasticity of the body, which as a physical structure remains much less malleable than many commentators suppose. Moreover, studying embodiment, and not just constructions of the body, could progress only by adopting the vantage point of the embodied worker and listening to their accounts of workplace experience 'from the inside'.

Still there are more modest research agendas that can be recommended. An important step would be to try to integrate data and debates on occupational health and safety more fully into both the sociology of the body and the sociology of work and employment, something that this book attempts only in a very fragmentary way. We also need to bring into the picture other areas of employment that I have not been able to address in this book, such as the sociology of scientific practice and human–technology interaction, where much relevant research is being undertaken. My own interest is in further homing in on the corporeality of workers' experience of employment in occupations that take the human body as their focus. As suggested in Chapter 7, though in the West there has been a downturn in manufacturing and other areas of industrial employment, a great many workers are still involved in complex practices that require embodied manual skills and capacities. Further studies of their activities could shed light on the 'everyday' experiences of the body that were alluded to at the beginning of this chapter.

I hope that Chapter 7 shows that a consideration of the encounters involved in what I have termed 'body work' provides a useful way of further exploring the body politics of work, and also generating ideas about less intimate bodily interactions in other kinds of work. Given our present state of knowledge, that chapter necessarily drew mainly on research data produced within the framework of the sociology of health and medicine, gender studies and social policy, rather than the sociology of employment as this is usually understood. What I would like to see is further studies that would enable us to better understand how body–work relations are shaped by the kinds of factors with which the sociology of employment is more usually concerned, for instance patterns of ownership, work systems, intensities and types of surveillance, and types of employment relation, for instance subcontracting, franchising and self-employment. As the example of sex work suggests, we also have to consider the relative intimacy of the encounter, the legal regulation to which it is subject, the relative status of the parties involved, and the actual and/or symbolic violence which it generates.

Much harder to conceptualise are the ways in which assumptions and experiences of embodiment shape work systems and all the other aspects of employment relations noted above. We saw in Chapter 3 that the development of scientific management involved rethinking the body, and this is no doubt the case in the development of human–technology interfaces more recently. But I wonder whether we know much about how people 'think' human bodies in these contexts, much less in fields in which the body is not so visibly present in the work relation. What do call centre companies think they gain by dispensing with the physical co-presence of customer services worker and customer, for instance, and what do hospital doctors feel they gain (or lose) when their caseload consists of test results rather than patients? And are these questions over which workers feel that they want more control? These kinds of investigation then need to feed back into a sociology of the body willing to take on board the very diverse implications and experiences of workers' embodiment.

References

Abel, E.K. and M.K. Nelson (1990) *Circles of Care: Work and Identity in Women's Lives*. Albany: State University of New York Press.

Acker, J. (1990) 'Hierarchies, Jobs, Bodies: A Theory of Gendered Organisations', *Gender and Society* 4 (2): 139–58.

Adams, K.M. and S. Dickey (eds) (2000) *Home and Hegemony: Domestic Service and Identity Politics in South and Southeast Asia*. Ann Arbor: University of Michigan Press.

Adkins, L. (2004) 'Reflexivity: Freedom or Habit of Gender?', in L. Adkins and B. Skeggs (eds) *Feminism after Bourdieu*. Oxford: Blackwell.

Adkins, L. (2002) *Revisions: Gender and Sexuality in Late Modernity*. Buckingham: Open University Press.

Adkins, L. (2001) 'Cultural Feminization: "Money, Sex and Power" for Women', *Signs* 26 (3): 669–95.

Adkins, L. (1995) *Gendered Work: Sexuality, Family and the Labour Market*. Buckingham: Open University Press.

Adkins, L. (1992) 'Sexual Work and the Employment of Women in the Service Industries', in M. Savage and A. Witz (eds) *Gender and Bureaucracy*. Oxford: Blackwell.

Adkins, L. and B. Skeggs (eds) (2004) *Feminism after Bourdieu*. Oxford: Blackwell.

Aglietta, M. (1979) *A Theory of Capitalist Regulation: The US Experience*. London: New Left Books.

Ahmed, S. (1998) 'Animated Borders: Skin, Colour and Tanning', in M. Shildrick and J. Price (eds) *Vital Signs*. Edinburgh: Edinburgh University Press.

Allvin, M. and G. Aronson (2003) 'The Future of Work Environment Reforms: Does the Concept of Work Environment Apply within the New Economy?', *International Journal of Health Services* 33 (1): 99–111.

Alvesson, M. and H. Willmott (1992) 'Critical Theory and Management Studies: An Introduction', in M. Alvesson and H. Willmott (eds) *Critical Management Studies*. London: Sage.

Andermahr, S., T. Lovell and C. Wolkowitz (2000) *A Glossary of Feminist Theory*. London: Arnold.

Anderson, B. (2000) *Doing the Dirty Work: The Global Politics of Domestic Labour*. London: Zed Books.

Anderson, B. and J. O'Connell Davidson (2002) *Trafficking: A Demand Led Problem?* Stockholm: Save the Children Sweden. Retrieved 22 May 2005, from http://www.jagori.org/pdf/3%20RB%202486%20-%20 The%20Demand%20Side.pdf

Anderson, B. and B. Rogaly (2004) 'Forced Labour and Migration to the UK', Study prepared by COMPAS in collaboration with the Trades Union Congress. Retrieved on 29 June 2005, from http://www.compas.ox. ac.uk/publications/papers/Forced%20Labour%20TUC%20Report.pdf

Annandale, E. (1998) *The Sociology of Health and Medicine: A Critical Introduction*. Cambridge: Polity Press.

Appleyard, D. (2001) 'My Domestic Army', *Daily Mail*, 6 March.

Archer, M.S. (2000) *Being Human: The Problem of Agency*. Cambridge: Cambridge University Press.

Archer, M.S. (1988) *Culture and Agency: The Place of Culture in Social Theory*. Cambridge: Cambridge University Press.

Arthur, A. (2004) 'Just Managing to Care'. Paper presented to the Work, Employment and Society Conference, Manchester, UMIST, September.

Ashforth, B.E. and R.H. Humphries (1993) 'Emotional Labour in Service Roles', *Academy of Management Review* 18 (1): 88–115.

Ashforth, B.E. and G.E. Kreiner (1999) 'How Can You Do It? Dirty Work and the Challenge of Constructing a Positive Identity', *Academy of Management Review* 24 (3): 413-34.

Atkinson, P. (1995) *Medical Talk, Medical Work: The Liturgy of the Clinic*. London: Sage.

Azaroff, L.S., M.B. Lax, C. Levenstein and D.H. Wegman (2004) 'Wounding the Messenger: The New Economy Makes Occupational Health Indicators Too Good to Be True', *International Journal of Health Services* 34 (2): 271-303.

Bahnisch, M. (2000) 'Embodied Work, Divided Labour: Subjectivity and the Scientific Management of the Body in Frederick W. Taylor's 1907 "Lecture on Management"', *Body and Society* 6 (1): 51-68.

Bakewell, J. (2005) 'Just 70', *Guardian* G2 Section, 15 April: 7.

Banta, M. (1993) *Taylored Lives: Productions in the Age of Taylor, Veblen and Ford*. Chicago: University of Chicago Press.

Barrett, M. (1991) *The Politics of Truth: From Marx to Foucault*. Cambridge: Polity Press.

Barry, K. (1995) *The Prostitution of Sexuality*. New York: New York University Press.

Barry, K. (1984) *Female Sexual Slavery*. New York: New York University Press.

Bartky, S.L. (1990) *Femininity and Domination: Studies in the Phenomenology of Oppression*. New York: Routledge.

Batchen, G. (1997) *Burning with Desire: The Conception of Photography*. Cambridge: MIT Press.

Battersby, C. (1997) *The Phenomenal Woman: Feminist Metaphysics and the Patterns of Identity*. Oxford: Polity.

Battersby, C. (1989) *Gender and Genius: Towards a Feminist Aesthetics*. London: Women's Press.

Batty, D. (2005) 'Q&A: MRSA', *Guardian* 7 June. Retrieved on 7 June 2005, from http://www.guardian.co.uk/uk_news/story/0,,1433104,00.html#article_continue

Baxter, L. and C. Hughes (2004) 'Tongue Sandwiches and Bagel Days: Sex, Food and Mind-Body Dualism', *Gender, Work and Organization* 11 (4): 363-80.

Bell, S. (1994) *Reading, Writing and Rewriting the Prostitute Body*. Bloomington: Indiana University Press.

Bell, V. (1999) *Feminist Imagination*. London: Sage.

Bell, V. (1993) *Interrogating Incest*. London: Routledge.

Bellaby, P. (1999) *Sick from Work: The Body in Employment*. Aldershot: Ashgate.

Bendelow, G. and Mayall (2000) 'How Children Manage Emotions in Schools' in S. Fineman (ed.) *Emotion in Organizations*. London: Sage.

Benjamin, B. and Wilkie, R. (1983) (eds) *Mining Photographs and Other Pictures 1948-1968*. Canada: The Press of Nova Scotia College of Art and Design and The University College of Cape Breton Press.

Benjamin, J. (1988) *The Bonds of Love: Psychoanalysis, Feminism and the Problem of Domination*. New York: Pantheon Books.

Beynon, H. (1973) *Working for Ford*. London: Allen Lane.

Beynon, H., D. Grimshaw, J. Rubery and K. Ward (2002) *Managing Employment Change: The New Realities of Work*. Oxford: Oxford University Press.

Bhavnani, R. (1994) *Black Women in the Labour Market: A Research Review*. Manchester: Equal Opportunities Commission.

Billig, M. (1999) 'Commodity Fetishism and Repression: Reflections on Marx, Freud and the Psychology of Consumer Capitalism', *Theory & Psychology* 9 (3): 313-29.

Birke, L. (2000) *Feminism and the Biological Body*. New Brunswick, NJ: Rutgers University Press.

Bishop, R. and L. Robinson (1998) *Night Market: Sexual Cultures and the Thai Economic Miracle*. New York: Routledge.

Black, P. (2004) *The Beauty Industry: Gender, Culture, Pleasure.* London: Routledge.

Black, P. (2002) '"Ordinary People Come through Here": Locating the Beauty Salon in Women's Lives', *Feminist Review* 71 (1): 2–17.

Black, P. and U. Sharma (2001) 'Men are Real, Women are "Made Up": Beauty Therapy and the Construction of Femininity', *Sociological Review* 49 (1): 100–16.

Blackburn, R.M. and M. Mann (1979) *The Working Class in the Labour Market.* London: Macmillan.

Blackmar, E. (2001) 'Modernist Ruins', *American Quarterly* 53 (2): 324–39.

Bland, L. (1992) 'Feminist Vigilantes of Late Victorian England', in C. Smart (ed.) *Regulating Womanhood: Historical Essays on Marriage, Motherhood and Sexuality.* London: Routledge.

Bolton, A., C. Pole and P. Mizen (2001) 'Picture This: Researching Child Workers', *Sociology* 35 (2): 501–18.

Bolton, S. (2005) 'Women's Work, Dirty Work: The Gynaecology Nurse as "Other"', *Gender, Work and Organization,* 12 (3): 169–86.

Bolton, S. and C. Boyd (2003) 'Trolley Dolly or Skilled Emotional Manager? Moving on from Hochschild's Managed Heart', *Work, Employment and Society* 17 (2): 289–308.

Bone, D. (2000) '"I Don't Have Time to Spend Like I Used To": Dilemmas of Emotional Work in Nursing under Managed Care', Emotional Labour 2000 Conference, South Bank University, London, July.

Bordo, S. (1993) 'Reading the Male Body', *Michigan Quarterly Review* (Special Issue edited by L. Goldstein) 32 (4): 696–734.

Bordo, S. (1990a) 'The Body and Post Modern Thought', in L. Goldstein (ed.) *The Female Body.* Ann Arbor: University of Michigan Press.

Bordo, S. (1990b) 'Reading the Slender Body', in M. Jacobus, E. Fox Keller and S. Shuttlewood (eds) *Body/Politics: Women and the Discourses of Science.* New York: Routledge.

Bordo, S. (1989) 'The Body and the Reproduction of Femininity: A Feminist Appropriation of Foucault', in A. Jaggar and S. Bordo (eds) *Gender/Body/Knowledge: Feminist Constructions of Being and Knowing.* New Brunswick: Rutgers University Press.

Boris, E. (1994) *Home to Work: Motherhood and the Politics of Industrial Homework.* Cambridge: Cambridge University Press.

Bourdieu, P. (2001) *The Male Domination.* London: Polity.

Bourdieu, P. (1990a) *The Logic of Practice.* Cambridge: Polity.

Bourdieu, P. (1990b) 'La domination masculine', *Actes de la Recherche en Sciences Sociales* 84: 2–31.

Bourdieu, P. and L.J.D. Wacquant (1992) *An Invitation to Reflexive Sociology.* Cambridge: Polity.

Boyd, C. (2002) 'Customer Violence and Employee Health and Safety', *Work, Employment and Society* 16 (1): 151–69.

Boyd, R. (1996) 'The Great Migration to the North and the Rise of Ethnic Niches for African American Women in Beauty Culture and Hairdressing, 1910–1920', *Sociological Focus* 29 (1): 33–454.

Braverman, H. (1974) *Labour and Monopoly Capital: The Degradation of Work in the Twentieth Century.* New York: Monthly Review Press.

Breman, J. and P. Shah (2004) *Working in the Mill No More.* New Delhi: Oxford University Press.

Brenner, J. and M. Ramas (1984) 'Rethinking Women's Oppression', *New Left Review* 144: 33–71.

Brewis, J. (2000) 'Foucault, Politics and Organization: Reconstructing Sexual Harassment', *Gender, Work and Organization* 8 (1): 37–60.

Brewis, J. and D. Kerfoot (1994) 'Selling Our Selves: Sexual Harassment and the Intimate Violations of the Workplace'. Paper presented to the 1994 Annual British Sociological Association Conference on Sexualities in their Social Context, University of Central Lancashire, Preston, March.

Brewis, J. and S. Linstead (2000) *Sex, Work and Sex Work.* London: Routledge.

Brook, B. (1999) *Feminist Perspectives on the Body.* London: Longman.

Brown, J. (1991) 'Beauty', in L. Goldstein (ed.) *The Female Body: Figures, Styles and Speculations.* Ann Arbor: The University of Michigan Press.

Brown, R.H. (ed.) (2003) *The Politics of Selfhood: Bodies and Identities in Global Capitalism*. Minneapolis: University of Minnesota.

Bunting, M. (2005) 'No More Dog-Eat-Dog', *Guardian*, 25 April. Retrieved on 26 April 2005, from http://money.guardian.co.uk/work/story/0,1456,1469476,00.html

Bunting, M. (2004) *Willing Slaves: How the Overwork Culture is Ruling our Lives*. London: HarperCollins.

Burawoy, M. (1979) *Manufacturing Consent: Changes in the Labor Process under Monopoly Capitalism*. Chicago: University of Chicago Press.

Burgin, V. (ed.) (1982) *Thinking Photography*. London: Macmillan.

Burkitt, I. (1999) *Bodies of Thought: Embodiment, Identity and Modernity*. London: Sage.

Burrell, G. (1992) 'The Organization of Pleasure', in M. Alvesson and H. Willmott (eds) *Critical Management Studies*. London: Sage.

Butler, J. (1993) *Bodies That Matter: On the Discursive Limits of 'Sex'*. London: Routledge.

Butler, J. (1991) 'Imitation and Gender Insubordination', in D. Fuss (ed.) *Inside/Out: Lesbian Theories, Gay Theories*. London: Routledge.

Butler, J. (1990) *Gender Trouble: Feminism and the Subversion of Identity*. London: Routledge.

Callan, A. (2005) 'Man or Machine: Ideals of the Labouring Male Body and the Aesthetics of Industrial Production in Early Twentieth Century Europe'. Paper presented to the Centre for the History of Medicine Conference on 'Corporealities: The Contested Body in 19th and 20th Century Medical Photography and Illustration', Kenilworth, 23 April.

Callinicos, A. (1989) *Against Postmodernism: A Marxist Critique*. Cambridge: Polity.

Canaan, J.E. (1999) 'In the Hand or in the Head? Contextualising the Debate about Repetitive Strain Injury', in N. Daykin and L. Doyal (eds) *Health and Work: Critical Perspectives*. Basingstoke: Palgrave Macmillan.

Cant, S. and U. Sharma (1999) *A New Medical Pluralism? Alternative Medicine, Doctors, Patients and the State*. London: UCL Press.

Carvel, J. (2005) 'MRSA Crisis Blamed on Tendering', *Guardian*, 10 January. Retrieved on 10 January 2005, from http://www.guardian.co.uk/uk_news/story/0,,1386497,00.html

Carvel, J. (2004) 'Nil by Mouth', *Guardian*, 27 August. Retrieved on 28 August 2004, from http://www.guardian.co.uk/analysis/story/0,,1291858,00.html

Casey, C. (2000) 'Sociology Sensing the Body: Revitalizing a Disassociative Discourse', in J.R. Hassard, R. Holliday and H. Willmott (eds) *Body and Organization*. London: Sage.

Casey, C. (1995) *Work, Self and Society: After Industrialism*. London: Routledge.

Cavendish, R. (1982) *Women on the Line*. London: Routledge & Kegan Paul.

Chambliss, D. (1996) *Beyond Caring: Hospitals, Nurses and the Social Organization of Ethics*. Chicago: University of Chicago Press.

Chapkis, W. (1997) *Live Sex Acts: Women Performing Erotic Labour*. London: Cassell.

Chaplin, E. (1994) *Sociology and Visual Representation*. London: Routledge.

Charlesworth, S. (2000) *A Phenomenology of Working Class Experience*. Cambridge: Cambridge University Press.

Chatterji, R.S., F. Chattoo and V. Das (1998) 'The Death of the Clinic? Normality and Pathology in Recrafting Aging Bodies', in M.Shildrick and J. Price (eds) *Vital Signs*. Edinburgh: Edinburgh University Press.

Cheng, S.J.A. (2004) 'Contextual Politics of Difference in Transnational Care: The Rhetoric of Filipina Domestics' Employers in Taiwan', *Feminist Review* 77: 46–64.

Clarke, D. and M. Neale (1998) '"Mums" and "Babes": Gendered Bodies and the Labour Process'. Paper presented at the Conference on 'Making Sense of the Body', Annual British Sociological Conference, Edinburgh, April.

Clarke, S. (1990) 'The Crisis of Fordism or the Crisis of Social Democracy', *Telos* 83: 71–98.

Clift, S. and S. Carter (eds) (2000) *Tourism and Sex: Culture, Commerce and Coercion*. London: Pinter.

Cockburn, C. (1991) *In the Way of Women*. Basingstoke: Macmillan.

Cockburn, C. (1986) 'The Materiality of Male Power', in Feminist Review (eds) *Waged Work: A Reader*. London: Virago.

Cockburn, C. (1983) *Brothers: Male Dominance and Technological Change*. London: Pluto.

Cohen, R. (2005) 'Working Time in Hairstyling: The Importance of Work Relations'. Paper presented at the International Labour Process Conference, Glasgow.

Collinson, D. (2003) 'Identities and Insecurities: Selves at Work', *Organization* 10 (3): 527–47.

Collinson, D. (1992) *Managing the Shopfloor: Subjectivity, Masculinity, and Workplace Culture*. Berlin: W. de Gruyter.

Collinson, D. and J. Hearn (1994) 'Naming Men as Men: Implications for Work, Organisation and Management', *Gender, Work and Organization* 1: 8–20.

Collinson, D.L., D. Knights and M. Collinson (1990) *Managing to Discriminate*. London: Routledge.

Connell, R.W. (2002) *Gender*. Cambridge: Polity.

Cooper, M. (2004) 'Being the "Go-to Guy": Fatherhood, Masculinity, and the Organization of Work in Silicon Valley', in M.S. Kimmel and M.A. Messner (eds) *Men's Lives* (sixth edition) Boston: Pearson.

Coover, R. (2004) 'Working with Images, Images of Work', in S. Pink, L. Kürti and A.L. Alfonso (eds) *Working Images*. London: Routledge.

Cornfield, D.B. and R. Hodson (eds) (2002) *Worlds of Work: Building an International Sociology of Work*. N.Y.: Kluwer Academic/Plenum Publishers.

Cottell, C. (2005) 'Is This the Way to Treat Nurses Who Want a Job?', *Guardian*, 5 February. Retrieved on 6 February 2005, from http://www.guardian.co.uk/guardian_jobs_and_money/story/0,,1405922,00.html

Cranny-Francis, A. (1995) *The Body in the Text*. Melbourne: Melbourne University Press.

Crick, A.P. (2004) 'Recruiting and Selecting Emotional and Aesthetic Labourers for the "Home Away from Home"'. Paper presented at the Work, Employment and Society Conference, UMIST, Manchester, September.

Crick, A.P. (2002) '"Glad to Meet You – My Best Friend": Relationships in the Hospitality Industry', *Social and Economic Studies*, 51 (1): 99–125.

Crompton, R. and F. Harris (1998) 'Gender Relations and Employment: The Impact of Occupation', *Work, Employment and* Society 12 (2): 279–316.

Crossley, N. (2001) *The Social Body: Habit, Identity and Desire*. London: Sage.

Crossley, N. (1996) *Intersubjectivity*. London: Sage.

Crossley, N. (1995) 'Body Techniques, Agency and Intercorporeality: On Goffman's *Relations in Public'*, *Sociology* 29 (1): 133–50.

Culley, L. (2001) 'Equal Opportunities Policies and Nursing Employment within the British National Health Service', *Journal of Advanced Nursing* 33 (1): 130–7.

Dale, K. and G. Burrell (2000) 'What Shape Are We In? Organizational Theory and the Organized Body' in J.R. Hassard, R. Holliday and H. Willmott (eds) *Body and Organization*. London: Sage.

Dant, T. and D. Bowles (2003) 'Dealing with Dirt: Servicing and Repairing Cars', *Sociological Review Online* 8 (2). Retrieved on 20 January 2005, from htttp://www.socresonline.org.uk/8/2/dant.html

Davidoff, L. (1988) 'Class and Gender in Victorian England' in J. Newton, M. Ryan and J. Walkowitz (eds) *Sex and Class in Women's History: Essays from Feminist Studies*. London: Routledge & Kegan Paul.

Davies, C. (2002) 'What about the Girl Next Door? Gender and the Politics of Professional Self-Regulation', in G. Bendelow, M. Carpenter, C. Vautier and S. Williams (eds) *Gender, Health and Healing: The Public/Private Divide*. London: Routledge.

Davis, M. (1993) 'The Dead West: Ecocide in Marlboro Country', *New Left Review* 1/200: 49–73.

Dawkins, H. (1987) 'The Diaries and Photographs of Hannah Cullwick', *Art History*, 10 (2): 154–87.

De Beauvoir, S. (1972) *The Second Sex*. Harmondsworth: Penguin.

Delbridge, R. (1998) *Life on the Line in Contemporary Manufacturing: The Workplace Experience of Lean Production and the 'Japanese Model'*. Oxford: Oxford University Press.

Delphy, C. (1984) *Close to Home: A Materialist Analysis of Women's Oppression*. London: Hutchinson.

Dembe, A. (1996) *Occupation and Disease: How Social Factors Effect the Conception of Work-Related Disorders*. New Haven: Yale University Press.

Dennis, N., F. Henriques and C. Slaughter (1956) *Coal is Our Life: An Analysis of a Yorkshire Mining Community*. London: Tavistock Press.

Department of Environment, Transport and the Regions (2000) *Revitalising Health and Safety - Strategic Statement*. Retrieved on 1 March 2005, from www.hse.gov.uk/revitalising/strategy/pdf

Dickenson, D. (1997) *Property, Women and Politics: Subjects or Objects*. Cambridge: Polity.

Doezema, J. (2001) 'Ouch! Western Feminists Wounded Attachment to the Third World Prostitute', *Feminist Review* 67: 16-38.

Doherty, J.L. (1981) *Women at Work: 155 Photographs by Lewis W. Hine*. New York: Dover Publications.

Douglas, M. (1966) *Purity and Danger*. London: Routledge.

Dunlop, M. (1986) 'Is a Science of Nursing Possible?', *Journal of Advanced Nursing* 11 (6): 661-70.

Durand, J.P. and N. Hatzfeld (2003) *Living Labour: Life on the Line at Peugeot France*. Basingstoke: Macmillan Palgrave.

Dyer, R. (1997) *White*. London: Routledge.

Eagleton, T. (2003) *After Theory*. London: Allen Lane.

Eagleton, T. (1993) 'It Is Not Quite True That I Have A Body, and Not Quite True That I Am One Either', *London Review of Books* 27 May: 7-8.

Ebert, T. (1996) *Ludic Feminism and After: Postmodernism, Desire and Labor in Late Capitalism*. Ann Arbor: University of Michigan Press.

Ebert, T. (1993) 'Ludic Feminism, the Body, Performance and Labor: Bringing Materialism Back into Feminist Cultural Studies', *Cultural Critique* 23: 5-50.

Edemariam, A. (2005) 'A Hard Day's Night', Parts 1 and 2, *Guardian*, 1 March. Retrieved on 1 May 2005, from http://www.guardian.co.uk/g2/story/0,,1427468,00.html

Edwards, P. (2003) 'The Employment Relationship and the Field of Industrial Relations', in P. Edwards (ed.) *Industrial Relations: Theory and Practice*. Oxford: Blackwell.

Edwards, P. and C. Wolkowitz (2002) 'The Sociology of Employment in Britain', in D.B. Cornfield and R. Hodson (eds) *Worlds of Work*. New York: Kluwer/Plenum.

Edwards, R.C., M. Reich and D.M. Gordon (1975) *Labour Market Segmentation*. Lexington: D.C. Heath.

Ehrenreich, B. (2003) 'Maid to Order' in B. Ehrenreich and A.R. Hochschild (eds) *Global Woman: Nannies, Maids and Sex Workers in the New Economy*. London: Granta.

Ehrenreich, B. (2001) *Nickel and Dimed: On (Not) Getting by in America*. New York: Henry Holt.

Ehrenreich, B. and A.R. Hochschild (eds) (2003a) *Global Woman: Nannies, Maids and Sex Workers in the New Economy*. London: Granta Books.

Ehrenreich, B. and A.R. Hochschild (2003b) 'Introduction', in B. Ehrenreich and A.R. Hochschild (eds) *Global Woman*. London: Granta Books.

Elias, N. (1978 [1939]) *The Civilising Process*. Oxford: Blackwell.

Elger, T. and C. Smith (2004) *Assembling Work: The Remaking of Work Regimes in Japanese Multinationals in Britain*. Oxford: Oxford University Press.

European Agency for Safety and Health at Work (2003) *Gender Issues in Safety and Health at Work: A Review*. Luxembourg: Office for Official Publications of the European Communities.

Evans, M. and E. Lee (eds) (2002) *Real Bodies: a Sociological Introduction*. Basingstoke: Palgrave.

Farr, J.M. and L. Ludden. (1999) *Best Jobs of the 21st Century*. Indianapolis: JIST Works.

Featherstone, M., M. Hepworth and B.S. Turner (eds) (1991) *The Body: Social Processes and Cultural Theory*. London: Sage.

Federman, M., D. Harrington and K. Krynski (2004) 'Vietnamese Manicurists: Displacing Natives or Finding New Nails to Polish'. Retreived on 4 September 2005, from http://hubcap.clemson.edu/~sauerr/seminar_papers/manicure.pdf

Ferguson, B. (2004) 'Sex Industry Streets No-Go Area for Women', *Scotsman Evening News*. 7 October. Retrieved on 20 November 2004, from http://news.scotsman.com/topics.cfm?tid+589&id+116.7842004

Fermi, R. and E. Samra (1995) *Picturing the Bomb: Photographs from the Secret World of the Manhattan Project*. New York: Harry N. Abrams Publishers.

Fineman, S. (2004) 'Getting the Measure of Emotion - and the Cautionary Tale of Emotional Intelligence', *Human Relations* 57 (6): 719–40.

Fineman, S. (2000) 'Emotional Arenas Revisited', in S. Fineman (ed.) *Emotion in Organizations*. Second edition. London: Sage.

Fineman, S. (ed.) (1993) *Emotion in Organizations*. First edition. London: Sage.

Fleming, P. and A. Spicer (2004) '"You Can Check out Anytime, but You Can Never Leave": Spatial Boundaries in a High Commitment Organization', *Human Relations* 57 (1): 75–94.

Fleming, P. and A. Spicer (2003) 'Working at a Cynical Distance', *Organization* 10 (1): 157–79.

Folbre, N. (2001) *The Invisible Heart: Economics and Family*. New York: The New Press.

Foner, N. (1994) *The Caregiving Dilemma: Work in an American Nursing Home*. Berkeley: University of California Press.

Forseth, U. (2005) 'Gender(ed) Bodies and Boundary Setting in the Airline Industry', in B. Brandth, E. Kvande and D. Morgan (eds) *Gender, Bodies and Work*. Aldershot: Ashgate.

Forseth, U. (2003) 'Individualization and "Incorporation" of Work in an Airline Carrier'. Paper presented to the Standing Conference on Organizational Symbolism, Cambridge, July.

Forseth, U. and B. Gullikstad (2005) 'Boundless Work: Discourses on Flexibility, Setting and Gender'. Paper to be presented to Women, Work and Health Conference, New Delhi, December.

Foucault, M. (1991) *Discipline and Punish: The Birth of the Prison*. London: Penguin.

Foucault, M. (1984) *The Foucault Reader,* ed P. Rabinow. London: Penguin.

Foucault, M. (1979) *The History of Sexuality, Volume 1: An Introduction*. London: Allen Lane.

Fox, N. (1999) *Beyond Health: Postmodernism and Embodiment*. London: Free Association Books.

Frank, K. (2002) 'Stripping, Starving and the Politics of Ambiguous Pleasure', in M.L. Johnson (ed.) *Jane Sexes It Up: True Confessions of Feminist Desire*. New York: Four Walls Eight Windows Press.

Fraser, L. (1993) 'Reflections on Carole Pateman's "Sexual Contract"', *Social Text* 37: 173–81.

Fraser, M. and M. Greco (2004) *The Body: A Reader*. London: Routledge.

Frenkel, S., M. Korczynski, K. Shire and M. Tan (1999) *On the Front Line: Organization of Work in the Information Society*. Ithaca: Cornell University Press.

Frith, G. (1995) 'Transforming Features: Double Vision and the Female Reader', in T. Lovell (ed.) *Feminist Cultural Studies Volume I*. London: Edward Elgar.

Frost, M. (2005) 'Designers Plunge into Upmarket Spa Scene', *Daily Express* 18 Jan.: 60.

Furman, F. (1997) *Facing the Mirror: Older Women and Beauty Shop Culture*. New York: Routledge.

Gabriel, Y. (2003) 'Organisations and their Discontents'. Paper presented to the Standing Conference on Organizational Symbolism, Cambridge, July.

Gallagher, C. (1993) *American Ground Zero: The Secret Nuclear War*. Boston: MIT Press.

Garland, D. (1990) *Punishment and Modern Society*. Oxford: Clarendon Press.

Gay, P. du (1996) *Consumption and Identity at Work*. London: Sage.

Giddens, A. (1991) *Modernity and Self-Identity*. Cambridge: Polity.

Gilligan, C. (1982) *In a Different Voice: Psychological Theory and Women's Development*. Cambridge, MA: Harvard University Press.

Gimlin, D.L. (2002) *Body Work: Beauty and Self-Image in American Culture*. Berkeley: University of California Press.

Gimlin, D.L. (1996) 'Pamela's Place: Power and Negotiation in the Hair Salon', *Gender and Society* 10 (5): 505–26.

Giobbe, E. (1993) 'Women Hurt in Systems of Prostitution Engaged in Revolt', *Trouble and Strife* 26: 22–7.

Giobbe, E. (1990) 'Confronting the Liberal Lies about Prostitution', in D. Leidholdt and J. Raymond (eds) *The Sexual Liberals and the Attack on Feminism*. Oxford: Pergamon.

Glassner, B. (1995) 'In the Name of Health', in R. Bunton, S. Nettleton and R. Burrows (eds) *The Sociology of Health Promotion: Critical Analyses of Consumption, Lifestyle and Risk*. London: Routledge.

Glenn, E.N. (1996) 'From Servitude to Service Work: Historical Divisions in the Racial Division of Paid Reproductive Labor', in C.L. Macdonald and C. Sirianni (eds) *Working in the Service Sector*. Philadelphia: Temple University Press.

Glucksmann, M. (2006) 'Shifting Boundaries and the Interconnections: Extending the "Total Social Organisation of Labour"' in L. Pettinger, J. Parry, R. Taylor and M. Glucksmann (eds) *A New Sociology of Work?* Oxford: Blackwell.

Glucksmann, M. (1995) 'Why Work? Gender and the Total Social Organisation of Labour', *Gender, Work and Organization* 2 (2): 63–75.

Glucksmann, M. (1990) *Women Assemble: Women Workers and the New Industries in Inter-War Britain*. London: Routledge.

Goffman, E. (1972) *Relations in Public: Microstudies of the Public Order*. Harmondsworth: Penguin.

Goffman, E. (1969) *The Presentation of Self in Everyday Life*. Harmondsworth: Penguin.

Goffman, E. (1963) *Stigma: Notes on the Management of Spoiled Identity*. New York: Prentice Hall.

Goldthorpe, J.H. (1982) 'On the Service Class, its Formation and Future', in A. Giddens and G. Mackenzie (eds) *Social Class and the Division of Labour*. Cambridge: Cambridge University Press.

Gottfried, H. (2003) 'Temp(t)ing Bodies: Shaping Gender at Work in Japan', *Sociology* 37 (2): 257–76.

Greed, C. (2000) 'Women in the Construction Professions: Achieving Critical Mass', *Gender, Work and Organisation* 7 (3): 181–96.

Gregson, N. and M. Lowe (1994) *Servicing the Middle Classes*. London: Routledge.

Grimshaw, D. (1999) 'Changes in Skill-Mix and Pay Determination', *Work, Employment & Society* 12 (2): 295–328.

Grint, K. (1991) *The Sociology of Work: An Introduction*. Cambridge: Polity.

Grosz, E. (1994) *Volatile Bodies: Toward a Corporeal Feminism*. Bloomington: University of Indiana Press.

Grosz, E. (1989) *Sexual Subversions: Three French Feminists*. Sydney: Allen & Unwin.

Guardian (2005) 'Friday Television', *Guardian* G2 Section, 15 April: 20.

Gubrium, J.F. (1975) *Living and Dying at Murray Manor*. N.Y.: St. Martin's Press.

Guerrier, Y. and A. Adib (2000) '"No, We Don't Provide That Service": The Harassment of Hotel Employees by Customers', *Work, Employment and Society* 14 (4): 689–705.

Ha, T. (2002) 'Immigrant Business Development: A Study of the Vietnamese Manicure Business', Southern Sociological Society, unpublished paper.

Haaken, J. (1996) 'The Recovery of Memory, Fantasy and Desire: Feminist Approaches to Sexual Abuse and Psychic Trauma', *Signs* 21 (4): 1069–94.

Hacker, B.C. (1992) *The Dragon's Tail: Radiation Safety in the Manhattan Project, 1942–1946*. California: University of California Press.

Hakim, C. (1996) *Key Issues in Women's Work*. London: Athlone Press.

Hales, P.B. (1997) *Atomic Spaces: Living on the Manhattan Project*. Urbana: University of Illinois Press.

Halford, S., M. Savage and A. Witz (1997) *Gender, Careers and Organisations: Current Developments in Banking, Nursing and Local Government*. Basingstoke: Macmillan.

Hancock, P., B. Hughes, E. Jagger, K. Paterson, R. Russell, E. Tulle-Winton and M. Tyler (eds) (2000) *The Body, Culture and Society: An Introduction*. Buckingham: Open University Press.

Hancock, P. and M. Tyler (2000a) 'Working Bodies', in P. Hancock, B. Hughes, E. Jagger, K. Paterson, R. Russell, E. Tulle-Winton and M. Tyler (2000) *The Body, Culture and Society: An Introduction*. Buckingham: Open University Press.

Hancock, P. and M. Tyler (2000b) '"The Look of Love": Gender and the Organisation of Aesthetics', in J.R. Hassard, R. Holliday and H. Willmott (eds) *Body and Organization*. London: Sage.

Hankins, J. (2005) 'In It for the Money', *Guardian* Weekend, 7 May: 2.

Haraway, D. (1991) *Simians, Cyborgs and Women: The Re-invention of Nature*. London: Free Association Books.

Harper, D. (2003) 'An Argument for Visual Sociology', in J. Prosser (ed.) *Image-Based Research*. London: Routledge.

Harper, D. (1987) *Working Knowledge*. Chicago: University of Chicago Press.

Harrington, M., A. Bookman, L. Bailyn and T. Kochan (2001) *Workforce Issues in the Greater Boston Health Care Industry: Implications for Work and Family*. Boston: MIT Sloan Working Paper 4472-01 and MIT Workplace Center Working Paper 0001. Retrieved on 18 December 2004, from http://ssm.com/abstract=511244

Harrison, B. (1996) *Not Only the Dangerous Trades: Women, Work and Health in Britain, 1880–1914*. London: Taylor & Francis.

Harrison, B. (1989) '"Some of Them Gets Lead Poisoned": Occupational Lead Exposure in Women, 1880–1914', *Journal for the Social History of Medicine* 2 (2): 171-95.

Hart, L. (1991) '"A Ward of My Own": Social Organization and Identity among Hospital Domestics', in P. Holden and J. Littlewood (eds) *Anthropology and Nursing*. London: Routledge.

Hartmann, H. (1979) 'The Unhappy Marriage of Marxism and Feminism: Toward a More Progressive Union', *Capitalism and Class* 8: 1-33.

Harvey, D. (1998) 'The Body as an Accumulation Strategy', *Environment and Planning D: Society and Space* 16: 401-21.

Harvey, D. (1990) *The Condition of Postmodernity: An Enquiry into the Origins of Social Change*. Oxford: Basil Blackwell.

Harvey, D. and D. Haraway (1995) 'Nature, Politics and Possibilities: A Debate and Discussion with David Harvey and Donna Haraway', *Environment and Planning D: Society and Space* 13: 507-27.

Hassard, J.R., R. Holliday and H. Willmott (eds) (2000) *Body and Organization*. London: Sage.

Hau, W.W. (2004) 'Caring Holistically within New Managerialism', *Nursing Inquiry* 11 (1): 2-13.

Health and Safety Commission (2004) *A Strategy for Workplace Health and Safety in Great Britain to 2010 and Beyond*. London: Health and Safety Commission.

Health and Safety Executive (2004) *Occupational Health Statistics Bulletin 2003/4*. Retrieved on 1 March 2005, from www.hse.gov.uk/statistics/overall/ohsb0304.pdf

Health and Safety Executive (c. 2001) *Statistics of Workplace Fatalities and Injuries in Great Britain: International Comparisons 2000*. Retrieved on 1 March 2005, from www.hse.gov.uk/statistics/pdf/eurocomp.pdf

Health & Safety Practitioner (1997) 'Help for Nursing Home Owners', 15 (7): 8.

Hearn, J. and W. Parkin (1995) *Sex at Work: The Power and Paradox of Organisation Sexuality*. Hemel Hempstead: Harvester Wheatsheaf/Prentice Hall.

Herzenberg, S.A., J.A. Alic and H. Wial (1998) *New Rules for a New Economy: Employment and Opportunity in Postindustrial America*. Ithaca: ILR Press.

Hester, M. and N. Westmarland (2004) *Tackling Street Prostitution: Towards an Holistic Approach*. London: Home Office.

Hiley, M. (1979) *Victorian Working Women: Portraits from Life*. London: Gordon Fraser.

Hill, Stephen (1976) *The Dockers: Class and Tradition in London*. London: Heinemann.

Hine, L.W. (1977) [1932] *Men at Work: Photographic Studies of Modern Men and Machines*. New York: Dover Publications.

Hochschild, A.R. (2003b) 'Love and Gold', in B. Ehrenreich and A.R. Hochschild (eds) *Global Woman: Nannies, Maids and Sex Workers in the New Economy*. London: Granta Books.

Hochschild, A.R. (2003b) *The Commercialization of Intimate Life: Notes from Home and Work*. Berkeley: University of California Press.

Hochschild, A.R. (2001) 'Global Care Chains and Emotional Surplus Value', in W. Hutton and A. Giddens (eds) *On the Edge: Living with Global Capitalism*. London: Random House Vintage.

Hochschild, A.R. (1997) *The Time Bind: When Work Becomes Home and Home Becomes Work*. New York: Henry Holt and Company/Metropolitan Books.

Hochschild, A.R. (1989) *The Second Shift*. New York: Avon Books.

Hochschild, A.R. (1983) *The Managed Heart: Commercialization of Human Feeling*. Berkeley: University of California Press.

Hoigard, C. and L. Finstad (1992) *Backstreets: Prostitution, Money and Love*. University Park: The Pennsylvania State University Press.

Holliday, R. and J. Hassard (2001) (eds) *Contested Bodies*. London: Routledge.

Holliday, R. and G. Thompson (2001) 'A Body of Work', in R. Holliday and J. Hassard (eds) *Contested Bodies*. London: Routledge.

Hollowell, P.G. (1968) *The Lorry Driver*. London: Routledge & Kegan Paul.

Holsopple, K. (nd) *Strip Club Testimony*, Minneapolis, MN: The Freedom and Justice Centre for Prostitution Resources. Retrieved on 10 January 2004, from http://www.ccv.org/images/strip_club_testimony_and_study.pdf

Home Office (2004) *Paying the Price: A Consultation Paper on Prostitution*. London: Home Office.

Howson, A. (2004) *The Body in Society*. Cambridge: Polity.

Hubbard, P. (1998) 'Sexuality, Immorality and the City: Red-Light Districts and the Marginalisation of Street Prostitutes', *Gender, Place and Culture* 5 (1): 55–76.

Hudson, D. (1972) *Munby: A Man of Two Worlds*. London: Gambit.

Hughes, C. (2002) *Key Concepts in Feminist Theory and Research*. London: Sage.

Hughes, E.C. (1984) *The Sociological Eye*. New Brunswick, Transaction Books.

Hunter, B. (2004) 'Conflicting Ideologies as a Source of Emotion Work in Midwifery', *Midwifery* 20 (3): 261–72.

Hyde, A. (1997) *Bodies of Law*. Princeton: Princeton University Press.

Irigaray, L. (1991) *The Irigaray Reader*, ed. M. Whitford. Oxford: Blackwell.

Jaggar, A. and S. Bordo (eds) (1989) *Gender/Body/Knowledge: Feminist Reconstructions of Being and Knowing*. New Brunswick: Rutgers University Press.

James, N. (1992) 'Care = Organisation + Physical Labour + Emotional Labour', *Sociology and Health and Illness* 14 (4): 488–509.

Jeffreys, S. (2003) 'Sex Tourism: Do Women Do It Too?', *Leisure Studies* 22 (3): 223–38.

Jeffreys, S. (1997) *The Idea of Prostitution*. North Melbourne: Spiniflex.

Jervis, L.L. (2001) 'The Pollution of Incontinence and the Dirty Work of Caregiving in a US Nursing Home', *Medical Anthropology Quarterly* 15 (1): 84–99.

Jewson, N. (1976) 'The Disappearance of the Sick-Man from Medical Cosmology, 1770–1870', *Sociology* 10 (2): 225–44.

Jones, P., P. Shears and D. Hillier (2003) 'Retailing and the Regulatory State: a Case Study of Lap Dancing Clubs in the UK', *International Journal of Retail and Distribution Management* 31 (4): 214–19.

Jordan, S. (2001) 'From Grotesque Bodies to Useful Hands: Idleness, Industry and the Laboring Class', *Eighteenth Century Life* 25: 62–79.

Kahn, R. (1989) 'Women and Time in Childbirth and During Lactation', in F.J. Forman with C. Sowton (eds) *Taking Our Time: Feminist Perspectives on Temporality*. Oxford: Pergamon.

Kang, M. (2003) 'The Managed Hand: The Commercialization of Bodies and Emotions in Korean Immigrant-owned Nail Salons', *Gender and Society* 17 (6): 820–39.

Kantola, J. and J. Squires (2004a) 'Prostitution Policies in Britain' in J. Outshoorn (ed.) *The Politics of Prostitution*. Cambridge: Cambridge University Press.

Kantola, J. and J. Squires (2004b) 'Discourses Surrounding Prostitution Policies in the UK', *European Journal of Women's Studies* 11 (1): 77–101.

Kelly, L. (2003) 'The Wrong Debate: Reflections on Why Force Is Not the Key Issue with Respect to Trafficking in Women for Sexual Exploitation', *Feminist Review* 73 (1): 139–44.

Kelly, L. and L. Regan (2000) 'Stopping Traffic: Exploring the Extent of and Responses to Trafficking in Women for Sexual Exploitation in the UK', Home Office: Police Research Series Paper 125.

Kempadoo, K. (ed.) (1999) *Sun, Sex and Gold: Tourism and Sex Work in the Caribbean*. Lanham, MD: Rowman & Littlefield.

Kempadoo, K. and J. Doezema (eds) (1998) *Global Sex Workers*. New York: Routledge.

Kerfoot, D. (2000) 'Body Work: Estrangement, Disembodiment and the Organizational Other', in J.R. Hassard, R. Holliday and H. Willmott (eds) *Body and Organization*. London: Sage.

Kingma, M. (2001) 'Nursing Migration: Global Treasure Hunt or Disaster-in-the-Making?', *Nursing Inquiry* 8 (4): 205–21.

Kofman, E. and P. Raghuram (forthcoming) 'Gender and Global Labour Migration: Incorporating the Skilled', *Antipodes*.

Korczynski, M. (2003) 'Communities of Coping: Collective Emotional Labour in Service Work', *Organization* 10 (1): 55–79.

Korczynski, M. (2002) *Human Resource Management in the Service Sector*. Basingstoke: Palgrave.

Kristeva, J. (1989) 'Women's Time', in C. Belsey and J. Moore (eds) *The Feminist Reader*. London: Macmillan.

Kuhn, A. (1985) *The Power of the Image*. London: Routledge & Kegan Paul.

Kunda, G. (1992) *Engineering Culture: Control and Commitment in a High-Tech Corporation*. Philadelphia: Temple University Press.

Lalvani, S. (1996) *Photography, Vision and the Production of Modern Bodies*. Albany: State University of New York Press.

Lan, P.C. (2003) 'Among Women: Migrant Domestics and their Taiwanese Employers', in B. Ehrenreich and A.R. Hochschild (eds) (2003) *Global Woman: Nannies, Maids and Sex Workers in the New Economy*. London: Granta Books.

Lash, S, and J. Urry (1994) *Economies of Signs and Spaces*. London: Sage.

Lawler, J. (ed.) (1997) *The Body in Nursing*. Melbourne: Churchill Livingstone.

Lawler, J. (1991) *Behind the Screens: Nursing, Somology and the Problem of the Body*. Melbourne: Churchill Livingstone.

Lawrence, F. (2005) 'The Precarious Existence of the Thousands in Britain's Underclass', *Guardian*, 10 January 2005. Retrieved on 28 February 2005, from http://www.guardian.co.uk/uk_news/story/0,,1386616,00.html

Lawton, J. (1998) 'Contemporary Hospice Care', *Sociology of Health and Illness* 2 (2): 121–43.

Leask, H. (2000) 'The Employment of Women in the British Meat Industry'. University of Warwick, unpublished PhD thesis.

Leder, D. (1990) *The Absent Body*. Chicago: University of Chicago Press.

Lee-Trewick, G. (1997) 'Women, Resistance and Care: An Ethnographic Study of Nursing Work', *Work, Employment & Society* 11 (1): 47–64.

Lee-Trewick, G. (1996) 'Emotion Work, Order and Emotional Power in Care Assistant Work', in V. James and J. Gabe (eds) *Health and the Sociology of Emotions*. Oxford: Blackwell.

Leslie, D. (2002) 'Gender, Retail Employment and the Clothing Commodity Chain', *Gender, Place and Culture* 9 (1): 61–76.

Levine, P. (1994) 'Venereal Disease, Prostitution and the Politics of Empire: The Case of British India', *Journal of the History of Sexuality* 4 (4): 579–602.

Liddle, J. and E. Michielsens (2000) 'Gender, Class and Political Power in Britain: Narratives of Entitlement', in S. Rai (ed.) *International Perspectives on Gender and Democratisation*. London: Macmillan.

Liepe-Levinson, K. (2002) *Strip Show: Performances of Gender and Desire*. London: Routledge.

Linstead, A. and J. Brewis (2004) 'Beyond Boundaries: Towards Fluidity in Theory and Practice', *Gender, Work and Organization* 11 (4): 355–62.

Lipietz, A. (1987) *Mirages and Miracles: The Crises of Global Fordism*. London: Verso.

Littlewood, J. (1991) 'Care and Ambiguity: Towards a Concept of Nursing', in P. Holden and J. Littlewood (eds) *Anthropology and Nursing*. London: Routledge.

Longhurst, R. (2001) *Bodies: Exploring Fluid Boundaries*. London: Routledge.

Lovell, T. (2004) 'Bourdieu, Class and Gender: The Return of the Living Dead', in L. Adkins and B. Skeggs (eds) *Feminism after Bourdieu*. Oxford: Blackwell.

Lovell, T. (2000) 'Thinking Feminism with and against Bourdieu', *Feminist Theory* 1 (1): 11–32.

Lowe, D.M. (1995) *The Body in Late-Capitalist USA*. Durham, NC: Duke University Press.

Lupton, D. (1996) 'Your Life in Their Hands', in V. James and J. Gabe (eds) *Health and the Sociology of Emotions*. Oxford: Blackwell.

Lutz, C.A. and J.L. Collins (1993) *Reading National Geographic*. Chicago: University of Chicago Press.

McCall, L. (2001) *Complex Inequality: Gender, Class, and Race in the New Economy*. London: Routledge.

McClintock, A. (1995) *Imperial Leather: Race, Gender and Sexuality in the Colonial Context*. London: Routledge.

McClintock, A. (1992) 'Screwing the System: Sexwork, Race and the Law', *Boundary 2* 19 (2): 70–95.

Macdonald, C.L. (1996) 'Shadow Mothers: Nannies, *Au Pairs* and Invisible Work' in C.L. Macdonald and C. Sirianni (eds) *Working in the Service Sector*. Philadelphia: Temple University Press.

Macdonald, C.L. and C. Sirianni (eds) (1996) *Working in the Service Sector*. Philadelphia: Temple University Press.

McDowell, L. (2002) 'Transitions to Work: Masculine Identities, Youth Inequalities and Labour Market Change', *Gender, Place and Culture* 9 (1): 39–59.

McDowell, L. (1997) *Capital Culture: Gender at Work in the City*. Oxford: Blackwell.

McDowell, L and G. Court (1994a) 'Missing Subjects: Gender, Power and Sexuality in Merchant Banking', *Economic Geography* 70 (3): 229–51.

McDowell, L. and G. Court (1994b) 'Performing Work: Bodily Representations in Merchant Banks', *Environment and Planning D: Society and Space* 12: 727–50.

McKeganey, N. and M. Barnard (1996) *Sex Work on the Streets: Prostitutes and their Clients*. Buckingham: Open University Press.

MacKinnon, C. (1994) *Only Words*. London: HarperCollins.

MacKinnon, C. (1987) *Feminism Unmodified: Discourses on Life and Law*. Cambridge, MA: Harvard University Press.

McNair, B. (2002) *Striptease Culture: Sex, Media and the Democratisation of Desire*. London: Routledge.

McNair, B. (1996) *Mediated Sex: Pornography and Postmodern Culture*. London: Arnold.

McNay, L. (2004) 'Agency and Experience: Gender as a Lived Relation', in L. Adkins and B. Skeggs (eds) *Feminism after Bourdieu*. Oxford: Blackwell.

McNay, L. (1999) 'Gender, Habitus and the Field: Pierre Bourdieu and the Limits of Reflexivity', *Theory, Culture and Society* 16 (1): 175–93.

McNay, L. (1992) *Foucault and Feminism: Power, Gender and the Self*. Cambridge: Polity.

McRobbie, A. (2004) 'Notes on *What Not to Wear* and Post-feminist Symbolic Violence', in L. Adkins and B. Skeggs (eds) *Feminism after Bourdieu*, Oxford: Blackwell.

McRobbie, A. (1997) 'A New Kind of Rag Trade?', in A. Ross (ed.) *No Sweat: Fashion, Free Trade, and the Rights of Garment Workers*. New York: Verso.

Madjar, I. (1997) 'The Body in Health, Illness and Pain', in J. Lawler (ed.) *The Body in Nursing*. Melbourne: Churchill Livingstone.

Marchington, M., D. Grimshaw, J. Rubery and H. Willmott (eds) (2005) *Fragmenting Work: Blurring Organizational Boundaries and Disordering Hierarchies*. Oxford: Oxford University Press.

Martin, E. (1996) 'The Body at Work: Boundaries and Collectivities in the Late Twentieth Century', in T. Schatzki and W. Natter (eds) *The Social and Political Body*. London: Guilford Press.

Martin, E. (c. 1994) *Flexible Bodies: Tracking Immunity in American Culture from the Days of Polio to the Age of AIDS*. Boston: Beacon Press.

Massey, D. (1996) 'Masculinity, Dualisms and High Technology', in N. Duncan (ed.) *Body Space: Destabilizing Geographies of Gender and Sexuality*. London: Routledge.

Mauss, M. (1973) 'Techniques of the Body', *Economy and Society* 2: 70–88.

Mavor, C. (1996) *Pleasures Taken: Performances of Sexuality and Loss in Victorian Photographs*. London: I.B. Tauris.

Meerabeau, L. and S. Page (1997) 'Getting the Job Done: Emotion Management and Cardiopulmonary Resuscitation in Nursing', in G. Bendelow and S. Williams (eds) *Emotions in Social Life*. London: Routledge.

Melosh, B. (1993) 'Manly Work: Public Art and Masculinity in Depression America', in B. Melosh (ed.) *Gender and American History since 1890*. London: Routledge.

Menzies-Lyth, I. (1988) *Containing Anxiety in Institutions: Selected Essays*. London: Free Association Press.

Merleau-Ponty, M. (1962) *The Phenomenology of Perception*. London: Routledge & Kegan Paul.

Merrell, F. (2003) *Sensing Corporeally: Toward a Posthuman Understanding*. Toronto: University of Toronto Press.

Messing, K. (1998a) 'Hospital Trash: Cleaners Speak of Their Role in Disease Prevention', *Medical Anthropology Quarterly* 12 (2): 168–87.

Messing, K. (1998b) *One-Eyed Science: Occupational Health and Women Workers*. Philadelphia: Temple University Press.

Messing, K., L. Dumais and P. Romito (1993) 'Prostitutes and Chimney Sweeps Both Have Problems', *Social Science and Medicine* 36 (1): 47–55.

Messing, K, L. Punnett, M. Bond, K. Alexanderson, J. Pyle, S. Zahm, D. Wegman, S.R. Stock and S. de Grosbois (2003) 'Be the Fairest of Them All: Challenges and Recommendations for the Treatment of Gender in Occupational Health Research', *American Journal of Industrial Medicine* 43 (6): 618–29.

Millett, K. (1971) *The Prostitution Papers*. New York: Palladin.

Mintel (2005) 'Spa Holidays'. Accessed on 9 February 2005, from http://www.mintel.com

Mintel (1999a) 'Report on the Market in Health and Beauty Treatments'. Accessed on 23 March 1999, from http://www.mintel.com

Mintel (1999b) 'Hairdressing Salons and Barber Shops'. Accessed on 24 June 1999, from http://www.mintel.com

Mintel (1998) 'Facial Skincare'. Accessed on 22 July 1998, from http://www.mintel.com

Moi, T. (1999) *What Is a Woman and Other Essays*. Oxford: Oxford University Press.

Monaghan, L. (2002a) 'Hard Men, Shop Boys and Others: Embodying Competence in a Masculinised Occupation', *Sociological Review* 50 (3): 334–55.

Monaghan, L. (2002b) 'Regulating "Unruly" Bodies: Work Tasks, Conflict and Violence in Britain's Night-Time Economy', *British Journal of Sociology* 53 (3): 403–29.

Montgomery, H. (1998) 'Children, Prostitution and Identity: A Case Study from a Tourist Resort in Thailand', in K. Kempadoo and J. Doezema (eds) (1998) *Global Sex Workers*. New York: Routledge.

Morgan, D. (1992) *Discovering Men*. London: Routledge.

Morgan, D. and B. Brandth (eds) (2005) *Gender, Bodies, Work*. Avebury: Ashgate.

Mort, F. (1996) *Cultures of Consumption: Masculinities and Social Space in Late Twentieth Century Britain*. London: Routledge.

Mort, F. (1987) *Dangerous Sexualities: Medico and Moral Politics in England since 1830*. London: Routledge & Kegan Paul.

Moss, S. (2005) 'Are You on the Guest List?', *Guardian* G2 Section, 15 April: 3.

Mulvey, L. (1975) 'Visual Pleasures and Narrative Cinema', in L. Mulvey, *Visual and Other Pleasures*. London: Macmillan.

Munro, A. (2001) 'A Feminist Trade Union Agenda? The Continued Significance of Class, Race and Gender', *Gender, Work and Organisation* 8 (4): 454–71.

Munro, A. (1999) *Women, Work and Trade Unions*. London: Mansell.

Murcott, A. (2002) 'Shouldering the Burden: The Case of Funeral Directing', in G. Bendelow, M. Carpenter, C. Vautier and S. Williams (eds) *Gender, Health and Healing: The Public/Private Divide*. London: Routledge.

Nagel, J. (2003) *Race, Ethnicity and Sexuality: Intimate Intersections, Forbidden Frontiers*. New York: Oxford University Press.

Natanson, N. (1992) *The Black Image in the New Deal: The Politics of FSA Photography*. Knoxville: University of Tennessee Press.

Nead, L. (1988) *Myths of Sexuality*. Oxford: Blackwell.

Neuberger, J. (2005) 'None of these Patients Should Be Getting a Dirty Bed', *Independent on Sunday*, 24 April: 15.

Newton, T. (2003) 'Truly Embodied Sociology: Marrying the Social and the Biological? The Sociological Review 51 (1): 20–42.

Newton, T. (1999) 'Power, Subjectivity and British Industrial and Organisational Society: The Relevance of the Work of Norbert Elias', *Sociology* 33 (2): 411–40.

Nichols, T. (1997) *The Sociology of Industrial Injury*. London: Mansell.

Nichols, T. and H. Beynon (1977) *Living with Capitalism: Class Relations and the Modern Factory*. London: Routledge & Kegan Paul.

Nickson, D. and C. Warhurst (2003) 'Workwear: Clothing within Corporations, Corporate Clothing, Employees and Company Image'. Paper presented to the 21st Standing Conference on Organizational Symbolism, University of Cambridge, July.

Nickson, D., C. Warhurst, A.M. Cullen and A. Watt (2002) 'Bringing in the Excluded: Aesthetic Labour, Skills and Training in the New Economy', Strathclyde, 20th Annual International Labour Process Conference.

Nickson, D., C. Warhurst, A. Witz and A.M. Cullen (2001) 'The Importance of Being Aesthetic: Work, Employment and Service Organisation', in A. Sturdy, I. Grugulis and H. Willmott (eds) *Customer Service: Empowerment and Entrapment*. London: Palgrave.

Nixon, S. (1996) *Hard Looks: Masculinities, Spectatorship and Contemporary Consumption*. London: UCL Press.

Nolan, P. (2004) 'The Changing World of Work', *Journal of Health Services Research and Policy*, 9 (Supplement to Issue 1): 3–9.

O'Connell Davidson, J. (2002) 'The Rights and Wrongs of Prostitution', *Hypatia* 17 (2): 84–98.

O'Connell Davidson, J. (1998) *Prostitution, Power and Freedom*. Cambridge: Polity.

O'Connell Davidson, J. (1997) 'Does She Do Queening? Prostitution, Sovereignty and Community', in L. Brace and J. Hoffman (eds) *Reclaiming Sovereignty*. London: Pinter.

O'Connell Davidson, J. (1995a) 'The Anatomy of Free Choice Prostitution', *Gender, Work and Organization* 2 (1): 1–10.

O'Connell Davidson, J. (1995b) 'British Sex Tourists in Thailand', in M. Maynard and J. Purvis (eds) *(Hetero)sexual Politics*. London: Taylor & Francis.

O'Connell Davidson, J. and J. Sanchez-Taylor (1999) 'Fantasy Islands: Exploring the Demand for Sex Tourism', in K. Kempadoo (ed.) *Sun, Sex and Gold: Tourism and Sex Work in the Caribbean*. Lanham, MD: Rowman & Littlefield.

Oerton, S. (2004) 'Bodywork Boundaries: Power, Politics and the Professionalism in Therapeutic Massage', *Gender, Work and Organizaion* 11 (5): 544-65.

Oerton, S. (1998) 'Life May Take It Out of You, But Touch Can Put It Back'. Paper presented to the British Sociological Association Annual Conference, Edinburgh, April.

Oerton, S. and J. Phoenix (2001) 'Sex/Bodywork: Discourses and Practices', *Sexualities* 4 (4): 387-412.

Ogasawara, Y. (1998) *Office Ladies and Salaried Men: Power, Gender and Work in Japanese Companies.* Berkeley: University of California Press.

O'Hagan, S. (2002) 'Focus: Meet Jo Vickers and Family' *Independent,* 24 November. Retreived on 4 September 2005, from the *Independent* archive on http://www.independent.co.uk

O'Kane, M. (2002) 'Mean Streets', *Guardian,* 16 September. Retrieved on 4 April 2004, from http://www.guardian.co.uk/g2/story/0,,792761,00.html

O'Neil, J. (1985) *Five Bodies: The Human Shape of Modern Society.* London: Cornell University Press.

O'Neill, M. (2001) *Prostitution and Feminism: Towards a Politics of Feeling.* Cambridge: Polity.

Outshoorn, J. (ed.) (2004) *The Politics of Prostitution: Women's Movements, Democratic States and the Globalisation of Sex Commerce.* Cambridge: Cambridge University Press.

Outshoorn, J. (2001) 'Debating Prostitution in Parliament: A Feminist Analysis', *European Journal of Women's Studies* 8 (4): 473-91.

Pace, P. (2002) 'Staging Childhood: Lewis Hine's Photographs of Child Labor', *The Lion and the Unicorn* 26: 324-52.

Pai, H.H. (2004a) 'The Gunpowder Plot', *Guardian,* 3 November. Retrieved 4 November 2004, from http://society.guardian.co.uk/societyguardian/story/0,,1341600,00.html

Pai, H.H. (2004b) 'The Invisibles: Migrant Cleaners at Canary Wharf', *Feminist Review* 78: 164-74.

Pandya, N. (2005) 'Sour Note for Whistleblowers: Unions Voice Concerns at Number of Workers Fired for Raising Safety Concerns', *Guardian,* 19 February. Retrieved on 28 February 2005, from http://www.guardian.co.uk/guardian_jobs_and_money/story/0,,1417505,00.html

Parker, J. (1997) 'The Body as Text and the Body as Living Flesh', in J. Lawler (ed.) *The Body in Nursing.* Melbourne: Churchill Livingstone.

Parreñas, R.S. (2001) *Servants of Globalization: Women, Migration and Domestic Work.* Stanford: Stanford University Press.

Pasko, L. (2002) 'Naked Power: The Practice of Stripping as a Confidence Game', *Sexualities* 5 (1): 49-66.

Pateman, C. (1988) *The Sexual Contract.* Cambridge: Polity.

Paule, G. (1996) 'Resisting the Symbolism of Service Among Waitresses' in C.L. Macdonald and C. Sirianni (eds) *Working in the Service Sector.* Philadelphia: Temple University Press.

Peck, J. (2004) 'Neo-liberalisms at work'. Paper presented at the Work, Employment and Society Conference, Manchester, UMIST, September.

Peck, J. (1996) *Work-Place: The Social Regulation of Labor Markets.* New York: The Guildford Press.

Peiss, K. (1998) *Hope in a Jar: The Making of America's Beauty Culture.* New York: Henry Holt.

Perrons, D. (2003) 'The New Economy, Labour Market Inequalities and the Work Life Balance' in R. Martin and P.S. Morrison (eds) *Geographies of Labour Market Inequality.* London: Routledge.

Pettinger, L. (2004) 'Brand Culture and Branded Workers: Service Work and Aesthetic Labour in Fashion Retail', *Consumption, Markets and Culture* 7 (2): 165-84.

Pettinger, L., J. Parry, R. Taylor and M. Glucksmann (eds) (2006) *A New Sociology of Work*? Oxford: Blackwell.

Pheterson, G. (c.1996) *The Prostitution Prism.* Amsterdam: University of Amsterdam Press.

Phillips, A. and B. Taylor (1986) 'Sex and Skill', in Feminist Review (eds) *Waged Work: A Reader.* London: Virago.

Phizacklea, A. (2005) 'Unfree Labour in the Twenty-first Century'. Paper presented at the Centre for the Study of Women and Gender, University of Warwick, March.

Phizacklea, A. (1996) 'Women, Migration and the State', in S. Rai and G. Lievesley (eds) *Women and the State: International Perspectives.* London: Taylor & Francis.

Phoenix, J. (1999) *Making Sense of Prostitution*. Basingstoke: Macmillan.

Pierce, J. (1996) 'Reproducing Gender Relations in Large Law Firms: The Role of Emotional Labour in Paralegal Work', in C.L. Macdonald and C. Sirianni (eds) *Working in the Service Sector*. Philadelphia: Temple University Press.

Pitts, V. (2003) *In the Flesh: The Cultural Politics of Body Modification*. New York: Palgrave Macmillan.

Pollert, A. (ed.) (1991) *Farewell to Flexibility?* Oxford: Basil Blackwell.

Pollert, A. (1981) *Girls, Wives and Factory Lives*. London: Macmillan.

Pollock, G. (1993) 'The Dangers of Proximity: The Spaces of Sexuality and Surveillance in Word and Image', *Discourse* 16 (2): 3–50.

Prasad, A. and P.K. Prasad (2003) 'Eat Like a Man: Strength, Virility and Muscular Nationalism in the Discourse of the Anglo-American Beef Industry'. Paper presented to the Standing Conference on Organizational Symbolism, Cambridge, July.

Pratt, G. (1998) 'Inscribing Domestic Work on Fillipina Bodies', in H. Nash and S. Pile (eds) *Places through the Body*. London: Routledge.

Price, J. and M. Shildrick (eds) (1999) *Feminist Theory and the Body: A Reader*. Edinburgh: Edinburgh University Press.

Pringle, R. (1989) *Secretaries Talk: Sexuality, Power and Work*. London: Verso.

Purser, G., A. Schalet and O. Sharone (2004) *Berkeley's Betrayal: Wages and Working Conditions at Cal*. 2nd edition. Berkeley, CA: University Labor Research Project. Retrieved on 1 March 2005, from http://www.berkeleybetrayal.org

Puwar, N. (2001) 'The Radicalised Somatic Norm and the Senior Civil Service', *Sociology* 35 (3): 651–70.

Puwar, N. and H. Crowley (2004) 'Introduction to the Special Issue on Labour Migrations', *Feminist Review* 77: 1–3.

Quinlan, M. (1999) 'The Implications of Labour Market Restructuring in Industrial Societies for Occupational Health and Safety', *Economic and Industrial Democracy* 20 (3): 427–60.

Quinlan, M. (1997) 'The Toll from Work Does Matter: Occupational Health and Labour History', *Labour History* 73: 1–29.

Quinlan, M. (ed.) (1993) *Work and Health: The Origins, Management and Regulation of Occupational Illness*. Melbourne: Macmillan.

Quinlan, M., C. Mayhew and P. Bohle (2001) 'The Global Expansion of Precarious Employment, Work Disorganization, and the Consequences for Occupational Health', *International Journal of Health Services* 31 (2): 335–414.

Reinarz, J. (2003) 'Uncommon Scents: Smell and Victorian England', in M. Bronwen and F. Ringham (eds) *Sense and Scent: An Exploration of Olfactory Meaning*. Dublin: Philomel.

Riley, D. (1988) *Am I That Name? Feminism and the Category of 'Women' in History*. Basingstoke: Macmillan.

Ritzer, G. (ed.) (1997) *The McDonaldization Thesis*. London: Sage.

Rivas, L.M. (2003) 'Invisible Labours: Caring for the Independent Person', in B. Ehrenreich and A.R. Hochschild (eds) *Global Woman: Nannies, Maids and Sex Workers in the New Economy*. London: Granta Books.

Roediger, D.R. (1999) *The Wages of Whiteness: Race and the Making of the American Working Class*. London: Verso.

Rollins, J. (1996) 'Invisibility, Consciousness of the Other, and Resentment among Black Domestic Workers', in C.L. Macdonald and C. Sirianni (eds) *Working in the Service Sector*. Philadelphia: Temple University Press.

Rollins, J. (1985) *Between Women: Domestics and their Employers*. Philadelphia: Temple University Press.

Rommi, S. (2005) 'There's the Rub', *Guardian*, 26 March. Retrieved on 27 March 2005, from http://www.guardian.co.uk/weekend/story/0,,1444864,00.html

Roper, M. (1994) *Masculinity and the British Organization Man since 1945*. Oxford: Oxford University Press.

Rose, G. (2001) *Visual Methodologies*. London: Sage.

Rose, M. (2000) 'Future Tense? Are Growing Occupations More Stressed Out and Depressed?'. Working Paper 5, ESRC Future of Work Programme. Swindon: ESRC.

Rose, N. (1989) *Governing the Soul*. London: Routledge.

Rotella, C. (2004) *Good with Their Hands: Boxers, Bluesmen and Other Characters from the Rust Belt*. Berkeley: University of California Press.

Rowland, D. (2005) 'In the Health Trade', *Guardian*, 20 January. Retrieved on 21 January 2005, from http://www.guardian.co.uk/analysis/story/0,,1394117,00.html

Salgado, S. (1993) *Workers: An Archaeology of the Industrial Age*. London: Phaidon.

Salmon, P. (2002) 'Being at the Receiving End: One Patient's Experience of Nursing Care', *Auto/Biography* 10 (12): 107–12.

Sanchez-Taylor, J. (2001) 'Dollars Are a Girl's Best Friend? Female Tourists' Sexual Behaviour in the Caribbean', *Sociology* 35 (3): 749–64.

Sanchez-Taylor, J. (2000) 'Tourism and Embodied Commodities: Sex Tourism in the Caribbean', in S. Clift and S. Carter (eds) *Tourism and Sex: Culture, Commerce and Coercion*. London: Pinter.

Sandal, J. (1999) 'The Paradox of the "Professional Ideal" and the "Second Shift"'. Paper presented to the conference on Gender, Health and Healing, in honour of Professor Meg Stacey, University of Warwick, April.

Sapper, G. (1999) *Blood in the Bank: Social and Legal Aspects of Death at Work*. Aldershot: Dartmouth Ashgate.

Sanders, M. (2000) 'Accidents of Production: Industrialisation and the Worker's Body in Early Industrial Fiction', in G.H. Klaus and S. Knight (eds) *British Industrial Fictions*. Cardiff: University of Wales Press.

Sassen, S. (1991) *The Global City*. Princeton: Princeton University Press.

Saunders, C., D.H. Summers and N. Teller (eds) (1981) *Hospice: The Living Idea*. London: Edward Arnold.

Sayer, A. and R. Walker (1992) *The New Social Economy: Reworking the Division of Labor*. Cambridge, MA: Blackwell.

Scarry, E. (1994) *Resisting Representation*. Oxford: Oxford University Press.

Scarry, E. (1985) *The Body in Pain*. Oxford: Oxford University Press.

Schatzki, T. and W. Natter (eds) (1996a) *The Social and Political Body*. London: The Guildford Press.

Schatzki, T. and W. Natter (1996b) 'Sociocultural Bodies, Bodies Sociopolitical', in T. Schatzki and W. Natter (eds) *The Social and Political Body*. London: The Guildford Press.

Scheper-Hughes, N. (2002) 'Bodies for Sale: Whole or in Parts', in N. Scheper-Hughes and L. Wacquant (eds) *Commodifying Bodies*. London: Sage.

Scheper-Hughes, N. (2001) 'Commodity Fetishism in Organ Trafficking', *Body and Society* 7 (2): 31–62.

Scheper-Hughes, N. (2000) 'Global Trafficking in Organs', *Current Anthropology* 41 (2): 191–224.

Scoular, J. (2004) 'The "Subject" of Prostitution: Interpreting the Discursive, Symbolic and Material Position of Sex/Work in Feminist Theory', *Feminist Theory* 5 (3): 343–55.

Segal-Horne, S. (1993) 'The Internationalization of Service Firms', *Advances in Strategic Management* 9: 31–55.

Sekula, A. (1982) 'On the Invention of Photographic Meaning', in V. Burgin (ed.) *Thinking Photography*. Basingstoke: Macmillan.

Sennett, R. (1998) *The Corrosion of Character: The Personal Consequences of Work in the New Capitalism*. New York: Norton.

Shakespeare, P. (2003) 'Nurses' Bodywork: Is There a Body of Work?', *Nursing Inquiry* 10 (1): 47–56.

Sharma, U. (1992) *Complementary Medicine Today*. London: Routledge.

Sharma, U. and P. Black (2001) 'Look Good, Feel Better: Beauty Therapy as Emotional Labour', *Sociology* 35 (4): 913–31.

Sharma, U. and P. Black (1999) 'The Sociology of Pampering: Beauty Therapy as a Form of Work'. Research paper, University of Derby.

Sherman, C. (1990) *Untitled Film Stills*. London: Cape.

Shildrick, M. and J. Price (eds) (1998) *Vital Signs*. Edinburgh: Edinburgh University Press.

Shilling, C. (2005) *The Body in Culture, Technology and Society*. London: Sage Publications.

Shilling, C. (1993) *The Body and Social Theory*. London: Sage Publications.

Shusterman, R. (1997) *Practicing Philosophy*. New York: Routledge.

Skeggs, B. (2005) 'The Making of Class and Gender through Visualizing Moral Subject Formation', *Sociology* 39 (5): 965-982.

Skeggs, B. (2004) 'Context and Background', in L. Adkins and B. Skeggs (eds) *Feminism after Bourdieu*. Oxford: Blackwell.

Skeggs, B. (2004a) 'Exchange, Value and Affect: Bourdieu and the "Self"', *The Sociological Review* 52 (2): 51-95.

Skeggs, B. (2004b) *Class, Self and Culture*. London: Routledge.

Skeggs, B. (1997) *Formations of Class and Gender: Becoming Respectable*. London: Sage.

Slapper, G. (1999) *Blood in the Bank: Social and Legal Aspects of Death at Work*. Aldershot: Dartmouth Ashgate.

Smart, C. (1996) 'Collusion, Collaboration and Confession: On Moving beyond the Heterosexuality Debate', in D. Richardson (ed.) *Theorising Heterosexuality*. Milton Keynes: Open University Press.

Smart, C. (1992) 'Disruptive Bodies and Unruly Sex', in C. Smart (ed.) *Regulating Womanhood*. London: Routledge.

Smart, C. (1989) *Feminism and the Power of Law*. London: Routledge.

Smart, C. (1985) 'Sexual Objects and Legal Subjects', in J. Brophy and C. Smart (eds) *Women in Law*. London: Routledge & Kegan Paul.

Smith, Clarissa (2002) 'Shiny Chests and Heaving G-Strings: A Night Out with the Chippendales', *Sexualities* 5 (1): 67-89.

Smith, D. (1988) *The Everyday World as Problematic*. Boston: Northeastern University Press.

Smith, D., T. Thompson and G. Hinsliff (2004) 'Sex Comes out of the City into Middle England', *Observer,* 18 April.

Smith, P. (1999) 'Logging Emotions', *Soundings* 11: 128-37.

Smith, V. and Gottfried, H. (1996) 'Flexibility in Work and Employment: The Impact on Women', Unpublished paper later published in B. Pfau-Effinger et al. (eds) *Feminist Research on Labor Market Theories*.

Sontag, S. (1979) *On Photography*. Harmondsworth: Penquin.

Sosteric, M. (1996) 'Subjectivity in the Labour Process: A Case Study in the Restaurant Industry', *Work, Employment and Society* 10 (2): 297-318.

Sound Ergonomics (2001) Retrieved on 21 February 2005, from http://www.soundergonomics.com/Pages/Articles/gbrownprecise.htm

Spongberg, M. (1997) *Feminizing Venereal Disease: The Body of the Prostitute in Nineteenth-Century Medical Discourse*. Basingstoke: Macmillan.

Stacey, J. (1997) *Teratologies*. London: Routledge.

Stacey, M. (1988) *The Sociology of Health and Healing*. London: Unwin Hyman.

Stanley, L. (ed.) (1984) *The Diaries of Hannah Cullwick: Victorian Maidservant*. London: Virago.

Steinberg, R. and D. Figart (1999) 'Emotional Labour since the Managed Heart', *The Annals of the American Academy of Political and Social Sciences* 561: 8-27.

Stetson, D.M. (2004) 'The Invisible Issue: Prostitution and the Trafficking of Women and Girls in the United States', in J. Outshoorn (ed.) *The Politics of Prostitution: Women's Movements, Democratic States and the Globalisation of Sex Commerce*. Cambridge: Cambridge University Press.

Stinson, K. (2001) *Women and Dieting Culture: Inside a Commercial Weight Loss Group*. New Brunswick: Rutgers University Press.

Strangleman, T. (2004) 'Ways of (not) Seeing Work: The Visual as a Blind Spot', *Work, Employment and Society* 18 (1): 170-92.

Sturdy, A. (2003) 'Knowing the Unknowable? A Discussion of Methodological and Theoretical Issues in Emotion Research and Organisation Studies', *Organisation* 10 (1): 81–105.

Sturdy, A. and S. Fineman (2001) 'Struggles for Control of Effect: Resistance as Politics and Emotion', in A. Sturdy, I. Grugulis and H. Willmott (eds) *Customer Service: Empowerment and Entrapment*. Basingstoke: Palgrave.

Sturdy, A., I. Grugulis and H. Willmott (eds) (2001) *Customer Service: Empowerment and Entrapment*. Basingstoke: Palgrave.

Sudbury, J. (2002) 'Celling Black Bodies: Black Women in the Global Prison Industrial Complex', *Feminist Review* 70 (1): 57–74.

Tagg, J. (1988) *The Burden of Representation: Essays on Photographies and Histories*. Basingstoke: Macmillan.

Tally, M. (2003) 'The Illnesses of Global Capitalism and the Meaning of Sick Leave' in R.H. Brown (ed.) *The Politics of Selfhood: Bodies and Identities in Global Capitalism*. Minneapolis: University of Minnesota.

Taylor, P. (2001) 'Attacking the Cultural Turn: Misrepresentation of the Service Encounter'. Paper presented to the Work Employment and Society Conference, Nottingham, September.

Taylor, P., C. Baldry, P. Bain and V. Ellis (2003) 'A Unique Work Environment: Health, Sickness and Absence Management in UK Call Centres', *Work, Employment and Society* 17 (3): 435–58.

Taylor, S. (1998) 'Emotional Labour and the New Workplace', in P. Thompson and C. Warhurst (eds) *Workplaces of the Future*. Basingstoke: Macmillan.

Thomas, C. (2002) 'The "Disabled" Body', in M. Evans and E. Lee (eds) *Real Bodies: A Sociological Introduction*. Basingstoke: Palgrave.

Thomas, C. (1993) 'Deconstructing the Concept of Care', *Sociology* 27 (4): 649–69.

Thompson, E.P. (1967) 'Time, Work-Discipline, and Industrial Capitalism', *Past and Present* 38: 56–97.

Thompson, P. (2003) 'Disconnected Capitalism: Or Why Employers Can't Keep their Part of the Bargain', *Work, Employment and Society* 17 (2): 359–78.

Thompson, P. (1989) *The Nature of Work: An Introduction to Debates on the Labour Process*. Basingstoke: Macmillan.

Thompson, P. and S. Ackroyd (1995) 'All Quiet on the Workplace Front? A Critique of Recent Trends in British Industrial Sociology', *Sociology* 29 (4): 615–33.

Thompson, P. and C. Warhurst (eds) (1998) *Workplaces of the Future*. Basingstoke: Macmillan.

Thorpe, C.R. and S. Shapin (2000) 'Who Was J. Robert Oppenheimer? Charisma and Complex Organisation', *Social Studies of Science* 30 (4): 545–90.

Thrift, N. (2005) *Knowing Capitalism*. London: Sage.

Tombs, S. (1999) 'Death and Work in Britain', *Sociological Review* 47 (2): 345–67.

Toynbee, P. (2003a) *Hard Work: Life in Low-Pay Britain*. London: Bloomsbury.

Toynbee, P. (2003b) 'Sexual Dealing', *Guardian*, 9 May. Retrieved on 10 May 2004, from http://www.guardian.co.uk/comment/story/0,,952285,00.html

Trachtenberg, A. (1989) *Reading American Photographs: Images as History*. New York: Hill & Wang.

Traweek, S. (1988) *Beamtimes and Lifetimes: The World of High Energy Physics*. Cambridge, Mass.: Harvard University Press.

Tredici, R. (1987) *At Work in the Fields of the Bomb*. London: Harrap.

Trethewey, A. (1999) 'Disciplined Bodies: Women's Embodied Identities at Work', *Organisational Studies* 20 (3): 423–50.

Treuherz, J. (1987) *Hard Times: Social Realism in Victorian Art*. London: Lund Humphries Publishers.

Tronto, J.C. (1993) *Moral Boundaries: A Political Argument for an Ethic of Care*. New York: Routledge.

Truong, T.D. (2001) 'Organised Crime and Human Trafficking', in E. Veriano (ed.) *Organised Crime: Myths and Profits*. Avebury: Ashgate.

Truong, T.D. (1990) *Sex, Money and Morality: Prostitution and Tourism in Southeast Asia*. London: Zed Press.

TUC (1999) *Violent Times*. London: TUC.

Tunstall, J. (1962) *The Fisherman*. London: McGibbon & Kee.

Turner, B.S. (1984) *The Body and Society*. Oxford: Blackwell.

Twigg, J. (2004) 'The Body, Gender, and Age: Feminist Insights in Social Gerontology', *Journal of Aging Studies* 18 (1): 59–73.

Twigg, J. (2000a) *Bathing: The Body and Community Care*. London: Routledge.

Twigg, J. (2000b) 'Carework as a Form of Body Work', *Ageing and Society* 20 (4): 389–41.

Tyler, M. and P. Abbott (1998) 'Chocs Away: Weightwatching in the Contemporary Airline Industry', *Sociology* 32 (3): 433–50.

Tyler, M. and P. Hancock (2001) 'Flight Attendants and the Management of Gendered "Organisational Bodies"', in K. Backett-Muilburn and L. McKie (eds) *Constructing Gendered Bodies*. London: Macmillan.

Tyler, M. and S. Taylor (2001) 'Juggling Justice and Care: Gendered Customer Service in the Contemporary Airlines Industry', in A. Sturdy, I. Grugulis and H. Willmott (eds) *Customer Service: Empowerment and Entrapment*. Basingstoke: Palgrave.

Ungerson, C. (2000) 'Thinking about the Production and Consumption of Long-term Care in Britain: Does Gender Still Matter?', *Journal of Social Policy* 29 (4): 623–43.

Valentine, G. (2002) 'In-corporations: Food, Bodies and Organizations', *Body and Society* 8 (2): 1–20.

Van Dongen, E. and R. Elema (2001) 'The Art of Touching: The Culture of "Body Work"', *Anthropology and Medicine* 8 (2/3): 149–210.

Vasselu, C. (1998) 'The Mouth and the Clinical Gaze', in M. Shildrick and J. Price (eds) *Vital Signs*. Edinburgh: Edinburgh University Press.

Wacquant, L. (2002) 'Whores, Slaves and Stallions: Languages of Exploitation and Accommodation among Professional Boxers', in N. Scheper-Hughes and L. Wacquant (eds) *Commodifying Bodies*. London: Sage.

Waerness, K. (1984) 'The Rationality of Caring', *Economic and Industrial Democracy* 5: 185–211.

Wainwright, D. and M. Calnan (2002) *Work Stress: The Making of a Modern Epidemic*. Buckingham: Open University Press.

Wajcman, J. (1998) *Managing Like a Man*. Oxford: Polity.

Walby, S. (1997) *Gender Transformations*. London: Routledge.

Walby, S. and J. Greenwell (1994) *Medicine and Nursing: Professions in a Changing Health Service*. London: Sage.

Walkowitz, J. (1984) 'Male Vice and Female Virtue', in A. Snitow, C. Stansell and S. Thompson (eds) *Desire: The Politics of Sexuality*. London: Virago.

Walkowitz, J. (1980) *Prostitution in Victorian Society* . Cambridge: Cambridge University Press.

Ward, L. (2005) 'Gender Split Still Thrives At Work', *Guardian,* 31 March. Retrieved on 31 March 2005, from http://www.guardian.co.uk/uk_news/story/0,,1448602,00.html#article_continue

Warhurst, C. and P. Thompson (1998) 'Hands, Hearts and Minds: Changing Work and Workers and the End of the Century', in P. Thompson and C. Warhurst (eds) *Workplaces of the Future*. Basingstoke: Macmillan.

Warhurst, C., D. Nickson and E. Dutton (2004) 'The View from the Front Line: Student Employees and Aesthetic Labour'. Paper presented to the Work, Employment and Society Conference, Manchester, September.

Warhurst, C., D. Nickson, A. Witz and A. Cullen (2000) 'Aesthetic Labour in Interactive Service Work', *Services Industries Journal* 20 (3): 1–18.

Watterson, A. and R. O'Neill (2004) 'The Decline and Immanent Fall of UK Occupational Health', *International Journal of Occupational and Environmental Health* 10: 340–342. Retrieved on 1 March 2005, from http://www.ijoeh.com/pfds/1003_Watter.pdf

Weeks, J. (1981) *Sex, Politics and Society: The Regulation of Sexuality since 1800*. Harlow: Longman.

Weitz, R. (ed.) (2003) *The Politics of Women's Bodies: Sexuality, Appearance and Behaviour*. Oxford: Oxford University Press.

Weitzer, R. (2000) *Sex for Sale: Prostitution, Pornography and the Sex Industry*. London: Routledge.

West, J. (2000) 'Prostitution: Collectives and the Politics of Regulation', *Gender, Work and Organization* 7 (2): 106–18.

West, J. and T. Austrin (2006) 'Markets and Politics: Public and Private Relations in the Case of Prostitution', in L. Pettinger, et al. (eds) *A New-Sociology of Work*. Oxford; Blackwell.

West, J. and T. Austrin (2002) 'From Work as Sex to Sex as Work: Networks, "Others" and Occupations in the Analysis of Work', *Gender, Work and Organization* 9 (5): 482–503.

Westwood, S. (1984) *All Day, Every Day: Factory and Family in the Making of Women's Lives*. London: Pluto.

Whitehead, A. (1984) ' "I'm Hungry, Mum": The Politics of Domestic Budgeting', in K. Young, C. Wolkowitz and R. McCullagh (eds) *Of Marriage and the Market; Women's Subordination in International Perspective*. London: Routledge & Kegan Paul.

Whyte, W.H. (2002 [1956]) *Organisation Man*. Philadelphia: University of Pennsylvania Press.

Williams, C. (2003) 'Sky Service: The Demands of Emotional Labours in the Airline Industry', *Gender, Work and Organisation* 10 (5): 513–50.

Williams, C. (1999) 'Danger: Bodies at Work', *Work, Employment and Society* 13 (1): 151–4.

Williams, C. (1997) 'Women and Occupational Health and Safety: From Narratives of Danger to Invisibility', *Labour History* 73: 30–52.

Williams, C. (1993) 'Class, Gender and the Body: The Occupational Health and Safety Concerns of Blue Collar Workers in the South Asian Timber Industry', in M. Quinlan (ed.) *Work and Health: The Origins, Management and Regulation of Occupational Illness*. Melbourne: Macmillan.

Williams, S. (2003) 'Marrying the Social and the Biological? A Rejoinder to Newton', The *Sociological Review* 51 (4): 550–61.

Williams, S. and G. Bendelow (1998) *The Lived Body: Sociological Themes, Embodied Issues*. London: Routledge.

Wills, J. (2005) 'The Geography of Union Organising in Low Paid Service Industries in the UK: Lessons from the T&G's Campaign to Unionise the Dorchester Hotel, London', *Antipode* 37 (1): 139–59.

Wills, J. (2001) 'Community Unionism and Trade Union Renewal in the UK', *Transactions of the Institute of British Geographers* 26 (4): 465–83.

Wilson, M.G. (1989) *Floridians at Work: Yesterday and Today*. Macon, GA: Mercer University Press.

Witz, A. (1994) 'The Challenge of Nursing' in J. Gabe, D. Kelleher and G. Williams (eds) *Challenging Medicine*. London: Routledge.

Witz, A., C. Warhurst and D. Nickson (2003) 'The Labour of Aesthetics and the Aesthetics of Organisation', *Organisation* 10 (1): 33–54.

Wokutch, R. (1992) *Worker Protection, Japanese Style: Occupational Health and Safety in the Auto Industry*. Ithaca: ILR Press.

Wolfenden, J. (1957) 'Report of the Committee on Homosexual Offences and Prostitution', Cmnd 247. London: HMSO.

Wolkowitz, C. (2004) 'Body Work and Postfeminist Crime Fiction'. Paper presented to the Work, Employment and Society Conference, Manchester, UMIST, September.

Wolkowitz, C. (2002) 'The Social Relations of Body Work', *Work, Employment and Society* 16 (3): 497–510.

Wolkowitz, C. (2001) 'The Working Body as Sign: Historical Snapshots', in K. Milburn-Backett and L. McKie (eds) *Constructing Gendered Bodies*. London: Macmillan.

Wolkowitz, C. (2000a) 'Nuclear Families: Women's Accounts of the Manhattan Project', in S. Ahmed, J. Kilby, C. Lury, M. McNeil and B. Skeggs (eds) *Transformations: Thinking through Feminism*. London and New York: Routledge.

Wolkowitz, C. (2000b) '"Papa's Bomb": The Local and the Global in Women's Manhattan Project Narratives', in M. Andrews, S. Day Sclater, C. Squire and A. Treacher (eds) *Lines of Narrative: Psychosocial Perspectives*. London and New York: Routledge.

Wood, E.A. (2000) 'Working in the Fantasy Factory: The Attention Hypothesis and the Enacting of Masculine Power in Strip Clubs', *Journal of Contemporary Ethnography* 29 (1): 5–31.

Wood, N. (1982) 'Prostitution and Feminism in 19th Century Britain', *m/f* 7: 61–78.

Woody, B. (1992) *Black Women in the Workplace: Impacts of Structural Change in the Economy*. New York: Greenwood Press.

Wouters, C. (1989) 'The Sociology of Emotions and Flight Attendants: Hochschild's Managed Heart', *Theory, Culture and Society* 6 (1): 95–123.

Wray-Bliss, E. (2001) 'Representing Customer Service: Telephone and Texts', in A. Sturdy, I. Grugulis and H. Willmott (eds) *Customer Service: Empowerment and Entrapment*. Basingstoke: Palgrave.

Wrench, J. (1995) 'Racism and Occupational Health and Safety: Migrant and Minority Women and "Poor Work". Centre for Comparative Labour Studies Working Paper no. 7, Department of Sociology, University of Warwick.

Wright, C. (2004) 'Consuming Lives, Consuming Landscapes: Interpreting Advertisements', *Journal of International Development* 16 (5): 665–80.

Yanarella, E. and H. Reid (1996) 'From "Trained Gorilla" to "Humanware": Repoliticising the Body-Machine Complex between Fordism and Post-Fordism', in T. Schatzki and W. Natter (eds) *The Social and Political Body*. London: The Guildford Press.

Yeates, N. (2004a) 'Global Care Chains: Critical Reflections and Lines of Inquiry', *International Feminist Journal of Politics* 6 (3): 369–91.

Yeates, N. (2004b) 'A Dialogue with "Global Care Chain" Analysis: Nurse Migration in the Irish Context', *Feminist Review* 77: 79–95.

Young, B. (2004) 'Global Governance of Privatisation: International Finance and the WTO'. Paper presented to the International Workshop on Gender, Governance and Globalisation, University of Warwick, September.

Young, I.M. (1990) *Throwing Like a Girl and Other Essays in Feminist Philosophy and Social Theory*. Bloomington: Indiana University Press.

Index